Single-Case Research Methods
for the Behavioral and Health Sciences

D1141795

Single-Case Research Methods
for the Behavioral and Health Sciences

David L. Morgan
Spalding University

Robin K. Morgan
Indiana University Southeast

Los Angeles • London • New Delhi • Singapore

For information:

SAGE Publications, Inc.
2455 Teller Road
Thousand Oaks, California 91320
E-mail: order@sagepub.com

SAGE Publications Ltd.
1 Oliver's Yard
55 City Road
London EC1Y 1SP
United Kingdom

SAGE Publications India Pvt. Ltd.
B 1/I 1 Mohan Cooperative Industrial Area
Mathura Road, New Delhi 110 044
India

SAGE Publications Asia-Pacific Pte. Ltd.
33 Pekin Street #02-01
Far East Square
Singapore 048763

Printed in the United States of America.

Library of Congress Cataloging-in-Publication Data

Morgan, David L. (David Lloyd), 1957-
Single-case research methods for the behavioral and health sciences/David L. Morgan, Robin K. Morgan.
    p.; cm.
Includes bibliographical references and index.
ISBN 978-1-4129-5039-8 (pbk.: alk. paper)
    1. Single subject research. 2. Social sciences—Research—Methodology. 3. Medical sciences—Research—Methodology. I. Morgan, Robin K., 1961- II. Title. [DNLM:
1. Behavioral Research—methods. 2. Health Services Research—methods. 3. Research Design. WM 20 M847s 2009]
BF76.6.S56M67 2009
150.72′2—dc22   2008011836

This book is printed on acid-free paper.

08   09   10   11   10 9 8 7 6 5 4 3 2 1

Acquisitions Editor:	Vicki Knight
Associate Editor:	Sean Connelly
Editorial Assistant:	Lauren Habib
Production Editor:	Karen Wiley
Copy Editor:	Kathy Anne Savadel
Typesetter:	C&M Digitals (P) Ltd.
Proofreader:	Caryne Brown
Indexer:	Gloria Tierney
Cover Designer:	Janet Foulger
Marketing Manager:	Stephanie Adams

CONTENTS

PREFACE

A decade ago, this book may have been seen as useful to only a small population of applied researchers, particularly applied behavior analysts. Because behavior analysts have been longtime supporters of single-case research, in both its basic and applied domains, the philosophy and design strategies discussed in this book will appear quite familiar to these professionals. But the increasing managed care landscape, coupled with multidisciplinary calls for evidence-based practice, has engendered substantial dialogue about and exploration of alternative research strategies. This change has been especially felt by practitioners who are being called upon to document the effectiveness of the health care interventions they deliver to clients. This requirement has historically gone unmet because the strategies and tactics of large group research designs have been unwieldy, if not impossible to implement in applied settings. We hope that the readers of this book will come to recognize that the goals of science and practice, so often and for so long viewed as disconnected, are in fact quite compatible. Indeed, even as this book was being written, numerous single-case studies were being published in professional journals in psychology, nursing, occupational and physical therapy, and social work. We think that you'll agree that this is a welcome development, not only for the sciences that inform professional practice but also for the citizens who ultimately stand to benefit from the establishment of evidence-based health care.

This book is the collaborative product of a great deal of work by some very talented people, including the very capable staff at Sage Publications. We would like to thank the following reviewers for investing both their time and intellectual energy in making this a much better book than it would have otherwise been: Neville Blampied, University of Canterbury, Christchurch, New Zealand; Maureen E. Angell, Illinois State University; and J. Michael Crowley, Oregon State University. We are especially grateful to Dennis McDougall at the University of Hawaii. With considerable diligence and a keen eye, Dennis went above and beyond the call of duty in providing editorial support, cogent recommendations, and suggested revisions through both drafts of the manuscript. Finally, we are fortunate to have worked with a supportive and professional editorial staff at Sage. Writing a textbook is an enormous challenge, requiring substantial coordination and timely correspondence with everyone involved. We are thankful to have had Lisa Cuevas-Shaw, Sean Connelly, Vicki Knight, and Karen Wiley onboard to make this process manageable and relatively anxiety free. We are especially indebted to Kathy Savadel, whose copyediting "magic" was rendered with great skill and professionalism, making the process much smoother than any author could anticipate.

For students and faculty: It would be hard to imagine more valuable feedback regarding this book than could be offered by those of you working in the trenches. Your comments and recommendations concerning this book would be greatly appreciated, and we welcome you to correspond with us at dmorgan@spalding.edu and rmorgan@ius.edu.

David L. Morgan, *Spalding University*
Robin K. Morgan *Indiana University Southeast*

Chapter 1

WHY SINGLE-CASE RESEARCH METHODS?

The methods of science have been enormously successful wherever they have been tried. Let us apply them to human affairs.

—B. F. Skinner (1953, p. 5)

These words, written a half century ago by America's leading behavioral scientist, reflect the purpose of this book. All around us, human service professionals—be they psychologists, nurses, rehabilitation specialists, or physical and occupational therapists—attempt to salve the aches, pain, and anxieties of being human in the 21st century. Increasingly, their efforts are being informed by the latest findings from the research-oriented disciplines of the behavioral and health sciences. As a consequence, it has become imperative that students in the human service fields acquire an understanding of and appreciation for the many philosophies and methods that characterize research in these areas. Indeed, being a competent professional in any field requires a working familiarity with the latest relevant research, particularly when this research bears important implications for applied interventions.

This book is intended as an introduction to the philosophical and strategic features of single-case research as conducted within the behavioral and health sciences. Single-case research represents a powerful and effective alternative to the large group designs that have characterized much of the history of behavioral science but that often prove impractical, particularly in the applied setting of the field or clinic. The flexibility and sensitivity of single-case designs to "local" factors offer substantial benefits to those charged with conducting research in clinical settings. Moreover, the single-case approach, in both spirit and practice, meshes well with the needs of professionals who are almost exclusively providing care for individual clients. We will be considering the philosophical underpinnings, historical development, design features and advantages, contemporary use, and future prospects of single-case research as conducted by psychologists, nurses, physical and occupational therapists, and other allied health scientists.

MANAGED CARE

Rising health care costs have changed the way health care practitioners offer their services and the ways in which they are reimbursed. **Managed care practices** affect the work of all health care providers in the United States in some way, whether they are psychologists, physicians, nurses, social workers, physical therapists, or occupational therapists. Given that approximately 170 million Americans subscribe to a managed care insurance plan (Kent & Hersen, 2000), health care providers are affected by the provisions set forth by their patients' managed care organizations. The managed care market is a product of free enterprise, and health care, like other systems, has not been spared the consequences of a competitive market.

The earliest recognized prepaid health care arrangement occurred in the early 20th century in the Pacific Northwestern portion of the United States with the development of the Western Clinic. The founders of the Western Clinic, physicians Thomas Curran and James Yocum, contracted with several lumber company representatives to provide comprehensive health care for their employees at the rate of 50 cents per employee per month. Curran and Yocum collected this fee independent of the number of patients they saw. The success of the Western Clinic inspired other physicians to build on this idea and to contract with employers from the railroad, mining, and lumber industries in the northwestern states, producing a rapid rise in such prepaid contacts between physicians and industry bosses. A second example of an early prepaid contract occurred in Texas in the early 1930s: Baylor Hospital contracted with 1,250 schoolteachers who agreed to prepay the hospital annual premiums in exchange for a set number of days of hospital care. This agreement is cited as the first group health insurance plan, eventually giving rise to Blue Cross (Rickel & Wise, 1999).

The Great Depression, with the uncertainties created by economic hardship, advanced early forms of managed care. More and more middle-class Americans wanted protection from the hardships brought on by an unexpected injury or illness. As a result, health care providers found more acceptance from Americans with strained incomes in changing their traditional ways of charging for their services.

Perhaps one of the best known and most successful of the Depression-era managed care arrangements came with the development of Kaiser Permanente, today's leading managed care organization with, as of the year 2004, over 7 million members (Moon, 2004). In 1931, Henry Kaiser and his business partners won a bid from the federal government to build Boulder Dam (now called Hoover Dam). For five cents per employee per work hour, Kaiser hired Sidney Garfield, and a group of physicians recruited by Garfield, to provide health care for his workers. As the dam's construction began, Kaiser built a 10-bed hospital on wheels that was pulled along in the direction of the construction. This early managed care structure possessed two features that are still found in today's **health maintenance organizations (HMOs)**: (1) prepaid arrangements and (2) group practice (Hendricks, 1993). Kaiser Permanente expanded its operations throughout the West Coast and eventually spread throughout the country, including states such as Texas, Ohio, and Maryland.

The success of Kaiser Permanente was due, in part, to the willingness of Americans to embrace these concepts. As Americans were becoming more technologically informed, they were generally not offended by the idea of their health statuses viewed as things to be "maintained," nor could they predict the mechanical approach to patient care that results in part from this philosophy of health (Hendricks, 1993). Interestingly, the American Medical Association (AMA) initially vehemently opposed such prepaid group plans for health care and advocated maintaining the traditional fee-for-service arrangements, for two reasons. First, the AMA argued that prepaid plans ethically compromised the patient–doctor trust. Second, the AMA stated that it would be impossible to hold a corporation accountable for breaches in standards of practice. Additionally, the AMA was disturbed by what it believed was intrusiveness into the lives of employees by their employers. In the early 1950s, the AMA argued against prepaid group health, claiming it was a form of "socialized medicine" (Hendricks, 1993). Despite these objections, prepaid group arrangements flourished.

For the most part, these early prepaid arrangements centered on the mission of providing affordable health care to the laborers of industrial companies. Employers typically provided workers a choice between traditional indemnity coverage and enrollment in an HMO. However, these early prepaid group plans served as models for the development of government-sponsored HMOs of the 1970s that led to the rapid growth of HMOs in the 1980s. Although HMOs in the 1980s were primarily involved in the private sector, they increasingly participated in publicly sponsored programs such as Medicare and Medicaid.

With the development of the social programs Medicaid and Medicare, the federal government fully stepped into the health insurance arena. Medicaid was established in 1965 by the federal government through Title XIX of the Social Security Act to provide health care to poor and disabled Americans (Spidle, 1999). It was modeled on the traditional Blue Cross/Blue Shield service benefits, thus emulating the private sector. Although Medicare was designed to be administered and handled by the federal government, Medicaid's budgetary spending was to be determined by state need, with each state government deciding how much it needed to spend. Historically, Medicaid has presented huge challenges to state budgets, leading an increasing number of states to look toward managed care operations to provide service for their Medicaid beneficiaries.

In the mid-1960s, President Lyndon Johnson made Medicare one of his administration's top priorities. By the early 1970s, the federal government spoke of a "national health care crisis." The Nixon Administration searched for ways to curtail what it perceived as the looming catastrophe associated with social welfare programs. Paul Ellwood, a Minneapolis physician, argued that the existing fee-for-service arrangements rewarded those physicians who kept their patients ill. He proposed a system in which the federal government rewarded physicians for maintaining health. Ellwood's model was based on the Kaiser Permanente models and led to the **HMO Act of 1973,** which provided economic incentives for the development of HMOs.

The creation of these HMOs was an effort to curtail the rising U.S. health and mental health care costs. The percentage of the gross national product spent on health care rose from 6% in 1963 to 10% in 1987 (Broskowski, 1994). Advancements in medical technology and pharmacology, although improving health and increasing the life span, cost the federal government more money. Finally, premiums for private insurance were also increasing.

Over the next several years, six amendments were made to the HMO Act of 1973 relaxing the requirements of the original act. The **1974 Employment Retirement Security Act (ERISA)** gave early HMOs a great boost by allowing employers an exemption to state laws requiring federally qualified HMOs to base premium rates on the health care costs of the entire community. By basing their premium costs solely on the health care of their employees, HMOs were able to reduce their premium rates, leading to a rapid expansion of HMOs in the 1980s (Zieman, 1998).

The HMO Act of 1973 was of particular interest to mental health providers. The legislation required provision of outpatient mental health care and referral services for drug and alcohol abuse. A 1976 amendment allowed HMOs to utilize clinical expertise of "other health care professionals," including clinical psychologists, rather than the traditional psychiatrists.

As noted earlier, both general health care and mental health care have experienced soaring costs in the last several decades. These high costs are frequently given as a rationale by insurance companies for increasing control over services provided by utilization review methods. Mental health professionals, embedded in today's managed care policies, work in an environment much different from the payment arrangements of the 1970s and a large portion of the 1980s. During those times, mental health professionals had more discretion in the types of treatments they chose for their clients. Often, they were not required to provide lengthy evidence and validation for the work they did in therapy. Mental health professionals who contract with HMOs earn a fixed amount per referral, regardless of the number of psychotherapy sessions required for treatment. Rickel and Wise (1999) wrote, "HMOs control costs by putting providers in a position to lose money by extensive or inefficient treatment, or having an unusually sick population" (p. 34). HMOs typically restrict their members' options for mental health care by limiting which mental health professional they will reimburse for services.

Preferred provider organizations (PPOs), compared with HMOs, are managed care structures that allow for a greater degree of flexibility in enrollees' choice of providers. When the member desires to see a mental health provider not on the PPO list of providers, the PPO typically reimburses the mental health provider by paying a percentage of the "usual, customary, and reasonable fee" for treatment.

Almost every managed care structure in which mental health providers (psychologists, social workers, occupational therapists, physical therapists, etc.) will be involved uses the practice of **utilization review** (management). This utilization review involves monitoring the treatment plan, including plans to help the client overcome the problem, diagnosis(es), previous treatments the client has received, and the time frame needed to achieve stated goals. The primary goal of such review is to limit costs that the insurance company must pay. Concerned about variations in practice, the health care community has focused on improving care as well as reducing costs by reviewing the empirical literature, developing protocols, and encouraging practitioners to voluntarily adopt the suggested treatment guidelines. In the early 1990s, for instance, a federal agency called the Agency for Health Care Policy and Research developed a series of treatment guidelines for various conditions (Clay, 2000). The primary treatments endorsed by managed care structures are solution-focused therapies; crisis interventions; group therapies; behaviorally oriented therapies; therapies that involve biopsychosocial assessments; and more recently, computer-assisted therapies.

The range of reactions to the advent of managed care from health care providers spans the gamut from denial and resistance, refusal to cooperate with utilization review demands, and career changes, to acceptance and adjusting and tailoring practices to fit managed care demands (Broskowski, 1994). Supporters of managed care policies assert that by requiring outcome research and the integration of physical and mental health care, managed care encourages the establishment of scientific foundations of practice (Sanchez & Turner, 2003). On the other hand, authors such as Hersch (1995) refer to managed care as "the most tangible and problematic manifestation of health care reform" (p. 16), and even "the corpse in the living room" (Pipal, 1995, p. 323).

Outcome measures, regardless of one's personal perspective, are becoming part of standard treatment in which service providers must demonstrate their efficacy as they are quantitatively being compared to one another. Cohen (2003) wrote:

> Outcome management serves several important functions in the mental health field, including evaluating and refining treatments, providing clear descriptions of therapeutic procedures, and enhancing the credibility of psychotherapy. The current marketplace of mental health care increasingly demands greater accountability of its practitioners. (p. 39)

Evidence suggests that outcome measures are valued by clinicians but are not widely used in practice. In the American Psychological Association's (APA's) 1998 Committee for the Advancement of Professional Practice survey on the effects of managed care on psychological practice, 29% of respondents reported that they used some type of outcome measure in their practice. Of these, 40% used a standardized method (e.g., administering the Beck Depression Inventory at multiple intervals), and the remaining 60% used nonstandardized methods of assessing client outcome (Phelps, Eisman, & Kohout, 1998). Hatfield and Ogles (2004) investigated provider factors associated with the use of outcome measures and concluded that clinicians are increasingly using outcome measures both because of the calls for accountability placed on practitioners by managed care and because of the usefulness of the information such measures can provide for treatment decisions.

EVIDENCE-BASED PRACTICE

Like nursing, medicine, social work, and other health care disciplines, psychology is struggling with **evidence-based practice (EBP)**. EBP has become a major movement calling on practitioners in all areas of health care, including mental health care, to use the best available scientific evidence as a basis for formulating treatments for individual clients. In cancer care, for example, EBP may mean informing patients about the most recent advances in chemotherapy and guiding them to the best type for their particular illness (DeAngelis, 2005). In psychology, Division 12 of the APA Task Force on the Promotion and Dissemination of Psychological Procedures created a firestorm when it published guidelines for evidence-based practice. The most recent update of the report (Chambless et al., 1998) lists 16 empirically supported treatments and 56 efficacious treatments (treatments supported, but with fewer studies). The empirically supported treatments (see Table 1.1 for a list) represent a range of orientations, including behavioral, cognitive, interpersonal, and family, although cognitive–behavioral and behavioral treatments are the most common. Each year's report has included a preamble that deals with issues related to the mandate of the task force or with reactions to its work. For example, the most recent report extended its review to include couples and family treatments for disorders, treatments for the severely mentally ill, and treatments within the field of health psychology. Critics of such EBPs argued that managed care companies could misuse findings to narrowly define EBPs and that the findings could give malpractice lawyers material with which to seek potential cases. In response, Levant (2005) wrote that by internally defining practice guidelines, psychologists can demonstrate their authority of the best treatments and avoid having them imposed by outside forces. Division 29 of the APA compiled a task force to examine empirically supported practices from a slightly broader perspective. Its findings emphasized the importance of considering the therapeutic relationship in research on empirically supported therapy (Ackerman et al., 2001). Elements of the therapeutic relationship that the committee found to be demonstratively effective include empathy, goal consensus between the therapist and the client, and collaboration.

Table 1.1 List of empirically supported treatments identified by Chambless et al. (1998)

Disorder	*Empirically Supported Treatments*
Anxiety and stress	Cognitive–behavior therapy for panic disorder with and without agoraphobia
	Cognitive–behavior therapy for generalized anxiety disorder
	Exposure treatment for agoraphobia
	Exposure/guided mastery for specific phobia
	Exposure and response prevention for obsessive–compulsive disorder
	Stress inoculation training for coping
Depression	Behavior therapy for depression
	Cognitive therapy for depression
	Interpersonal therapy for depression
Health problems	Behavior therapy for headache
	Cognitive–behavior therapy for bulimia
	Multicomponent cognitive–behavior therapy for pain associated with rheumatic disease
	Multicomponent cognitive–behavior therapy with relapse prevention for smoking cessation
Problems of childhood	Behavior modification for enuresis
	Parent training programs for children with oppositional behavior
Marital discord	Behavioral marital therapy

Source: Adapted from Chambless et al. (1998).

One problem that arises with conducting studies that determine EBPs is the incompatibility of psychological studies with research designs. The Food and Drug Administration uses randomized, double-blind placebo control group designs to determine which drugs will meet approval. This method has become the standard in fields as diverse as medicine, agriculture, and education. In fact, Chambless et al. (1998) argued that rigorous research methods are required to demonstrate treatment efficacy and document that any benefits observed may be reasonably attributed to the effects of the treatment and not to chance or confounding factors such as passage of time, the effects of psychological assessment, or unique client characteristics. In Chambless and Hollon's (1998) view, efficacy is best demonstrated in **randomized controlled trials (RCTs),** or carefully controlled *single-case research designs* and their group analogues.

Unfortunately, the limitations of RCTs have become increasingly apparent. Wampold and Bhati (2004), for instance, wrote that placebo-controlled groups are not suited for psychotherapy research because it is impossible for them to be blind; the psychologist would necessarily have to be aware of the treatment being administered during psychotherapy sessions. They also suggested that a psychologist who is assigned the noneffective placebo control cannot avoid communicating cues about his or her belief in the treatment. DeAngelis (2005) presented a compelling argument that such RCTs may present problems in **external validity**, that is, the ability of a treatment to work in real-life settings. RCTs' greatest strength is in demonstrating that a given intervention leads to a certain outcome by controlling for client characteristics and randomizing clients to different treatments. This methodological restriction, though, produces a very homogeneous client profile, resembling very little of the client variability often seen in practice. The unique client characteristics encountered by professionals poses serious problems for the generalizability of RCT findings.

In the subsequent chapters of this book we argue that single-case research offers substantial advantages over large-group designs, especially for scientists and practitioners working in applied behavioral and health care settings. Although single-case research has been enthusiastically endorsed by a number of professionals in psychology (Blampied, 1999, 2000; Kazdin, 1981, 1982b; Morgan & Morgan, 2001), nursing (Elder, 1997; Sterling & McNally, 1992), and rehabilitation science (Gill, Stratford, & Sanford, 1992; Gonnella, 1989; Joshi, 2000; Ottenbacher, 1990a; Zhan & Ottenbacher, 2001), the method has yet to be widely adopted within these professions. This reluctance may stem from several factors, perhaps the most important being that such professionals probably received the same training in research methods that their professors received, dominated by a focus on large-group research designs. Fortunately, research methodologists have reopened a considerable dialogue on the questionable hegemony of traditional large-group research designs (Cohen, 1990, 1994; Loftus, 1993, 1996; Wilkinson & The Task Force on Statistical Inference, 1999) and have encouraged the development of alternative strategies. Among these alternatives, single-case designs hold out unique promise for those charged with evaluating clinical interventions.

INTERIM SUMMARY

Managed care systems have changed the nature of insurance in the United States. Such systems have impacted consumers as well as health care providers, leading to a situation in which many practitioners are asked to justify the procedures they use with their clients. EBP encourages practitioners to utilize treatments that have been shown to be most effective by research and to collect outcome measures documenting that the treatment provided is effective. Traditional large-group research designs, however, are a poor fit with the practice of health care practitioners. Fortunately, single-case research designs offer with practical and valid strategies for empirically validating clinical interventions.

CONTEMPORARY THEMES IN SINGLE-CASE RESEARCH

In a perfect world, interventions delivered by health care professionals would be directly informed, perhaps even dictated by, current findings from basic research. Perfect worlds, of course, exist only in utopian novels, and the actual relationship between science and practice can be described only as an uneasy alliance. Although professional training programs profess commitment to the ideal of science-informed practice, practitioners report an altogether different reality. Psychologist Joseph Matarazzo, a recognized scientist and clinician, claimed some time ago that "few of my research findings affect my practice. Psychological science per se doesn't guide me one bit" (Bergin & Strupp, 1972). Such a statement is an alarming claim coming from such a notable **scientist–practitioner**, but it sheds important light on the contentious nature of the science–practice relationship and confirms what has become a widespread concern among professionals (Barlow, 1981; Stricker, 1992; Stricker & Trierweiler, 2006). This reluctance on the part of many health care providers to embrace EBP may be due to many factors. For example, the "clinical wisdom view" of practice has frequently been based on what the AMA Evidence-Based Practice Working Group (1992) referred to as (a) unsystematic observations from clinical experience, (b) valuing common sense over empirical findings, (c) a belief that clinical training and experience lead to effective practice, and (d) an assumption that wiser and more experienced clinicians are available for consultation. Unfortunately, all of these assumptions are grounded in a paradigm that tends to be subjective and is most often clinician rather than client focused.

Statistical Versus Clinical Significance

Perhaps one of the most salient factors leading to this disconnect between science and practice is the research training received by behavioral and health care professionals. This training has been dominated by the conventions of large group research design and the statistical methods used in such research. Of particular value to those professionals in training who will be delivering services to clients in applied settings is the distinction between statistical and clinical significance. Statistical significance, as we discuss in Chapter 2, refers to a specific probability that a calculated value of a test statistic, such as reflected in the difference between two group means on a dependent variable, is due to chance. If this probability is very low (usually 5% or less) and the study was conducted in a methodologically sound manner, then the results are said to be **statistically significant**, leading to the inference that the group difference was due to the independent variable.

For many practicing professionals, however, an intervention is significant, or important, to the extent that it produces a noticeable, real world change in functioning for the client. This standard, known as **clinical or practical significance**, has been recommended as a more relevant criterion for evaluating change than the purely mathematical criterion of statistical significance. There are, however, various ways to conceptualize clinical significance, and there exists no standard measure for evaluating treatment effectiveness in this manner. Despite this ongoing challenge, many applied researchers have argued forcefully for pursuing measures of clinical significance as being more appropriate and relevant than statistical significance within the clinical domain. As we discuss further in Chapter 4, single-case researchers have been frequent contributors to the dialogue on statistical versus clinical significance and have offered promising methods for assessing clinical or practical significance (Barlow & Hersen, 1984; Hayes, 1981).

External Validity and Traditional Large-Group Research Designs

In traditional large-group research designs, it is standard to assume that the research findings will generalize to people similar to the ones included in the study. For example, if a study examined 3,500 depressed women, then we take for granted that the results of the study would apply to a depressed woman encountered in another setting. However, this is not necessarily the case, because of the manner in which data in such studies are analyzed and interpreted. In traditional large-group research designs, researchers usually calculate group statistics by aggregating the data across all subjects, ordinarily producing group means. Separate means for experimental and control groups are then compared statistically to determine whether the clinical intervention was effective. However, these results, calculated at the group level, are meaningful only when applied to the larger population from which the subjects were sampled; thus, the study's group means are used to draw inferences about the means of the population. The results may or may not have any relevance for a particular client, and this is the dilemma faced by the practicing clinician. Even in a large group, individual clients will respond differentially to any treatment. The individual practitioner, whether psychologist, nurse, or occupational or physical therapist, is in no position to assume that an intervention shown to produce an effect at the group level will produce an identical effect for a particular client. To the extent that the findings of such a study possess external validity, such validity can be interpreted only at the level of the group, not the individual.

External Validity and Single-Case Research

Single-case researchers confront a slightly different issue regarding external validity. On the one hand, it might appear intuitive that the findings from a particular single-case study would have very little external validity, or applicability to other cases or settings. This characteristic of single-case designs is, in fact, frequently identified by authors of methodology textbooks as the most conspicuous shortcoming of single-case research methods. We tend naturally to be distrustful of small numbers, and so we might logically question whether the results of an intervention for one client would have any bearing on the effects of the intervention on other clients.

However, our ability to apply or generalize the results of any study is dependent on a number of factors, sample size being only one of these. Inevitably, questions about external validity often come down to such nuances as participant characteristics, such as age, gender, and ethnicity, and procedural details, such as the length, intensity, and competence with which the intervention was delivered. Many of these issues are as relevant to single-case research as they are to large-group research, although they are handled quite differently within these separate research traditions. Because single-case researchers tend to make little use of probability theory and statistical inference, their approach to establishing the external validity of a finding is quite disparate from the tradition embraced by group researchers. Single-case researchers, in keeping with the conventions of the natural sciences, endorse replication as the primary mechanism for establishing the generality of an empirical finding. Indeed, as we will see throughout much of this book, many of the designs used by single-case researchers are in part defined by strategies for conducting replications, both across multiple subjects and within the same subject over time. Replications of large group studies are difficult to conduct and require both considerable resources and time. The inherent flexibility of single-case research, however, makes replication quite feasible, and, as we will see in later chapters, most single-case designs derive their rigor from the ways in which such replications are conducted.

INTERIM SUMMARY

The distinction between statistical and clinical significance has been a contentious issue for decades, and it has very real implications for professionals delivering clinical services in the current managed care landscape. Single-case researchers have argued that this science-versus-practice gap has resulted largely from the conventional group research training received by most applied professionals. External validity, the extent to which research findings can be applied to subjects and/or settings beyond a particular study, constitutes a substantial challenge for any researcher. Group researchers tend to address this challenge through the use of large, representative samples of subjects or clients, whereas single-case researchers view replication as the most powerful and efficient method for ensuring the generalizability of findings.

KEY TERMS GLOSSARY

Managed care practices Any system of health care delivery aimed at controlling costs. Managed care systems typically rely on a primary care physician who acts as a gatekeeper through whom the patient has to go to obtain other health services, such as specialty medical care, surgery, or physical therapy.

Health maintenance organizations (HMOs) A type of managed care organization that provides health insurance coverage through contracted hospitals, doctors, and other providers. Unlike traditional insurance, the care provided generally follows a set of guidelines, typically allowing for a lower monthly premium.

HMO Act of 1973 This act provided economic incentives for the development of HMOs.

1974 Employment Retirement Security Act (ERISA) This law boosted HMOs by allowing employers an exemption to state laws requiring federally qualified HMOs to base premium rates on the health care costs of the entire community.

Preferred provider organizations (PPOs) Similar to HMOs; however, in a PPO care is paid for as it is received instead of in advance in the form of a scheduled fee, which may lead to more flexibility by allowing for visits to out-of-network professionals at a greater expense. Visits within the network require only the payment of a small fee. A primary physician within the network handles referrals to specialists covered by the PPO. After any visit, the policy holder must submit a claim and will be reimbursed for the visit minus his or her copayment.

Utilization review A process for monitoring the use and delivery of services, especially one used by a managed care provider to control health care costs.

Outcome measures Evaluate the success of a treatment by comparing the patient's behavior or progress with behavior at the beginning of treatment or at first assessment.

Evidence-based practice (EBP) Advocates using the best available scientific evidence as a basis for formulating treatments for individual clients.

Randomized controlled trials (RCTs) A study in which subjects are allocated at random (by chance alone) to receive one of several clinical interventions. One of these interventions is the standard of comparison or control. The control may be a standard practice, a placebo (e.g., "sugar pill"), or no intervention at all.

External validity When the findings of a study can be applied in other settings, under different conditions, or with different participants.

Scientist–practitioner A model of training and education leading to professional practice in which practitioners adhere to scientific methods, procedures, and research in their day-to-day practice.

Statistically significant A result is said to be statistically significant when the result would occur less than 5% of the time if the populations were really identical.

Clinical (practical) significance When a noticeable, real-world change in client symptoms or behavior is produced.

Replication The repetition of a research study to determine whether the basic findings of the original study can be generalized to other participants and circumstances

SUPPLEMENTS

Review Questions

1. Identify and describe two historical factors in the development and proliferation of managed care systems.

2. How did the HMO Act of 1973 and the 1974 Employment Retirement Security Act (ERISA) impact managed care?

3. What is EBP, and why is it so controversial?

4. What is the difference between clinical and statistical significance? Provide an example of how this might impact a health care provider.

5. Describe three problems with the use of large-group research for health care providers. How might single-participant research designs address these problems?

SUGGESTED READINGS/HELPFUL WEB SITES

http://www.pohly.com/terms.html
This Web site has a very comprehensive glossary for managed care terms.

http://healthlinks.washington.edu/index.jsp?id=e64464ae-50e1-4b89-b1d0-6c58f01b017f
This Web page is devoted to many issues relevant to evidence-based practice. Many links offer access to ways to calculate evidence measures, issues relevant to research methodology, and research centers that specialize in evidence-based practice.

Chapter 2

COMPARING GROUP AND SINGLE-CASE DESIGNS

Throughout the behavioral and health sciences, correlational and experimental studies dominate the research design landscape. Although differing from one another both with respect to the ability to control relevant variables and in terms of the kinds of inferences supported by the method, correlational and experimental designs share one very important feature: Both tend to employ large numbers of subjects or research participants. For this reason, both kinds of research strategy can be referred to as **group designs**. In group designs, the analysis of data (group means and correlation coefficients) and conclusions, or inferences, drawn from the study occur at the level of the group, not individual participants. In this chapter, we consider the history and underlying logic of group designs as used in behavioral and health science. We also begin to consider the ways in which group designs differ from single-case designs, the latter being the major focus of this book.

GROUP DESIGN METHODOLOGY

To illustrate the research process that ordinarily characterizes group designs, we describe a research project conducted by clinical psychologists. Zabinski, Wilfley, Calfas, and Winzelberg (2004) were interested in whether an online psychoeducational intervention would be effective in treating women identified to be at risk for an eating disorder. They began by screening female college students for eating disorder risk; students who met diagnostic criteria for an eating disorder were not chosen for participation but were referred to appropriate mental health professionals. A total of 60 students were eventually identified to be at risk of developing a disorder, and these students were randomly assigned to either a treatment group or a control group. Random assignment of participants to groups is important because it allows researchers to be fairly certain that the groups do not differ systematically on any important feature, such as intelligence, class rank, family background, and so on. The logic behind random assignment is that these other variables, which might impact the outcome or dependent variables, will be equally distributed across both groups. Thus, any difference between the groups on outcome measures should reflect only the effects of the independent variable, in this case the online intervention.

In many applied studies in health-related disciplines, clinical treatments serve as independent variables, factors intentionally manipulated or controlled by the researchers. The 30 participants in Zabinksi et al.'s (2004) treatment group took part in a psychoeducational program delivered on the Internet. These participants were provided with readings that covered important diet and other health-related topics, as well as weekly homework assignments built around this information, and they participated in a chat room discussion with other participants. The researchers anticipated that a combination of factual information and social support, the latter primarily generated through the chat room dialogue, would assist these students in reducing their risk of developing an eating disorder.

The second group of 30 participants served as a wait-list control group; that is, they did not receive the Internet intervention during the study, but they were eligible to receive the treatment after the study was terminated. To evaluate whether the Internet intervention was effective in reducing eating disorder risk, the researchers collected measures on several aspects of behavior and psychological functioning from both the experimental group and the control group at various stages during the study. Dependent variables measured during the study included self-report measures of behaviors predictive of eating disorders, self-esteem, and perceived social support. Because both groups contained many students, the researchers' first order of business was to find a way to summarize all of these numbers. This is ordinarily done through a simple mathematical calculation by adding all the scores together and dividing by the number of scores in the group. This procedure produces an arithmetic average, known as a **mean**. Then, because the researchers were interested in knowing whether the Internet treatment was effective in reducing eating disorder risk, the two groups' scores on the various dependent measures had to be compared. The answer to the study's question, as with so many studies carried out by behavioral scientists, comes down to this between-groups comparison.

Of course, we do not expect the two groups to have identical scores on any of the dependent measures (e.g., social support, self-esteem), any more than we would expect any two groups of people, chosen at random, to be the same on any particular characteristic, including intelligence, income, amount of formal education, and so on—that is, we cannot expect the two group means to be equivalent, *even if the independent variable (Internet treatment) had no effect whatsoever!* What we want to know, then, is just how big a difference there is between the groups, and how likely this difference would be to occur merely by chance, even if study method had no effect. The formal machinery for answering this question developed within the behavioral sciences in the first few decades of this century and has long since become the standard for designing and analyzing experiments in these disciplines. The general methodological framework for conducting science in this way is often referred to as **null hypothesis significance testing,** or **NHST** research. A discussion of this research tradition can hardly ensue without introducing R. A. Fisher, whose scientific contributions to behavioral science are considered unparalleled.

FISHER AND CROP YIELDS

During the 1920s and 1930s, Sir Ronald Fisher, a scientist trained in biology and mathematics, became enthralled by the mathematical regularities that seemed to characterize much of the natural world. One of the most important of these regularities, observed by many scientists even before Fisher's time, was that certain characteristics distribute themselves in nature in a highly orderly and predictable manner. For instance, suppose we were to measure height, in inches, in a large sample of, say, just over 1,000 adult women. After measuring this variable in all of our participants, we might want to know the typical, or "average" height of participants in our sample. As we saw previously, we can acquire this basic kind of quantitative information by calculating a simple mean for the variable of height. The purpose of this measure is to summarize the information we obtained. We wish, in other words, to boil down a large number of observations to a reasonable and interpretable number. As a single number that we can use to represent an entire sample, the mean is useful for this purpose.

Such statistics are frequently reported in summarized presentations of information. Suppose you were intending to relocate to another city in a different part of the country. You would probably be interested in learning something about the community and region to which you were moving. If you were to contact the Chamber of Commerce for that city, it would probably supply you with abundant information, some of it in quantitative form, describing the community and local region. You might, for example, learn that the average temperature during the month of July is 85° and that the region receives an average yearly snowfall of 65 inches. You might also discover that the average income for residents of this city is $22,500 per year. Of course, you recognize that these are just representative numbers. They don't describe specific instances of these phenomena with precision, only general tendencies. Nevertheless, the information helps you to familiarize yourself with some of the general features of the new region and perhaps helps you to prepare for the relocation.

Suppose, in the preceding example, we were to discover that the average woman in our sample stood 64 inches (5 feet, 4 inches) tall. This number clearly does not represent every person in the group. In fact, it is possible, because the mean is a mathematically derived number, that no single person in the group stands exactly 64 inches tall. What we would expect to find, however, is that a relatively large percentage of persons in our sample will be close to 64 inches in height, some slightly taller, some slightly shorter. In fact, most members of our sample will probably fall within a couple of inches above or below the mean of 64 inches. However, as we move further away from this mean height, we will encounter fewer members. In other words, although we expect that many women stand 65 or 66 inches tall, as we approach 70 inches (5 feet, 10 inches), we expect fewer. Once beyond 6 feet (72 inches), very few members of our sample should remain. The same is true, of course, on the other end of the spectrum. Although we would anticipate some of our group to stand less than 64 inches, the further below this mean we go, the fewer women we expect to encounter.

What we eventually end up with in this kind of exercise is a variable—in this case, adult female height—that distributes itself in a fairly symmetrical manner about a mean of 64 inches. This symmetrical distribution, characteristic of many features observed in nature, is referred to as a **normal curve, or normal distribution.** As you can see in Figure 2.1, the majority of participants in our sample fall close to the mean of 64 inches, and as we move further away from this mean on either side, the number and proportion of participants become fewer. This is an important feature of normal distributions because it allows us to determine how likely, or probable, any particular measure is in the distribution. For example, 65 inches is just one inch beyond our mean, and because it represents a small departure from the average height, we see this as a fairly likely outcome. Thus, being 65 inches tall is a fairly probable event, and we would expect perhaps several observations of women this tall. On the other hand, a height of 75 inches is markedly different from our mean. Consequently, the probability that any one member of our sample is 75 inches tall is very low, because this is an unlikely, though not impossible, occurrence.

One of the advantages of normally distributed variables is that we can calculate the likelihood, or probability, of obtaining any particular measurement from our sample. Obviously, the further away from the group mean a particular score is, the less probable its occurrence. Essentially the same logic is used in group research designs when comparing participants in experimental and control groups on some outcome or dependent measure. Although the details of doing so get somewhat more complex than this, we still end up utilizing the properties of the normal curve

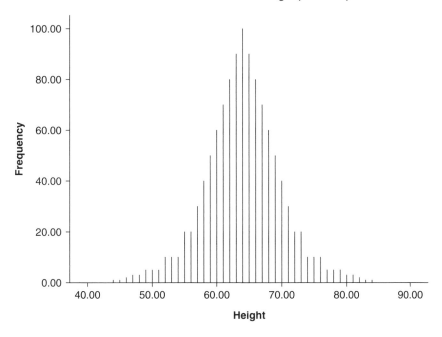

Figure 2.1   Normal curve of adult female height

to draw conclusions about the effects of independent variables. The larger the difference between group means, the less probable this outcome and the more convinced we are that the difference is due to our independent variable, as opposed to mere chance or random error. Thus, the normal curve has proved to be an immensely useful tool in the conduct of research in the behavioral sciences.

Among the first applications of the normal curve to scientific research was Fisher's application to agricultural science. Fisher and his colleagues devised several statistical tests, all founded on the basic properties of the normal curve, that allowed agriculturists to study the effects of numerous variables, such as soil characteristics, fertilization, watering schedule, and so on, on crop productivity. In such research, two crops containing the same plant (e.g., corn) would be grown under identical conditions with the exception of the independent variable of interest; that is, one crop might be treated with a new fertilizer while the other crop received no special fertilization at all. At some predetermined time, the crops would be compared with respect to yield. Of interest in such a comparison is the overall or total yield of a particular crop, not comparisons of individual plants. It makes sense that an agriculturist would benefit from information about how to increase crop yield through changes in fertilization, watering practices, and so on.

THE NULL HYPOTHESIS

Other researchers came to see the value of the statistical methods used in agricultural research and considered how they might be applied as well to the behavioral sciences. By the late 1930s, the formal research design and decision-making machinery introduced by Fisher had become a mainstay of psychology and related fields. Although today's researchers have at their disposal an array of statistical tools (particularly in the form of high-powered computer programs) that would have been the envy of Fisher and his contemporaries, the formal logic driving data analysis in the behavioral sciences has not changed since Fisher's revolutionary contributions.

Whether comparing crop yields—or, in our case, group means on a scholastic test—data analysis in the Fisherian tradition reduces to evaluation of the researcher's hypothesis about the subject matter. A **hypothesis** is a testable statement about the relation between variables. The purpose of conducting a formal research project in the Fisherian tradition is to assess whether one's formal hypothesis is tenable. In the case of the Internet eating disorder treatment study, the researchers' hypothesis suggests that measures of social support, self-esteem, and eating disorder risk will be related to the independent variable (treatment or no treatment) in some systematic way. We can, of course, propose as specific a hypothesis as we feel confident in making. For instance, perhaps the researchers believe that students who receive the Internet treatment will demonstrate higher self-esteem after treatment than those in the control group. We would therefore expect that the mean self-esteem score for the Internet treatment group would be higher than the mean self-esteem score for the control group.

In the Fisherian tradition, the results of the Internet treatment study will be evaluated not against any specific experimental hypothesis but against the **null hypothesis**, which suggests that there will be no difference between the groups on any of the dependent measures, such as self-esteem or eating disorder risk. In other words, the null hypothesis states that treatment will have no effect on the various outcome measures. Clearly, the researchers believe otherwise, or they would have no reason to conduct the study in the first place. Researchers, then, are in reality attempting to reject the null hypothesis, or show it to be false. In doing so, they provide support for the original research hypothesis, that Internet treatment will influence outcome or dependent measures.

In actuality, the null hypothesis doesn't really refer to what the researchers would expect to find among their specific sample of students. Instead, it refers to the entire population from which the sample has been selected, all college students. Researchers operate as if the study were actually being carried out on the complete population of college students, which would probably number in the hundreds of thousands. This is important, because the researchers obviously are not conducting the study because they believe their results are meaningful only to their students. Instead, they think that online interventions may prove effective in reducing eating disorder risks in large numbers of people and that this knowledge may be very broadly applied. The null hypothesis states that, at the population level, there would be no difference between groups on the dependent variable as a function of treatment versus no treatment. In demonstrating that their sample means are in fact different, the researchers are in effect casting doubt on the validity of this null hypothesis.

STATISTICAL INFERENCE

Testing the null hypothesis is a formal procedure that allows us to state, with some degree of confidence, that our independent variable had an effect on the dependent variable. If this turns out to be the case, then we will use the quantitative measures obtained from our study sample to draw conclusions about the effects of the independent variable at the population level. The act of using sample data to infer certain characteristics of a population is referred to as **statistical inference**. So how are such decisions made? Remember that in an experiment such as the one on eating disorder risk, we would not necessarily expect the group means to be identical if the independent variable (Internet treatment) had no effect. What statistical decision making comes down to is determining how likely it is that any particular difference between means would have occurred by chance, that is, not as a result of the independent variable but simply as a result of measurement error and individual differences. Researchers use probability theory and knowledge of the normal curve to make such decisions. Statisticians have created numerical tables containing distributions of test statistics reflecting differences in group means and their specific probabilities of occurrence. If consultation of these tables reveals a difference between group means that would occur by chance less than 5% of the time, then most researchers consider this to be sufficient as a scientific criterion for drawing conclusions. Such a result allows the researcher to be confident that the difference in means obtained in the study was not due to random error or chance, that is, the difference is considered to be *statistically significant*. Finally, if the study was conducted in a methodologically sound manner, eliminating alternative explanations, then the most probable interpretation is that the difference was in fact brought about by the independent variable (Internet treatment).

Needless to say, the actual statistical mechanics of testing the null hypothesis entail more detail than this account describes. Such detail, however, is not the primary focus of this book. Just about any basic book on statistics found in your college library or local bookstore will have adequate coverage of this material. The purpose of describing these features of group designs is to provide a benchmark against which single-subject designs can be compared.

INTERIM SUMMARY

Traditional group designs involve data collection from many subjects, often in the hundreds, and the use of inferential statistics to draw conclusions about group differences. This statistical strategy involves formal testing of the null hypothesis, which states that no differences exist between the groups. The purpose of statistical inference is to determine whether the null hypothesis can be rejected, thus indicating that differences between the groups were statistically significant. If the study was conducted according to strong methodological standards, then rejection of the null hypothesis leads to the conclusion that differences between groups were due to the independent variable.

SHORTCOMINGS OF GROUP DESIGNS

Group designs and statistical decision making have influenced the research process in the behavioral and health sciences for many decades, ever since Fisher introduced the logic of NHST. As a result, generations of social and behavioral scientists have cut their methodological teeth on the logic and tactics of null hypothesis testing. One unfortunate consequence of this fact, however, is that contemporary researchers tend to be somewhat myopic about research design, viewing NHST as the only way to conduct scientific research. Despite being a time-honored method of research in the behavioral sciences, NHST has its detractors, and research methodologists have directed increasing attention to the shortcomings of null hypothesis testing as well as the advantages of alternative data collection and analysis strategies (Cohen, 1990, 1994; Loftus, 1993, 1996). In fact, psychologists' discontent with NHST has reached such a fever pitch that a symposium was held at the annual convention of the American Psychological Association (Wilkinson & The Task Force on Statistical Inference, 1999) in 1996 to consider whether significance tests should be banned from their journals! No resolutions emerged from this provocative meeting, but a clear signal was sent that perhaps better methods might be available to behavioral researchers. Let's consider for a moment what all the fuss has been about.

The Meaninglessness of the Null Hypothesis

Many critics charge that the null hypothesis as a standard of comparison is of little value to researchers because it is almost invariably false anyway (Loftus,

1993, 1996; Meehl, 1978; Michael, 1974). Remember, the null hypothesis states that the population means, from which the researcher has obtained the observed group means, are equal. It is, in fact, nearly impossible that population means would be precisely equal, even if an independent variable had no effect on a dependent variable. Thus, we know that the null hypothesis is almost necessarily false, and this means that proving it to be so is not a very impressive scientific achievement. Indeed, psychologist Geoffrey Loftus (1996) claimed that rejecting the null hypothesis in most psychological research is like "rejecting the proposition that the moon is made of green cheese. The appropriate response would be 'Well, yes, okay . . . but so what?'" (p. 163). Moreover, a number of controllable factors influence how readily the null hypothesis can be proved false, the most salient of which is simply increasing sample sizes, which explains why traditional group researchers have historically paid so much attention to sample size.

You may recall, too, that rejecting the null hypothesis simply means that the difference we obtained between our group means is unlikely to be due to chance. Rejecting the null hypothesis *does not* tell us how large our effect is or whether this effect would make a difference in the real world. For this reason, critics of null hypothesis testing argue that we often end up asking the wrong question about our subject matter, especially when you consider that we pretty much know beforehand what the answer will be. Thus, Loftus (1996) suggested that the use of null hypothesis testing and statistical inference is "akin to trying to build a violin using a stone mallet and a chain saw. The tool-to-task fit is not very good, and, as a result, we wind up building a lot of poor quality violins" (p. 161). Some research methodologists believe that research in the behavioral sciences has placed too much emphasis on the goal of rejecting the null hypothesis at the expense of asking the more relevant question of "How big is the difference between group means, and what implications might this have for the real world?" Highly celebrated clinician and researcher Paul Meehl (1978) was perhaps most critical of psychology's dependence on significance tests and the null hypothesis testing tradition:

> I believe that the almost universal reliance on merely refuting the null hypothesis as the standard method for corroborating substantive theories in the soft areas is a terrible mistake, is basically unsound, poor scientific strategy, and one of the worst things that ever happened in the history of psychology. (p. 817)

The Limited Information Value of Aggregated Data

Perhaps the most conspicuous characteristic of group designs is the fact that the primary data in such studies are dependent variables summarized across many subjects. As we have seen, the most common such measure is the group mean.

There is no question that a group mean, or *arithmetic average*, is easy to calculate and makes the business of evaluating many data points more manageable, but researchers often forget that sample statistics, such as group means, should not be used to predict or draw inferences about individual behavior. The group means calculated in such studies are interpreted as estimates of the population group means only. They are not, nor should they be taken as, indicative of the behavior of any one person, even a member of the group on which the mean was calculated. As we have already seen, means can be quite unrepresentative of the individuals who comprise the group, and this is especially true when groups exhibit considerable variability.

Unfortunately, the temptation to use group means as representative of individual behavior, or as some kind of comparison or standard measure, is irresistible. For example, a typical textbook in developmental psychology may state that the "average" infant is able to walk unsupported at approximately 14 months. This fact may be viewed, especially by anxious first-time parents, as a rigid criterion or temporal milestone that must be achieved by all normal infants. Deviation from this mean, which is actually quite common, may be an additional source of stress or worry to the parents. At such times, it may be helpful to remind ourselves that a mean is simply a mathematical shortcut or economical way of reducing the variability that characterizes all natural phenomena. The biologist Stephen Jay Gould (1996) suggested that scientists are often too quick to render their observations in manageable, summarized form, while in the process neglecting to appreciate the inherent complexity and variability of the natural world. As a case in point, Gould pointed to the domain of evolutionary theory, in which genetic variability, produced both by sexual recombination and mutation, plays an essential role. Genetic variability is the raw material on which natural selection operates, and in its absence the very process of evolution would be unthinkable. Nevertheless, recognizing the importance of variability required a historic shift in perception, according to Gould:

> What can be more discombobulating than a full inversion, or "grand flip," in our concept of reality: in Plato's world, variation is accidental, while essences record a higher reality; in Darwin's reversal, we value variation as a defining (and concrete earthly) reality, while averages (our closest operational approach to "essences") become mental abstractions. (p. 41)

Gould reminded us that mathematical averages are convenient abstractions that allow us to make sense of large amounts of data but that often distort or misrepresent the individual case. The world is full of rich variation that often goes unappreciated in our haste to reduce multiple observations to singular, discrete measures.

Limitations of Single or Few Measures of the Dependent Variable

Clearly, a defining feature of group designs is the use of large samples of subjects, sometimes numbering in the hundreds. This ordinarily means that it would be impractical to take more than one or two measures of the dependent variable from each subject, because doing so would take unreasonable amounts of time and effort. As a consequence, group researchers ordinarily measure the dependent variable, after manipulating the independent variable, one time in each experimental and control subject. Even this practice can prove Herculean, depending on the nature of the dependent variable and the size of the sample. Recall, though, that the dependent variable is most likely to be an outcome measure of behavior or psychological functioning. Although perhaps unintentionally, group researchers, by measuring the dependent variable once, are treating the variable as a discrete, singular phenomenon (much like Fisher's measure of crop yield).

However, the subject matters of the behavioral and health sciences are anything but discrete. Behavior and psychological and physical functioning are highly dynamic and time-dependent phenomena, continuously waxing and waning from one moment to the next. In other words, we must ask how well a continuous subject matter can be circumscribed by so few observations (usually only one or two). Imagine, if you will, walking into a busy preschool for the purpose of observing the interaction between the children and the teacher and to get a feel for the overall ambience of the environment. Suppose you were allotted only a brief period in which to observe, say, the first 15 minutes of the day. To your considerable dismay, what you witness is utter chaos, with children running about the room, discarding coats and hats here and there, singing, and playing tag, all the while oblivious of the teacher's instructions to sit down and be quiet. Having made your observation, you bid the teacher good-bye (and, perhaps, "Good luck"), and leave the room. The important question now becomes *How do you summarize your observation of the classroom? What conclusions will you draw about the teacher–child interaction and the climate in the classroom?*

Perhaps more important, let's consider the teacher's perspective on this observation. Is there any reason for the teacher to be concerned about the conclusions that you might draw from your observation? Of course! First, she might be rather disappointed that you showed up at the beginning of the day, shortly after both she and the children had arrived. This is ordinarily a very busy, often frantic time, when children are making the transition from the home environment to the school. Lunch boxes need to be put away, coats hung up, greetings made, and other sundry matters attended to before settling down into a daily routine. In other words, the first few minutes of the school day may be the absolute worst time to be observing, *if one is interested in obtaining a representative picture of the behavior of interest*. The teacher no doubt would want you to hang around a bit longer to observe a larger sample of behavior and obtain a more representative picture of her interactions with the students and the overall classroom climate.

What this example suggests is that brief, discrete observations of behavior are likely to offer a distorted or, at best, incomplete picture of the subject matter. This is the case simply because behavior changes, sometimes quite dramatically, over time, and it is difficult to appreciate this natural ebb and flow if your measurement strategy does not allow for prolonged or repeated observations. The use of large numbers of subjects in group designs often precludes making multiple or long-term measures of the dependent variable. Were we not dealing with a continuous phenomenon that exhibits serial dependence and cyclic trends, this would not be problematic, but behavior, unlike crop yield, is a dynamic, continuous phenomenon whose natural dimensions seem to call out for continuous or repeated measurement. The structure of group designs ordinarily renders continuous measurement unmanageable.

Studying Numbers Rather Than People

Whatever else could be said about them, statistical significance tests are, in essence, devices used by researchers to help in decision making. We want to know whether an independent or treatment variable had an effect on some dependent or outcome variable. Much of the current controversy swirling around hypothesis testing and statistical inference has to do with whether these methods contribute positively to the business of scientific decision making. Jack Michael (1974) offered a very compelling argument that statistical techniques actually impair good decision making, in part because more intellectual effort is expended on evaluating the properties of the significance tests themselves than paying attention to the actual subject matter. Michael claimed that inordinate amounts of time are spent in professional and graduate education, training researchers in the intricacies of hypothesis testing, probability theory, and statistical significance, when this time could be spent putting the student into better contact with the actual phenomenon of interest. In addition, today's high-powered computer programs may offer a seductive alternative to the painstaking work of conceptualizing, operationalizing, observing, and measuring behavior. It is quite easy for today's scientists to get caught up in the bells and whistles of powerful and convenient statistical analysis while forgetting why the analysis is being conducted in the first place. Thus, some researchers may become more infatuated with the behavior of numbers than the behavior of organisms. The situation is analogous to the "gadget fanatic" who simply delights in any new technology, regardless of whether the technology proves helpful in completing a task or solving a problem. Much of this could be forgiven if statistical inference proved to be an indispensable tool for drawing conclusions in the behavioral sciences. This is clearly not the case, however, as attested to by the ongoing dialogue among research methodologists.

The limitations of group designs and the NHST strategy are by now quite apparent to many researchers in psychology and the behavioral sciences. Nevertheless, group methodology remains predominant in the behavioral sciences because most researchers were trained in its use and continue to teach the methods to their students. Researchers, like everybody else, get used to doing things the way they have always done them, and breaking habits and exploring new ways of doing things is always a challenge. Avoiding this challenge would be understandable if, in fact, there existed no alternative research strategy to group designs and NHST. This is not the case, however, as we will soon see.

INTERIM SUMMARY

Despite dominating the behavioral science research landscape for more than six decades, group design and its attendant data analysis strategies possess serious limitations. In particular, the improbability of the null hypothesis makes its rejection a rather weak benchmark of scientific progress. Also, the practice of summing behavioral measures across subjects and calculating group averages may produce artificial descriptions that misrepresent the degree of variability characterizing behavior. Finally, the practices of statistical inference have taken on a life of their own in the behavioral sciences, and some scientists believe that unjustifiable amounts of time and effort are spent training researchers on these questionable decision-making criteria, when instead more time should be devoted to learning about the subject matter relevant to one's profession.

PHILOSOPHY OF THE SINGLE-CASE ALTERNATIVE

Among the more fruitful outcomes of the recent dialogue concerning NHST research is an enhanced willingness by researchers to consider alternative research strategies. One such alternative, and the major subject of this book, is the *single-case research design*, also referred to variably as *single-subject, small n,* and *N = 1* designs. We use the moniker *single-case design* to describe this class of research strategies because, depending on the context, a *case* may refer to a particular client, a social unit, such as a family or a support group, or even to an institutional or organizational body, such as a group of employees. In most health care environments, the "case" would in fact be a client receiving some kind of medical or health-related service.

Although the single-case method represents one alternative to the NHST strategy, it is anything but a newcomer. In fact, single-case research was in use in the behavioral sciences long before the development of group designs and statistical inference, and it continues to make important contributions to the study of behavior, particularly in applied settings (Blampied, 1999, 2000, 2001; Blampied, Barabasz, & Barabasz, 1996; Morgan & Morgan, 2001). There is much more, however, to this research strategy than simply choosing to measure variables at the level of the individual instead of the group. In fact, single-case research design differs from traditional group designs along several dimensions, and these differences are reflected in all aspects of the research design, from observation and measurement, to manipulation of independent variables, to data analysis and interpretation, to the drawing of conclusions. Although we will have a chance later to examine these differences in detail, let's take a brief look at the more fundamental assumptions that inform single-case research.

Behavior as an Individual Organism Phenomenon

The pursuit of any scientific enterprise begins with some basic assumptions about the phenomenon of interest. How scientists view their subject matter has important consequences for methodological practices, including measurement, research design, and the drawing of inferences or conclusions. Among the most fundamental assumptions guiding single-case research is the recognition that behavior is a natural phenomenon that takes place at the level of the individual organism. Although we can speak of abstractions such as *groups*, *communities*, *societies*, and the like, much of what interests us about behavior is readily observed at the individual level. Individual organisms, after all, must solve certain problems in order to survive, including the acquisition of food and water, safety from predators or the elements, and selection of a mate for purposes of reproduction. These are universal requirements of all biological creatures, and while you and I as humans may achieve them through very different means than do other animals, we all do so only through behaving or acting on the world around us.

The study of human behavior is necessarily an enormous undertaking because it includes every activity imaginable, from simplistic actions, such as reflexively blinking when encountering a bright light, to complex activity, such as programming a computer. The entirety of human experience, including all of our thoughts, emotions, and actions, is open to investigation. However, it is essential to understand that our unit of analysis, *at least within the behavioral sciences*, is the individual. Even when we study group behavior, such as decision making in a jury, most of our observations will be made initially at the level of the individual—and it is at precisely this level that most human service personnel intervene in human behavior. The clinical psychologist treating a client's snake phobia, the home care nurse teaching a patient to operate his or her own intravenous equipment, and the physical therapist assisting an accident victim in relearning physical movements are all contributing to the adaptive behavior of their individual clients.

Keep in mind, too, that behavior is a fairly inclusive concept. Although for methodological reasons many behavioral scientists have restricted their observations to overt, readily observable behavior, we well recognize the importance of the less conspicuous processes of thinking, imagining, and feeling. Over the years, researchers have developed some ingenious ways of enhancing the accessibility to scientific scrutiny of these covert processes, referred to by Skinner (1953) as *private events*. Through self-report instruments, explicit training in self observation and self-monitoring, and even through sophisticated scanning technology, previously hidden dimensions of behavior have increasingly been opened up to analysis. An important point about all of these developments, however, is that they reflect advances in our ability to observe, measure, and record activity at the level of the individual organism.

Clearly, the most apparent feature of single-case research is that observation and measurement always take place at the level of the individual subject. Of course, this is also true of group designs. Except under highly unusual circumstances—perhaps if one is measuring, in decibels, the total noise level of a crowd—most observation and measurement in the behavioral and health sciences are initially conducted at the level of the individual subject. It is common, however, in group designs, to combine the individual data from all participants in the research, usually by calculating means or other quantitative summary measures. These aggregate measures are then treated statistically during the data analysis phase of the study. Finally, in such research it is understood that the conclusions are to be applied only at the group level, not to individuals. For example, in the experiment on eating disorder risk, the results demonstrated that the group of participants who received the Internet treatment improved on several dependent measures relative to members of the control group. This improvement, however, manifested itself only in differences between the group means on relevant measures, such as self-esteem and social support. These group differences do not allow the researchers to make any specific statements about individuals within the groups. In other words, just because the treatment group showed increased self-esteem after treatment does not mean that every person in that group benefited from treatment on this measure or that members of the control group did not evidence increases in self-esteem.

Unlike group designs, single-case research designs do not involve aggregation of data across multiple participants for the purpose of creating group statistics. Data collection, analysis, and presentation are all conducted on individual data only, and summary measures are not calculated across subjects. In this way, single-case designs avoid the problem of referring to the "average" subject, because this label is understood to reflect only the abstract consequence of a somewhat arbitrary mathematical calculation.

It is important to keep in mind that the phrase *single-case research* does not mean that only *one* subject participates in the study. The designation *single case* simply means that all data collection and analysis are conducted on the data from individual subjects, not at the group level. Actually, several subjects may serve in a single-case research study and, in fact, most single-case research studies include more than one subject. The participation of more than one subject is crucial if researchers are to reach conclusions that can be broadly applied. Only when the effect of an independent variable can be shown over and over again, through experimental replication, will such an effect take on the status of a general principle or law. Science relies quite heavily on the replication of important findings. We will have more to say later on the special place of replication in single-case research.

Measurement Must Be Sensitive to Behavioral Continuity

In addition to occurring at the individual level, behavior also manifests itself continuously. Learning to ride a bicycle, writing a term paper, discussing discipline with a teenager, studying for an exam, and practicing therapeutic exercises are all quite difficult to conceive of as discrete events, and for very good reason: They are not discrete, one-time occurrences but dynamic events that unfold and change, sometimes dramatically, over time. It makes sense, then, to expect observational and measurement strategies within the behavioral sciences to take the temporal and serial dependence of behavior into account. Unfortunately, this has not been the case historically. A discrete group mean, measured at only one point in time, regardless of how many participants' data contributed to the calculation, does not adequately reflect behavior's continuous nature. Instead, it is a little like looking at a single snapshot of a gymnast, frozen in time in the middle of a routine. The picture does little to portray the complexity and drama of the rapid changes of pace and sequential transitions from one difficult move to the next that characterize the full routine. For this reason, single-case researchers believe the discrete measurement practices of group designs are ill founded within the behavioral and health sciences, not because such measurement is inherently poor but because it does not sufficiently map onto a continuous, dynamic phenomenon such as behavior.

The logic of single-case research mandates that researchers observe and measure behavior as continuously as possible within the practical constraints of any particular study. Continuous measurement is advantageous for several reasons, perhaps the most important being the fact that many variables, including those that might be explicitly manipulated by the researcher, affect behavior differently with continued exposure. Many therapeutic regimens, in particular, produce their effects unevenly over the course of treatment. As a result, the nature and intensity of the treatment itself may have to be adjusted in response to the client's level of improvement. Such moment-to-moment adjustments are not possible in designs that employ single outcome measures.

Continuous measurement also serves the purpose of ensuring the representativeness of our data. Many natural phenomena, including behavior, exhibit cycles or fluctuations over time (Beasley, Allison, & Gorman, 1997). For example, suppose a corporate executive named Bob, on the advice of his physician, decides to begin an exercise regimen. He decides to walk a trail near his workplace during each day's lunch break and to walk in his neighborhood on weekends. Unfortunately, standard meetings that occur every Tuesday and Thursday prevent walking on those days. Therefore, a graph of the number of miles Bob walked each day over a 2-week period might look something like Figure 2.2. Notice that the distance walked ranges from a low of 0 miles to a high of 4 miles. This means that if we were to take any one day's measure as an accurate representation of the typical amount of walking Bob has done, we would have to conclude that he either walks a good deal (2–4 miles) or not at all. Neither of these single measures seems to do a very good job of capturing or representing the behavior of interest. On the other hand, measuring and recording the behavior every day allows us to follow the natural pattern this behavior exhibits and to appreciate the typical fluctuations that characterize any behavior when viewed through a temporal window. This measurement scheme helps us to see the process by which behavior change comes about, not just the end product. Also, this fairly refined observational strategy often proves useful in identifying naturally occurring moderating variables, some of which may serve as independent variables in a treatment regimen.

Participants Serve as Their Own Controls

Remember that in group designs the effects of a manipulated independent variable are assessed by comparing group means on the dependent variable of interest. This between-groups comparison is evaluated statistically to determine whether such a difference could have occurred by chance, or if something other than chance was operating. If all procedural aspects of the study, including the elimination of extraneous variables, were properly conducted, then that something else, within a certain degree of probability, was the independent variable.

In single-case research, group means are not even calculated, so between-group mean comparisons are not possible. What are available, however, are several

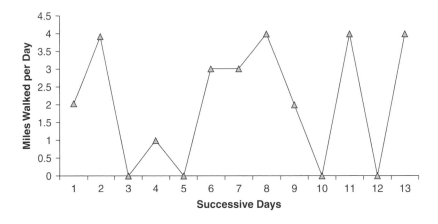

Figure 2.2   Bob's walking distance

measures of the dependent variable for each subject, obtained both prior to and during or after intervention. Thus, the meaningful comparison in this type of design is between the same person's behavior at different times. To some extent, single-case designs resemble, in logic, the before-and-after portraits of patients presented in testimonials or advertisements for weight loss, hair replacement, and other clinical treatment programs. Because different patients begin such a program at different levels of the dependent variable (e.g., different weights), simply calculating a group mean can be somewhat misleading. A weight loss of 18 pounds may be rather inconsequential to someone who begins a program at 350 pounds but considered quite respectable for someone who begins the program at 169 pounds. Collecting the data for each individual and having each person serve as the benchmark against which to measure his or her own amount of change offer a more refined assessment than that provided by group averages. There will, of course, be differences between subjects on any measure of change, but such differences are at least easily observed in single-case designs. They are obscured by group averages in group designs, and only a purposeful analysis of individual data will reveal these differences in such a study.

Drawing Inferences in Single-Case Research

In group designs we wish to draw conclusions about the larger population from which our sample was taken. We do so using statistical tests that take advantage of well-known mathematical properties of normal curves. It is important to understand, however, that the inferences we draw hold true only at the group level; that is, if the study on eating disorder risk demonstrates improvement for participants who received the Internet treatment, then we can infer that such an outcome would hold true at the population level. In other words, we could conclude that the mean differences in improvement between the treatment and control groups in Zabinski et al.'s (2004) study are reflective of a similar mean difference in the population. This difference attends only to the group mean or average, though, not to individuals. As a consequence, we cannot really recommend the Internet treatment to any person at risk of developing an eating disorder, because the data do not allow inferences about individual behavior. We are on safe ground only so long as we discuss average group differences.

Because in single-case studies individuals are compared only with themselves under different experimental conditions, the most meaningful inference pertains to that subject. Instead of asking whether the difference between two calculated group means is larger than would be expected by chance, we want to know whether an individual's behavior following an experimental treatment is noticeably different from its pretreatment level. Although statistical techniques can be of assistance in making such decisions (Jones, Vaught, & Reid, 1975; Kazdin, 1976), single-case researchers seldom call on statistical inference to interpret data. Instead, the plotting of data on real-time charts, and pre- and posttreatment comparisons of variability and upward and downward trends in data, serve as the primary vehicle for data interpretation in this research tradition (Parsonson & Baer, 1986; Sidman, 1960). This graphic display of data is more reminiscent of the data analysis methods of the natural sciences than of the behavioral sciences. Indeed, B. F. Skinner (1956), among the most influential proponents of single-case research, often contended that the study of behavior was in fact a specialized branch of biological science.

Of course, at some level, single-case researchers want to draw the same conclusions desired by group design researchers. We are always interested in whether a particular finding will extend beyond our study sample, whether that sample included a handful or 1,000 subjects. The question of whether an empirical finding exhibits **generality**, or applies to subjects or settings beyond a particular research project, is a difficult one to answer. In general, the size of a study's sample will have little bearing on establishing the generality of a particular finding. Only through *replication*, the systematic repetition of a study, can the generality of a phenomenon be seriously confirmed or disconfirmed (Cohen, 1990; Sidman, 1960). In other words, both group and single-subject researchers must rely on the logic of replication to establish the widespread reliability of a behavioral phenomenon.

INTERIM SUMMARY

Single-subject research is informed by certain basic assumptions about the subject matter of the behavioral sciences, including the claim that behavior is best understood as a phenomenon that occurs at the level of individual organisms. Consequently, the single-subject method places a premium on observation and measurement of behavior in individual subjects. An additional assumption is that behavior is a continuous phenomenon, changing dynamically with time, thus justifying a continuous measurement strategy. Measuring behavior at the individual level also allows the subject to serve as his or her own comparison because behavioral measures can be taken prior to, during, and after manipulation of a variable or treatment. Finally, conclusions drawn from single-subject research seldom rely on statistical criteria, but instead on real-time data displayed graphically for each subject.

A BRIEF HISTORY OF SINGLE-CASE RESEARCH

We have already seen that single-case research actually predated the large-group research designs that would eventually become the norm in the behavioral sciences. This is particularly true of psychology, which was, prior to the turn of the century, closely aligned with experimental physiology. In its infancy, psychological science was a staunchly laboratory-oriented discipline because its practitioners were adamant about distinguishing the young science from the "armchair thought" experiments of philosophy. Only by adopting the trappings of "real science," including laboratory preparations, instrumentation, and objective empiricism, could psychology be taken seriously as a scientific discipline. In addition, many of psychology's early pioneers were trained in the scientific methods of biology and physiology.

Early Experimental Psychology

Among the earliest formal psychological experiments were studies of the various human senses and their capabilities. Two German scientists, Ernst Weber (1795–1878) and Gustav Fechner (1801–1887), established many of psychology's first quantitative principles by mapping out the sensory thresholds for vision, audition, and touch. Because such studies require the presentation of various amounts of stimulation to the subject over lengthy experimental sessions, large-group studies are often impractical. Indeed, the study of sensory thresholds, known as **psychophysics**, is still dominated by single-case designs. Among the fascinating topics being addressed by contemporary psychophysicists are the sensory capacities of many nonhuman animals, as well as the practical benefits accruing from such knowledge. A case in point is the government and/or police trained canine whose tremendous olfactory abilities allows it to detect minuscule amounts of illicit drugs like cocaine, heroin, and marijuana; materials used in explosives; and even the ink on illegal bank notes. Using single-case methodology and a sophisticated combination of psychophysical techniques and operant conditioning, scientists have trained dogs to identify illegal substances and, perhaps just as important, disregard irrelevant stimuli, in such busy environments as schools, airports, and office buildings. These animals are so well trained and so skilled that they often thwart ingenious criminals, such as the smugglers who placed heroin inside concrete statues (Wren, 1999). In fact, these animals have proven to be both more sensitive and more reliable in detecting substances than are computerized electronic detectors (Wren, 1999).

The first laboratory-based study of human memory can also be traced to Germany and the work of Hermann Ebbinghaus (1850–1909). Ebbinghaus (1885/1913) created the nonsense syllable, three-letter nonword combinations (*dal, fep, bil, hos,* etc.) that possessed no pre-experimental meaning. This was an important methodological innovation because Ebbinghaus was interested in how novel material is processed in memory, and conventional words would have been contaminated by previous associations and usage.

Ebbinghaus then rehearsed a series of such nonsense syllables until he could recite the list without error. Thus, he could quantify how frequently a list of given length had to be rehearsed in order to commit the list to memory. Ebbinghaus also studied how learning one list affected the learning of subsequent lists, leading to the discovery of what is referred to today as *interference effects*. He was also able to track the amount of forgetting that occurs as a function of time, length of list, and other variables. Ebbinghaus's research, carried out in the 1880s, represented the first systematic effort to identify the lawful properties of human memory, and he served by himself as the sole subject in this research. Indeed, for this reason his research program may represent the most pure instance of single-case research in psychology's history. Impressively, many of Ebbinghaus's basic findings hold up remarkably well more than a century later, serving as ample testimony not only to his scientific ingenuity and rigor but also to the strength of the single-case method.

Behavior Analysis and Cognitive Psychology

Although eclipsed in popularity by large-group research and statistical inference during the 1920s and 1930s, the single-case method retained a strong cadre of proponents and practitioners within psychology. Particularly ardent support for the method would come from the field of behavior analysis and its articulate and influential spokesman, B. F. Skinner (1904–1990). As a psychology graduate student at Harvard in the late 1920s, Skinner wrestled with the problem of research design in psychology as he studied fundamental learning processes in nonhumans. A wonderful, often-humorous account of Skinner's (1956) development as a scientist includes a description of the various laboratory instruments this eminent scholar created to study learning in individual organisms, including the famous instrument which bears his name, the Skinner box. Skinner eventually became frustrated not only by the impracticality of monitoring the behavior of many different subjects during learning experiments but also by psychology's growing tendency to group data from many subjects together for the purpose of calculating average scores. Skinner was of the opinion that this aggregation of data actually obscured the nature of the learning process by producing smooth, gradual learning curves that failed to represent the complexity of learning. Arguing that psychology was a natural science, Skinner chose instead to observe and record the behavior of a single subject over the course of long experimental sessions, both prior to and after the manipulation of experimental variables.

Over the course of several decades, Skinner and his students accumulated large amounts of data representing the orderly effects of independent variables on various dimensions of behavior. Despite the orderliness of the data and the rigorous experimental conditions under which they were collected, Skinner and his colleagues had difficulty getting their work published in major psychological journals, largely because of the reluctance of editors to publish reports of studies based on data from single subjects. By the 1930s and 1940s, null hypothesis testing and statistical inference were standard aspects of most psychological research, and the idea of conducting an experiment with fewer than 30 or 40 subjects was viewed with considerable disdain. In response to this rather politicized climate of scientific publishing, Skinner and his colleagues established the *Journal of the Experimental Analysis of Behavior* (*JEAB*) in 1958. *JEAB* eventually became one of experimental psychology's most prestigious journals. To this day, *JEAB* remains the primary outlet for research on operant behavior (e.g., reinforcement, punishment, extinction, stimulus control) and publishes only articles in which the data from individual organisms are presented without aggregation.

Behavior analysts have not been alone in their endorsement of single-case research within psychology. In 1972, Newell and Simon published a landmark book in cognitive psychology, *Human Problem Solving*, which outlined both a theory and detailed methodological strategies for studying problem solving. An interesting feature of their method was the intense analysis of individual subjects attempting to solve an experimenter-imposed problem. Newell and Simon used a process known as **protocol analysis**, in which a participant verbalized his or her moment-to-moment decisions and strategies throughout a problem-solving session. Thus, a written transcript of the participant's verbalizations served as the primary data in this research and, for obvious reasons, Newell and Simon refrained from combining the transcripts of multiple participants for purposes of analysis.

Protocol analysis represents an important example of how researchers must develop observational and measurement strategies that respect the natural dimensions of their subject matter. Newell and Simon were not merely interested in whether their participants solved the problem; instead, they wished to examine the thoughts, decision criteria, and detailed strategies the participants used throughout the experiment. In other words, they were interested in studying the process, not product, of problem solving. This required a data collection procedure that allowed for ongoing measurement, because problem solving is inherently a continuous process, in which responses and decisions made at one juncture affect later responses and options. Rather than producing a discrete and uninformative group mean, *protocol analysis* offers a refined and detailed account of the dynamic interplay between the subject and the problem space. Protocol analysis would eventually become a standard procedure for the study of human problem solving (Ericsson & Simon, 1984).

Case Studies and Clinical Psychology

A focus on the individual case has played an integral role in the health sciences, particularly psychiatry and clinical psychology. Serving an especially instructive role in the professional literatures of these disciplines is the **case study**, a detailed description of diagnosis, treatment, and outcome for a particular client. Information in a case study is often very thorough, including family background, history of illness, possible precipitating factors, and other information that helps to provide context for understanding the specific case. Also, case studies are often presented for cases that appear quite novel or unique in terms of symptoms, or that prove challenging or unresponsive to treatment. In general, case studies are usually published for their educational value and are often considered invaluable by individuals training in medicine and other health sciences.

It is important to note, however, that a case study is not, first and foremost, a research endeavor; that is, such written accounts ordinarily do not entail formal research design, manipulation of variables, and data analysis and interpretation consistent with that encountered in the scientific research literature. Nor is the purpose of a case study to discover some invariant principle of physical or psychological pathology or the causal relationship between a given treatment regimen and clinical outcome. Case studies are important to the extent that they help inform the practicing clinician of certain features of a disorder or its treatment that *may* be of relevance or help shed light on similar cases in the future. The primary limitation of case studies, at least from a scientific standpoint, is not that they represent a single case but that strong conclusions regarding cause and effect are not possible because of a lack of rigor in research design. In this sense, case studies are to be distinguished from the single-case research designs that are the focus of this book. As Aeschleman (1991) pointed out, single-case designs are experimental research designs that allow for a significant amount of control over relevant variables and consequently support scientifically sound inferences. Also, most single-case studies do not use only one subject. The relevant independent variables are manipulated, and data collected and analyzed, at the level of individual subjects, but in most cases several subjects serve in such studies.

INTERIM SUMMARY

The single-case research strategy has played a historically important role in the behavioral and health sciences. Indeed, much of the work conducted by pioneering experimental psychologists, prior to the advent of Fisherian designs and statistical inference, used single-case designs. More recently, both behavioral and cognitive psychologists, despite divergent worldviews, have benefited from studies of individual participants. A focus on the single case has also characterized the work of clinicians in both psychology and medicine, particularly in the form of case studies. In Chapter 3, we continue our discussion of single-case designs by focusing on observation. Systematic observation, frequently overlooked, is one of the most fundamental and critical components of the scientific enterprise.

KEY TERMS GLOSSARY

Group designs Studies in which data are aggregated across many subjects and inferences are drawn on the basis of between-group comparisons.

Mean An arithmetic average calculated by adding scores together and then dividing this sum by the number of scores added.

Normal curve A probability distribution of scores on a variable in which scores are symmetrically distributed about a sample mean.

Hypothesis A testable statement about a relationship between two variables.

Null hypothesis The hypothesis that no relationship exists between the independent and the dependent variables in a study. In a particular study, for example, sample data, usually in the form of experimental and control group means, are being evaluated against the null hypothesis that there is no difference between population group means.

Null hypothesis significance testing (NHST) A procedure whereby the null hypothesis is either rejected or accepted according to whether the value of a sample statistic yielded by an experiment falls within a certain predetermined "rejection region" of possible values.

Statistical inference The act of drawing conclusions about a population based on observed sample statistics.

Generality The extent to which the findings of a particular study can be extended to, or are representative of, the larger population from which subjects were sampled.

Psychophysics The study of sensory thresholds and stimulus discrimination in humans and nonhuman animals.

Protocol analysis A data collection strategy in which research participants describe, in written or verbal form, their strategies in real time during problem-solving tasks.

Case study A common nonexperimental practice in medicine in which detailed information is collected from a patient before and during the course of treatment.

SUPPLEMENTS

Review Questions

1. In group research, what is the purpose of comparing the experimental group with the control group? Also, how are group means calculated?

2. What does the phrase "Intelligence is normally distributed" mean? Why is the normal curve of use to researchers?

3. Suppose a researcher is studying a new anti-anxiety medication in a large group of people with social phobia. The researcher will be comparing a control group that receives a placebo with the experimental group that receives the new medication. What would the null hypothesis be in this study?

4. Why is the calculation of group means and the aggregating of data across subjects incompatible with the study of behavioral continuity? How do single-case researchers assess behavioral continuity?

5. What does it mean to say that subjects in single-case studies "serve as their own controls"? Describe how this concept would be exhibited in a single-case drug study similar to that described in Question 3.

6. A cognitive psychologist is using protocol analysis to study how children solve logic problems. Why would the psychologist not aggregate or sum together the data from several children for purposes of analysis?

7. How are case studies in medicine and psychiatry different from the single-case research designs described in this text?

SUGGESTED READINGS/HELPFUL WEB SITES

Leary, M. R. (2004). *Introduction to behavioral research methods* (4th ed.). Boston: Pearson.

This text is a very readable introduction to research methods in the behavioral sciences. The general logic of experimental design and null hypothesis testing is described.

www.tushar-mehta.com/excel/charts/normal_distribution/
This Web page offers descriptions and explanations of the normal distribution and its contribution to research methodology. The page uses Microsoft Excel exercises to demonstrate the normal curve and its relationship to such statistics as the mean and standard deviation.

Skinner, B. F. (1956). A case history in scientific method. *American Psychologist, 11,* 221–233.

In this engaging and at times humorous article, Skinner describes his development as a scientist, some of the apparatus which he created to study learning, and his rationale for developing single-case methods for studying behavior change.

Newell, A., & Simon, H. A. (1972). *Human problem solving.* Englewood Cliffs, NJ: Prentice Hall.

This groundbreaking work by two pioneers in cognitive psychology describes the use of protocol analysis to collect and analyze individual subject data. The book is important in arguing for a method of data analysis appropriate to behavior that changes over time (problem solving) and in recognizing the limitations of traditional group designs and null hypothesis testing.

Chapter 3

OBSERVATIONAL STRATEGIES

- A young child, home from school in the afternoon, lies in a field of grass and watches, with great attention, the varying cloud shapes passing overhead, imagining this one to be a rabbit, this one a dragon, this one a puppy dog, and so on.
- A corporate lawyer, sitting in traffic on the way home from work, gazes inconspicuously at the young couple on the park bench, noting both their devotion to one another and their indifference to the outside world.
- Standing frozen in time, a lone backpacker in Yellowstone National Park spies a grizzly sow and her cubs frolicking in a high alpine meadow.

These scenarios depict neither scientists nor activities that you would probably consider to be scientific or research oriented. Yet, in one very important sense, each person described was engaged in a behavior so fundamental to the scientific enterprise that it often goes overlooked: **observation**. All science and research begin with observation, and all observation comes down to seeing, hearing, or otherwise making contact with the world through our senses. In fact, the other business of science, from data collection and analysis to theory construction and the drawing of conclusions, would simply be unthinkable without observation. Of course, different branches of science utilize varying strategies and technologies for conducting observation. The biologist's microscope, the nurse's blood pressure cup, the neuroscientist's collection of imaging technologies, including functional magnetic resonance image or positron emission tomography, and the child psychologist's digital recorder are all specialized instruments developed for the sole purpose of observing some aspect of human behavior or physiology. In this chapter, we consider the kinds of strategies and technologies available to researchers in the behavioral and health sciences, as well as the many decisions that researchers must confront in order to render valid observations.

OPERATIONAL DEFINITIONS AND DIMENSIONS OF BEHAVIOR

The cloud-watching child, the couple-watching lawyer, and the bear-watching hiker were all engaged in observing their world, but their observations fall somewhat short of what we would expect from a scientist. First, all of these scenarios represent fairly spontaneous activity, not planned, organized efforts at observing or studying some aspect of nature. Scientific observation, on the other hand, is anything but spontaneous. Indeed, one of the central features of any research project is the amount of time and effort expended in determining both the conditions under which observations will be made and specific methodology or instrumentation that will be employed in the observation. Thus, scientific observation distinguishes itself from casual observation primarily in the degree of planning and organization it entails.

Operational Definitions

Part of the planning that goes into scientific observation revolves around the question "What will I be observing?" This may seem a simple question at first blush, but in practice it often bedevils even the most experienced of researchers. This is because while you and I observe and talk about the world on a daily basis, usually in casual conversations with friends, we are not often required to provide justifications for or detailed accounts of our observations. The scientist, however, is not so lucky. Because the results of a particular scientific study may influence institutional or government policy, public opinion, or the development of new technology, researchers are required to be very specific in describing their observational rationale and methods. In addition, clear descriptions of observation and measurement practices are essential if the study is to be replicated or reproduced by other scientists. This means that the researcher has an obligation, prior to conducting the research, to specify the manner in which variables will be defined, observed, and measured in the study.

The major vehicle used by researchers to meet this important requirement is the **operational definition**, a description of a concept or variable based on how it will be measured in the current study. Operational definitions differ in important ways from the formal or conceptual definitions familiar to you. For example, let's consider the concept of "aggression." *Random House Webster's College Dictionary* (1997) says that to *aggress* is "to commit the first act of hostility or offense; attack first" (p. 25). Although you might not find any glaring fault with this definition, it may not be very useful in a research study, because the actions to which the term refers are too ambiguous to observe and measure with any precision. Interpreting any particular behavior as aggressive using this definition requires that we understand the separate meanings of *unprovoked*, *attack*, and *hostility*. Let us consider some of the difficulties that arise in the process of using a definition like this for research purposes.

Suppose a child psychologist is involved in a study of aggressive behavior in preschool children. As a scientific enterprise, the observations that the researcher will be making must be clear and concise, not ambiguous or unclear. This precision is necessary if the scientist wishes to render the observations in a numerical or quantitative format. Science, of course, finds numbers very handy, in part because math represents a universal symbol system that can be understood regardless of the idiosyncrasies of a particular subject matter. In addition, math brings a certain precision to our observations that is lacking in ordinary language. You might, for instance, look askance at the politician who claims that the average family income in her district has "skyrocketed" during her tenure. Suppose that having looked at the actual numbers, you know that income has increased during this time period, but by a modest 1%, a fact that leads the incumbent politician's opponent to refer to the increase as "minuscule and unimportant." Sometimes numbers talk more clearly, if not more loudly, than words.

Let us assume that in conducting the study of aggression in preschoolers, the psychologist comes up with the following operational definition: "Aggressive behavior will include any open-fist hitting, shoving, or kicking directed toward any other child." The advantage of this definition is that it informs the researcher about the specific behaviors to be looking for during the study. In addition, because the behaviors are fairly discrete (a single punch or shove is pretty easy to identify separately), observation could readily provide simple counts or frequencies of the behaviors. The clarity of the definition and the ease with which observations can be quantified represent the primary strength of operational definitions. Moreover, the definition is simple enough that additional researchers wishing to replicate the study would probably have little difficulty doing so.

The following are some examples of operational definitions employed by psychologists, nurses, and occupational and physical therapists in actual research projects.

- Meza, Powell, and Covington (1998) studied *non-nutritive sucking* in a 17-day-old premature infant. Using a specially adapted nipple that was connected to a pressure transducer, the researchers were able to measure the *force with which the infant sucked* during different phases of the experiment.
- Hinderer and Liberty (1996) were interested in whether baclofen, an antispasticity medication, might impair *cognitive functioning* in spinal cord injury patients. Several cognitive tasks served as dependent variables, including one

in which patients were required to *count out loud consecutive integers as quickly as possible for 10 seconds.* Researchers recorded both the highest number reached and the number of errors made by the patient.

- Mattacola and Lloyd (1997) studied the effects of a strength training program on *dynamic balance* in patients with ankle injuries. Dynamic balance was measured using a single-plane balance board on which patients were to stand. The board could rotate around a half-round wood fulcrum, and the *number of times either side of the board touched the floor during an observation period* represented the dependent variable.
- Lejuez, Zvolensky, and Eifert (1999) studied the ongoing development of *anxiety* in participants who were exposed to unsignaled presentations of a noxious stimulus. Participants *self-reported their level of anxiety, from 0* (no anxiety) *to 8* (extreme anxiety) *using the Anxiety Sensitivity Index* (Reiss, Peterson, Gursky, & McNally, 1986).
- *Self-control* is often defined as the ability to forgo a small, but immediately available, reinforcer for a more preferred, but delayed, reinforcer (Logue, 1988; Mischel & Mischel, 1983). For instance, a child who *chooses not to eat a single cookie made available at the beginning of an experiment while waiting for three cookies at the end of the experiment,* would be said to be exhibiting more self-control than a child who impulsively eats the single, immediately available cookie.
- Tiger, Bouxsein, and Fisher (2007) measured the *latency* (amount of time elapsing between a prompt and initiation of the target behavior) in a patient with Asperger syndrome when given various verbal prompts.

Limitations of Operational Definitions

Operational definitions serve important observational, measurement, and communicative functions in science, but they are not without their shortcomings. It is pretty easy to see that in creating an operational definition, researchers end up balancing the benefits of precision against a loss of breadth or inclusiveness; that is, by declaring only certain behaviors as aggressive for this particular study, we necessarily omit other behaviors that might be considered aggressive, not only to other scientists but to nonscientists as well. No operational definition could possibly enumerate *all* of the behaviors in which a person could engage that might be interpreted as aggression. Suppose that a child was observed, with a mischievous smile on his face, pulling a chair out from under another child who had just begun to sit down in the chair. Would the behavior of the first child be counted as an instance of aggression in the study? Not according to the operational definition, it wouldn't. It is in fact seldom possible to create operational definitions that adequately capture all instances of behavior that are circumscribed by the more casual, ordinary language term. This is, of course, what gives ordinary language its beauty and power; words often denote a much larger universe of things than could possibly be observed or recorded precisely in a particular study. The use of operational definitions and technical terms within science is an attempt to provide scientific communication a clarity that is not always apparent in the vernacular, but it does so at some cost.

The specificity of operational definitions can have negative consequences beyond the confines of a particular study. If many researchers are simultaneously studying aggression, for instance, and each scientist employs a slightly different operational definition, comparing the various studies and reaching general conclusions becomes more difficult. Also, when scientists communicate their findings to the general public, confusion may arise if operational definitions bear little resemblance to the concept as it is understood by nonscientists. This fact may be partly responsible for the common criticism that scientific research seldom has any bearing on the "real world." Though perhaps a bit harsh, this reaction serves to remind scientists of the importance of attending to language and its implications for disseminating their work.

Dimensions of Behavior

The behavior of an organism is that portion of the organism's interaction with its environment that is characterized by detectable displacement in space through time of some part of the organism and results in a measurable change in at least one aspect of the environment. (Johnston & Pennypacker, 1993b, p. 23)

Contributing to the difficulty of fashioning useful operational definitions is the tremendous variability that makes up subject matter in the behavioral and health sciences. We are addressing, after all, everything that people think, feel, and do, and this covers an enormous amount of territory. Fortunately, in any particular study, only a small sample from this larger domain of activity will be the focus of attention, so the field gets narrowed pretty early on. In addition, behavior manifests itself along several dimensions, not all of which are relevant or even meaningful in every study. Nevertheless, it is important that the researcher give prior consideration to those dimensions of behavior that will be the focus of observation and measurement. Let us now consider what some of these dimensions are and how they affect observation and measurement practices in research.

Frequency and Rate. As we have already seen, one of the advantages of discrete operational definitions is that they allow us to count or give some numeracy to the observations we make. Giving mathematical or quantitative form to our observations makes for useful comparisons, whether they are being made within the same study or between different studies. The frequency with which a particular behavior occurs is but one dimension of behavior, but it is often a critical one. Sometimes what matters most about a behavior is how often it does or does not occur. In fact, frequency is often an attribute that helps us separate "normal," or adaptive, behavior from "abnormal," or maladaptive, behavior. For instance, we might expect people to wash their hands several times a day, especially after using the restroom or prior to eating or handling food. We do not, however, consider it necessary, or even healthy, to wash one's hands dozens or even hundreds of times a day. Yet this is precisely what happens for some individuals, diagnosed with obsessive–compulsive disorder, who harbor a severe fear of contamination. Such individuals will wash their hands so often that they remove the natural oils from their skin, often resulting in cracking and open wounds on their hands. This amount of hand washing clearly is not adaptive. It is not that the behavior itself is inherently problematic; in fact, it is an important component of personal hygiene. What makes the behavior problematic in this clinical syndrome is the sheer frequency of its occurrence.

You can appreciate the importance of frequency in much of your behavior. Missing work or showing up late is generally not cause for alarm, so long as it doesn't occur with great frequency. Parents often lament the fact that they seldom hear from their children who go off to college. It is not that any parents desire a daily phone call—imagine the effect on the phone bill—but neither do they expect to lose contact for the entire school year. Similarly, the extent to which diets or exercise regimens are effective strategies in improving health depends, at least in part, on their consistent application. Occasional deviations from a healthful diet are probably nothing to worry about, but if such deviations occur with sufficient frequency they will tend to negate the benefits of the diet. Similarly, engaging in aerobic exercise once a month is not likely to produce long-lasting or significant increases in cardiovascular health. In sum, many kinds of behavior take on their importance in proportion to how frequently they occur, and for this reason many applied interventions directly target this dimension of behavior for change.

By itself, simple frequency is not a very meaningful dimension of behavior. Knowing that a person washed his or her hands 100 times or that you missed work 3 times tells us very little, unless we know the time frame within which this frequency was generated. In practice, researchers do not merely count how often a behavior occurs (i.e., simple frequency or occurrences); they do so within a specific unit of time. This measure, calculated as a ratio of responses per unit of time, is referred to as a **response rate**. Washing one's hands 100 times over the course of a month would probably not be considered unusual, but doing so in a single day is another matter altogether. Similarly, missing work 3 days in a calendar year might not get you into hot water, but missing 3 days in one week could prove troublesome. Many research projects, both basic and applied, utilize response rate as a fundamental measure of behavior.

Duration. In addition to being countable, behavior can be thought of as taking up time; that is, we can consider the amount of time that elapses from when a particular behavior begins (onset) and when it ends (offset), a dimension we refer to as **duration**. Naturally, attending to the duration of a behavior implies not only that we have a good operational definition but also that we can readily identify when the behavior begins and when it ends. In addition, our observation and measurement strategy must be continuous, because we are trying to evaluate a fundamentally temporal dimension of behavior.

There are many circumstances in research, particularly in applied settings, where duration looms as the most important dimension of behavior. Developmental psychologists, for example, have long wondered what impact television viewing might have on the cognitive, social, and emotional development of children. In such studies, television viewing usually serves as the independent or predictor variable, and it is typically measured in hours of viewing per week or month. In many such studies, parents or children are simply asked to estimate a child's average amount of viewing per unit of time, which represents the behavior at a fairly global level. Nevertheless, reporting that a child watches approximately 13 hours of television per week presumes that the observer (parent or child) has sampled numerous "bouts" of viewing and has a good sense of how long each "bout" was. After all, the specific duration of a particular program will differ from that of another, depending on the type of program (e.g., half-hour situation comedy, hourlong documentary, 2-hour movie, etc.). Reporting an overall "amount" of television viewing means that the observer has summed all of these unequal time periods to produce a total measure of duration for the designated observation period.

Notice that what matters in many studies of television viewing is the overall number of hours watched, not how many times (number of occurrences) the person watches television. One child may watch television every weekday morning, but for only half an hour each day, whereas another child may watch only on Saturdays, but do so all day, from 8:00 in the morning until 8:00 at night! In a study measuring total duration, we would be attending to an irrelevant aspect of behavior if we simply counted how many times each child watched television during the week. On the basis of a frequency measure, the child who watched television every weekday would be seen as watching more television than the child who watched television only on Saturdays. However, if we attend to total hours, we would note that Saturday's child actually watched more than four times the amount of television than did the first child. The point is that researchers must decide, before implementing a study, which of several dimensions of behavior would be most meaningful for the particular study. In the present case, overall duration seems to better reflect "amount of television viewing" than does a frequency or rate measure.

From a strategic standpoint, the challenge of measuring the duration of a behavior lies in being able to recognize when a behavior begins and when it ends. In the preceding example, this may not be too difficult. For example, our operational definition might dictate that the behavior begins when the child turns on the television and ends when the television is turned off. Of course, observation and measurement are rarely this simple in practice. Prior to conducting the study, we would expect the researcher to decide how to deal with possibly ambiguous circumstances that could influence measurement. For instance, if the child leaves the room during a program to use the restroom or answer the phone, should recording of the behavior be paused? In other words, is this time period going to be added to or omitted from the overall duration measure? Similarly, in many homes the television is left on virtually throughout the day, for no apparent reason other than to provide background noise. How will this situation be treated for measurement purposes, particularly if a child moves in and out of the television room, unsystematically, remaining for varying periods of time?

There are no hard-and-fast rules for making these decisions. What matters is that researchers consider these kinds of issues seriously before beginning the study and that they apply their decision rules consistently throughout the study. If researchers fail to anticipate these types of events when operationally defining behaviors and developing systems to measure those behaviors, then substantial measurement errors and problems are likely to occur, and the integrity of the study may be severely compromised.

Latency. Another temporal aspect of behavior is **latency**, the amount of time that elapses between a particular stimulus event and the behavior. This particular dimension of behavior proves adaptive in many ordinary circumstances. For instance, the amount of time it takes you to get out of bed after the alarm clock goes off has implications for whether you get to work or school on time. Indeed, an alarm clock is a behavior management device the sole purpose of which is to help us coordinate our own behavior with respect to time requirements. Also, many contemporary hotels now utilize room keys that resemble credit cards. Opening your room door requires that you insert the key in a slot and, when a small light on the slot illuminates, operating the door latch. If you wait too long, the light goes out, and the door will not open. Thus, timing your behavior with respect to the light is essential to getting into the room. Finally, authority figures in many settings make requests of their charges, and prompt compliance with such requests is generally deemed desirable. The parent asking a child to pick up his or her shoes, or the teacher requesting term papers to be handed in, both expect compliance within short latencies. Failure to comply promptly with such requests from teachers, parents, or bosses can have untoward consequences for any of us.

The practical issues that arise when considering latency as a measurable dimension of behavior are similar to those that attend to duration. Both the onset of the stimulus that begins the interval and the occurrence of the behavior must be unambiguous. In addition, continuous measurement is presumed, because the temporal relationship between the stimulus and the target behavior cannot be assessed in its absence. Finally, as with any other measurement practice, operational definitions and specific observational and measurement decisions must be agreed on prior to beginning observation.

Intensity. One feature of behavior that ordinarily calls attention to itself is the strength or **intensity** with which it manifests itself. It is amazing, for example, how much difference modulating the volume of one's voice has on the likelihood that others will respond to what one says. Every parent has probably noticed that a simple instruction or reprimand offered to a child may go unheeded if delivered at a volume consistent with everyday speech. On the other hand, the same request presented at substantial volume may produce remarkable compliance. This is of course unfortunate, and few parents are proud of the fact that they may on occasion raise their voices to their children. Nonetheless, the lesson is a powerful one: Intense behavior gets our attention. Of course, the reverse can be the case as well. A wise preschool teacher may purposefully speak at a barely audible whisper in order to quiet down an otherwise-raucous group of students.

There are numerous other examples of everyday behavior in which the intensity or magnitude of a response may have important implications. Most of the time, we bring our cars to a stop by gradually depressing the brake pedal. However, stepping vigorously on the brakes may be necessary if the vehicle in front of you stops unexpectedly or if a child runs in front of your vehicle. Although other factors make their own contribution, how hard you swing a golf club has some relationship to the direction and distance the ball travels. The winning team on a tug-of-war match will be the one that exerted the most force on its end of the rope. A painter can change the width and texture of a brush stroke by varying the amount of pressure put on the brush. All of these examples testify to the importance of intensity as a fundamental dimension of behavior.

Although the intensity of a particular behavior is ordinarily conspicuous, its measurement is not always effortless, in part because behavior can differ in magnitude along several dimensions. Consider the example of the parent instructing or reprimanding the child and the counterpart of the preschool teacher trying to get students' attention. In both cases, the volume of the adult's voice could be measured on a decibel scale because this is a standard unit of measure for this particular dimension of sound. The other examples, however, allude to properties of behavior other than acoustic ones. A golfer, for instance, swings a golf club with a measurable force, and the braking, tug-of-war, and painting examples all allude to behavior in which varying degrees of pressure or *force* are exerted in pushing or pulling objects. These are clearly relevant dimensions of behavior that may partly determine whether behavior is adaptive or maladaptive in a particular setting. Measuring such properties of behavior, however, especially in nonlaboratory settings, is not always easy. Fortunately, technological advances have in recent years made possible more mobile and flexible measurement instruments, many of which are easily utilized in nonlaboratory settings.

Environmental By-Products or Permanent Products. Among the most important features of the definition of behavior offered by Johnston and Pennypacker (1993b) is the claim that behavior brings about changes in the environment. This may be so fundamental a point as to go unnoticed. Behavior, after all, is how all animals go about meeting their needs, from basic physiological requirements, such as food and water, to higher order accomplishments, such as earning a college degree. None of this would be possible without the ability to interact effectively with both the animate and inanimate features of the surrounding environment. It is in fact difficult to imagine any behavior that does not have some impact on the environment. The animal in the wild foraging for food will, over time, deplete a particular food patch, making additional foraging necessary. An infant kicking the side of his crib may cause the mobile overhead to move, then enthusiastically repeat the action dozens of times. Even simple, thoughtless actions, such as turning on a light switch or the television, putting food into a pet's bowl, and throwing trash out of the window of a moving car, all bring about consequences, or effects on the environment, that are of at least momentary importance to either the person engaging in the behavior or others.

On occasion, the activities of an individual will produce relatively lasting and noticeable effects on the surrounding world, effects we refer to as **environmental by-products or permanent products**. Although not behavior themselves, these by-products may prove useful to researchers as indirect representations of behavior, and they may be invaluable when the actual behavior of interest is inaccessible to observation and measurement. There are, in fact, many categories of behavior that may not lend themselves readily to direct measurement yet produce a tangible record of their occurrence. Littering is an example of a behavior that, because of its reprehensible nature, seldom occurs in the presence of onlookers. Nevertheless, the resulting refuse is not only visually conspicuous (this is in fact part of the problem associated with this behavior) but also easily collected and measured along numerous dimensions, including weight or volume. Many other unfortunate human actions, including pollution of the environment and vandalism, leave similar tell-tale signs of their occurrence. Directly measuring these behaviors is seldom possible, which also reduces any chance of attributing the behavior to specific individuals. As a result, research in which these kinds of by-products are measured is seldom idiographic in nature; instead, the collection of data is understood to reflect large group or nomthetic trends.

Behavioral by-products can, under certain circumstances, be a reasonable measure of behavior in individuals. An intervention by a health psychologist to assist a patient in smoking cessation will require some deliberation over the definition, observation, and measurement of smoking. The psychologist could, for instance, have the client count bouts of smoking, but how would this dimension be specified? Number of puffs? Number of cigarettes actually lit, regardless of how many puffs occur on each? Clearly, identifying the elements of "smoking" becomes a challenge, one that must be adequately met prior to beginning the formal study.

There is another possibility, though. A smoked cigarette, in the form of a butt in an ashtray, is a definite result or by-product of smoking. In a study of this nature, the researcher, or the smoker him- or herself, could simply count the number of cigarette butts lying in ashtrays at the end of a specified time period. This strategy is, of course, not without its limitations. If the client smokes in different environments—say, at home and at work—then measurement would have to occur in both settings. Similarly, if other individuals in the client's environment smoke, then some method will need to be developed to distinguish between the by-products of the client's smoking and those of others. This may not be too difficult if the client is the only person in that environment who smokes a particular brand of cigarette. In addition, one can utilize various marking procedures (e.g., a dab of paint or ink on the filter of each cigarette) that will make for more valid measurement. Finally, the researcher would have to realize that simply counting cigarette butts represents a somewhat crude measure of smoking, because such a measure cannot distinguish between which cigarettes were actively smoked (puffed on) and those that may have been left in an ashtray to burn down.

The purpose of this discussion of behavioral dimensions was to highlight the fact that even simple actions may possess numerous measurable attributes. Deciding on any particular dimension as the focal point of a specific study is crucial to the success of the research enterprise. There are seldom hard-and-fast rules for making these measurement decisions. From a clinical standpoint, measurement should be relatively easy to accomplish and consistent with treatment goals. From a research perspective, it is important that measurement decisions be made prior to formal data collection. Failure to do so weakens the integrity of the measurement process and severely limits the kinds of inferences that can be drawn from the resulting data.

INTERIM SUMMARY

Behavior is an enormously complex subject matter, in part because it manifests itself along many separate dimensions. Using operational definitions, researchers make explicit which dimensions of behavior will be observed and measured in a particular study. A common dimension of behavior is its countability, ordinarily expressed as response rate, which is the frequency of occurrence over time. However, there are times when temporal aspects of behavior are most significant. Measures of duration, or length of behavior from onset to offset, and latency, the amount of time that elapses between a stimulus and behavior, may prove more useful for certain research purposes. Behavior also varies in its intensity and often produces noticeable by-products that may be relevant to particular research questions.

THE PRACTICALITIES OF OBSERVATION

In addition to arriving at a manageable operational definition as well as the appropriate behavioral dimension to be studied, researchers must make decisions regarding the time and place that actual observation and data collection will occur. Such decisions are driven not solely by the empirical question at hand but by real-world practical matters over which the researcher seldom has control. Much of this lack of control has to do with the fact that applied studies are typically conducted in the environment of the subject or client, not an environment designed and built for the convenience of the researcher. Thus, observation may take place in a hospital, nursing home, or other health care facility, in the workplace, at home, or at school. Among the first issues to be resolved is whether the researcher will have easy access to the environment or certain restrictions will be placed on when and where observation will be allowed. This decision often is not up to the researcher but to the director or other authority figure within the institution; consequently, researchers must carefully design their observational strategy around any such limitations.

Because of observational limitations, all research projects operate with something less than all of the relevant information; that is, we put ourselves in the best possible position to acquire a useful sample of behavior, but we recognize it as a sample from a much larger domain of activity. What we are after is a representative picture or portrayal of the behavior of interest, and all of the decisions made regarding when, how, and under what conditions to observe should bear on this issue. When data collection is completed, we wish to be sure that we have adequately sampled the relevant behavior in our target subject or client and that the conclusions we draw are pertinent to this sampled behavior. In essence, research entails the act of periodically dipping into the continuous behavior stream and pulling out observations that will then be used to make decisions about the stream in its entirety. Let us consider how this is done in practice.

Interval Recording

Among the most common strategies for observing and recording behavior is a method known as **interval recording**, in which a specified time period is subdivided into shorter blocks and observation occurs systematically for each block. For example, suppose we were conducting a study of an office worker suffering from a severe case of carpal tunnel syndrome, a physical ailment involving damage to the nerves in the forearm, resulting in pain and restricted movement. Part of the rehabilitation program for this individual might be use of a wrist brace, which maintains the hand in straighter alignment with the forearm. Because the brace is effective only when worn consistently, we are interested in observing and recording whether the individual adheres to the treatment recommendation. Because we may not be able to observe the individual continuously throughout her workday, we establish an interval recording strategy for making the observation.

We begin by identifying a block of time during which observation will occur, perhaps from 9:00 until 10:00 on a particular morning. Then, this 1-hour block is subdivided into brief intervals, perhaps 30 seconds each. For each interval, the researcher simply records whether the brace is being worn or not. In other words, measurement is discrete; the target behavior is observed to either occur or not during each interval. For purposes of interval recording, researchers usually construct a simple recording sheet that contains boxes representing each interval placed side by side (see Figure 3.1). Recording of behavior is as simple as placing a check mark inside any interval box in which a behavior was observed to occur. At the end of the larger time block (1 hour), we will have numerous observational intervals, each depicting either the occurrence or nonoccurrence of the targeted behavior.

Depending on the goals of a particular study, a researcher may choose between two interval recording strategies: (1) *whole interval* recording and (2) *partial interval* recording. In whole interval recording, the behavior is scored as occurring only if it occupies the entire interval; that is, if the behavior occurs continuously throughout the interval, it is scored as an occurrence. The primary advantage of whole interval recording is that because the behavior occurs throughout the interval,

Client/Subject:

Observer:

Place/Time of Observation:

Target Behavior Operationally Defined:

Successive 30-second intervals

	:30	:30	:30	:30	:30	:30	:30	:30	:30	:30
9:00–9:05										
9:05–9:10										
9:10–9:15										
9:15–9:20										
9:20–9:25										
9:25–9:30										
9:30–9:35										
9:35–9:40										
9:40–9:45										
9:45–9:50										
9:50–9:55										
9:55–10:00										

Figure 3.1   Sample interval recording sheet

it is possible to also estimate the overall duration of the behavior. Thus, the whole interval scoring method gives only an estimate of duration, and obviously requires greater vigilance and sustained attention, because the observer must look for the behavior throughout the entire interval. In contrast, in *partial interval* recording the behavior is scored if it occurs at any point during the observational interval, but it does not have to occur continuously throughout the interval.

There are important limitations on the kinds of statements that can be made based on data obtained through interval recording. For both whole interval and partial interval recording, we cannot add intervals in which the behavior occurred to get a measure of duration. Nor can number of occurrences simply be added to calculate a frequency or rate measure. Instead, we must characterize the results in terms of the number or percentage of intervals in which the target behavior occurred. For example, if we observed the office worker in the current example to be wearing the wrist brace during 90 of the 120 thirty-second intervals, we could conclude only that the behavior was observed to occur in 75% of the intervals.

Because any interval recording strategy involves selecting a particular block of time in which to conduct the observation, we are necessarily limiting the breadth of our observational strategy and thus possibly limiting the representativeness of our observation. If circumstances permit, however, the researcher can opt for a strategy referred to as **time sampling**, in which several blocks of observation periods, alternating with nonobservation periods, are distributed over a longer period of time. In *momentary time sampling*, observations occur at systematic times according to an agreed-on schedule. In the office worker example, if we have the opportunity to make observations throughout the entire workday, we might decide to observe and record the target behavior every other hour, beginning in the morning and ending at the end of the workday. Perhaps our observational blocks will occur at 9:15, 11:15, 1:15, and 3:15. Each block will last for 15 minutes and will be subdivided into brief intervals (perhaps 30 seconds) during which a discrete measure will be recorded. In *momentary time sampling*, actual observation and discrete categorization of behavior (occurrence vs. nonoccurrence) occurs at the very end of each interval. Depending on the needs or practicalities of observation, observation intervals can also be signaled by devices worn by the observer. For example, observers can use a watch as a visual cue to remind them when to observe, or they can use commercially available devices that emit either tactile cues by vibrating (e.g., the MotivAider) (Levinson, Kopari, & Fredstrom, 2002), or brief auditory signals. Although simple to use, these devices are quite sophisticated and can be set to emit cues on either fixed or random schedules over the course of a prolonged observation period. The observer can then record the occurrence or nonoccurrence of the target behavior whenever the signal occurs.

Time sampling is a frequently preferred recording strategy in applied settings, because it does not require continuous observation of behavior. The strategy is especially useful when dealing with behaviors that might be expected to fluctuate in occurrence over long time periods. A time sampling strategy would, for instance, tell us whether the individual tended to wear the brace more in the morning than in the afternoon, whereas an interval recording strategy, if applied only in the morning, would fail to identify this variability.

The decision to use interval recording or time sampling is driven both by practical limitations and by the desire to acquire a representative picture of the behavior. It is important to keep in mind that the overall accuracy of the measurement strategy is also impacted by the dimension of behavior chosen for study. For instance, deciding simply to record the occurrence or nonoccurrence of a target behavior within a given interval is different from recording the frequency or rate of occurrence during the interval. A discrete unit of measure (occurrence–nonoccurrence) tends to underestimate how often the behavior occurs, particularly for a behavior that occurs at a high rate during any given interval. For this reason, if the behavior is known to occur at a high rate, shorter intervals are preferable to longer intervals. Similarly, discrete measures fail to capture temporal characteristics of behavior, such as duration and latency, unless these dimensions are explicitly included in the study's operational definition.

Clearly, the gold standard for behavioral observation and measurement is continuous observation. Although this observation strategy might be possible, such as when the participant is trained to self-monitor and record his or her own behavior, or when continuous videotaping is feasible, continuous observation is, more often than not, a luxury unavailable to applied researchers. Consequently, the observation strategy is most likely to involve some variation on interval recording. Fortunately, research has demonstrated that when intervals are kept quite short, in general 20 seconds or less, interval recording can produce **reliability** approaching that of continuous observation (Gunter, Venn, Patrick, Miller, & Kelly, 2003; Powell, Martindale, & Kulp, 1975; Saudargas & Zanolli, 1990). This is a good illustration of how, in any given study, measurement decisions can strike a reasonable balance between the pragmatic limitations on observation posed by the setting and the scientific need to produce accurate and relevant measures of the target variables.

Observation in the Behavioral and Health Sciences

Because science relies so heavily on measurement, researchers take very seriously those aspects of their study that bear on the accuracy and reliability of their measurement system. Measurement strategies or instruments that prove unreliable are of little use to anybody, especially the scientist. Imagine stepping on your bathroom scale early one morning and discovering that you weigh 172 pounds (you'll have to determine whether this hypothetical amount is an insult or wishful thinking for you!). You step off the scale for a few brief moments and then step back on. The second reading: 188 pounds. You conduct this mini-experiment one more time by stepping off and then back onto the scale. The third reading registers at 127 pounds. You likely will draw several conclusions from this experience, one of which is you have no idea how much you really weigh. The scale has shown itself to be a very poor measurement instrument, providing wildly fluctuating and, therefore, unreliable measures that you know are simply not possible. You may not know exactly why the readings were amiss. Perhaps the batteries have run low if it's a modern electronic scale with a digital readout, or maybe the spring mechanism has malfunctioned if it's an older instrument. It does not really matter to you, though. The important point is that the scale is providing a distressingly unreliable measure of your weight and is therefore no longer useful as a measurement instrument.

Regardless of what aspect of nature is being measured and for what purpose, measurement strategies or instruments must be **reliable**; that is, they must provide consistent and accurate readings over time. In many basic areas of research, and especially in laboratory-based studies, measurement reliability is seldom problematic, for two reasons. First, the dimensions of the phenomenon being measured are well understood, and standardized units of measure have long been available to scientists. In the preceding example, weight served as a measurable variable. It does not really matter whether we are talking about weighing ourselves at home or weighing various metals in a laboratory. Standard units of weight, such as grams, ounces, and pounds, are utilized by many researchers. More important, a pound in New York City is the same as a pound in Albuquerque, or Vancouver for that matter. This means that one scientist attempting to communicate his or her findings to other scientists does not need to worry about disagreements or confusions regarding measurement. This is true, of course, not only for weight but also for other physical properties, such as volume, speed, distance, and height. Standardized units of measure allow researchers who may be studying very different kinds of phenomena to speak at least a similar measurement language.

Second, the process of measuring phenomena in these standard units is made possible by innumerable instruments, including the increasingly sophisticated high-tech devices found in most modern laboratories. Such advanced machinery allows for amazingly precise, refined, and consistent measurement. The "gadgetry" of science comes readily to mind when people are asked to envision scientists, but advanced technology is hardly a requirement for reliable measurement. Indeed, many eminent scientists, including Newton, Farraday, Harvey, Kepler, Mendel, and others made their mark in history without the aid of computers, oscilloscopes, particle accelerators, and imaging devices such as MRIs. Carl Sagan (1980) told of the Egyptian philosopher and scientist Eratosthenes, who lived 300 years before the birth of Christ and who used little more than knowledge of basic geometric principles and observation of shadows cast at different times of the day to calculate the Earth's circumference, resulting in a measure of approximately 25,000 miles:

> This is the right answer. Eratosthenes' only tools were sticks, eyes, feet and brains, plus a taste for experiment. With them he deduced the circumference of the Earth with an error of only a few percent, a remarkable achievement for 2,200 years ago. He was the first person accurately to measure the size of a planet. (p. 15)

It is important to understand that good science requires reliable and accurate measurement but that such measurement is not the sole domain of sophisticated electronic equipment. The standard ruler or yardstick, thermometer, bathroom scale, and other such instruments to be found in most homes all serve important measurement functions. As attested to by the story of Eratosthenes, it is the purposes to which these instruments are put that defines their scientific importance, and this has more to do with the ingenuity and insight of the scientist than any properties of the instruments themselves.

Measurement decisions in any science should be informed by the specific research question being asked and by the inherent dimensions of the phenomenon of interest. Within the behavioral and health sciences, research questions ordinarily address some activity or behavior on the part of the subject that has implications for that subject's adaptive functioning or physical well-being. Thus, the researcher's tasks include not only deciding which specific dimension of behavior to measure but also deciding how to collect such measures. For example, the researcher must decide whether or not to use automated, precision-based equipment for measurement purposes.

Automation. Depending on the specific behavioral dimension being studied and the setting of the study, researchers may be able to use automated instruments to collect data. Such measures have historically characterized laboratory and basic research. Experimental psychologists, for instance, have for many years utilized electronic equipment to present controlled visual and auditory stimuli to subjects and to record and measure subjects' responses. An early device called the *tachistoscope* (or T-scope) projected visual stimuli onto a white screen for very brief periods of time (i.e., milliseconds). The T-scope was most often used for studies of sensory processing and brief memory. Verbal learning and memory research also utilized the *memory drum*, a cylindrical platform on which various visual stimuli, especially words, could be printed. By way of a small motor, the memory drum rotated at standard time increments, exhibiting each stimulus through a small viewing window. This allowed the rate of presentation to be precisely controlled. Once standard equipment in the psychology laboratories of the 1940s through the 1960s, the T-scope and memory drum have long since joined the abacus and the slide rule in the graveyard of antique measurement instruments.

Today, the computer is the most widely used instrument in scientific research. In fact, you would probably be challenged to find a laboratory anywhere in the world and in any discipline from biology to psychology that did not contain one or more computers. The computer has truly revolutionized the practice of science, and its capabilities have been exploited in countless ways in the pursuit of answers to a dizzying array of scientific questions. Within the behavioral and health sciences, computers are often used to generate experimental conditions. A participant in a perception experiment, for example, may be asked to respond on the computer keyboard as various visual stimuli are projected on the monitor. In such an experiment, the computer serves several functions. In addition to presenting the stimulus conditions to which the participant responds, it records the relevant dimensions of the subject's response, such as reaction time (latency) or whether a response was correct or incorrect. Finally, researchers often use computers to analyze data from experiments and to formulate conclusions.

The computer, then, is a multifaceted research tool whose importance to modern science would be difficult to overstate. Moreover, recent advances in technology have allowed for the design of smaller computers that are nonetheless more powerful than the bulky room-size computers of the 1970s. As a result of these developments, computer technology is no longer restricted to laboratory environments but pervades nearly every aspect of our everyday lives. Many people avail themselves daily of such mobile devices as laptop computers, PDAs, iPods, cell phones, and other powerful yet diminutive electronic tools. The cars we drive, the video cameras we use to record family events for posterity, even the small key-chain games given away by fast-food restaurants rely increasingly on the seeming magic of computer circuitry. Within the behavioral sciences, new computer programs come along at a striking rate, many of which allow data collection and analysis through software programs and hand-held pocket computers already familiar to many of us (Dixon, 2003; Kahng & Iwata, 1998). Technological development has enormous, though perhaps not yet realized, implications for scientists who conduct research in applied settings.

Another high-tech device that has proved immensely helpful to behavioral observation and scoring in recent years is the videotape machine (Miltenberger, Rapp, & Long, 1999). Videotapes can record session data and produce a permanent record. Today's videotape devices, including digital camcorders, are smaller and less cumbersome to use, yet much more sophisticated than those of a generation ago. In addition, video recording devices, digitized or otherwise, can produce high-resolution images. These devices also offer considerable flexibility in zooming in or out, and built-in timers allow for precise scoring of response classes, including temporal characteristics such as duration or latency. Finally, video recording devices can play an especially critical role in training human observers, as we discuss in the following section.

The advantages of automated measurement in scientific research are not difficult to discern. Because such equipment is built to rather exacting mechanical or electronic standards and because a particular instrument was devised for a very specific measurement purpose, the quality of measurement produced tends to be quite high. Of course, equipment can break down, producing significant measurement error, but such error is usually easily detected given the precision characterizing the measures prior to the breakdown. Moreover, many instruments today, including the relatively inexpensive digital bathroom scales owned by many of us, possess built-in sensors that detect problems with the equipment (e.g., warning lights indicating low battery charge).

The most important advantage that automated equipment provides the researcher is the capacity for prolonged and precise measurement, unaffected by such human attributes as fatigue, inattention, or bias. A motion detector, for instance, situated next to your garage door and designed to turn on a light when an animal or person approaches your house, is always on duty. You could, of course, sit up all night and assume guard duties yourself, but this would be a rather extreme exercise, especially if repeated night after night. Unlike the simple motion detector, you would probably fall asleep, or your attention would drift. Such problems are eliminated or minimized with automated equipment, and this is why such instruments play a role not only in scientific research but increasingly in our everyday lives as well.

Humans as Observers. It is not always possible to use automated equipment for measurement purposes. In many applied settings, such devices would prove overly cumbersome or disruptive to the natural flow of events. Far more common in the behavioral and health sciences is the fact that precision instruments simply do not exist to measure such variables as aggression, suicidal ideation, self-efficacy, treatment compliance, and many behaviors that interest us. In our discussion of operational definitions, we talked about the inherent difficulty in unambiguously identifying "aggressive" behavior. Research on aggression usually requires some "unpacking" (Harzem, 1985) of the concept and clear delineation of what kinds of behaviors will or will not count as aggressive in a particular study. Clearly, there could be no measurement instrument that would be expected to recognize the varying classes of behavior identified by different researchers as aggressive. This does not mean that researchers cannot study aggression. It means that the process of observing and measuring the relevant variables will probably come to rely less on sophisticated electronics and more on the human optical system.

Fortunately, human beings have been observing behavior as a subject matter for longer than we can imagine, certainly much longer than the microscope or the video camera have been in existence. We are all quite practiced, in fact, at this business of people watching. Our success as a social species owes a good deal to our ability to differentiate, say, a smile from a frown. We can easily observe and readily interpret many features of behavior, and doing so requires no special credentials in behavioral science. Any one of us can, on the basis of a very brief glance at another person, recognize such common human activities as writing a letter, playing golf, giving a lecture, playing a video game, scolding a child, reading a book, or eating a cookie. In fact, many contemporary psychologists believe that humans, having evolved as a social species, possess special hardwired brain centers whose sole purpose is to attend to and make sense of other people's behavior (Cosmides & Tooby, 1992; Pinker, 1997). In other words, we may be especially primed to observe the actions of those around us, and this predisposition may serve us well in the scientific study of behavior.

None of this is to say that we are unerring recorders of what happens around us, for surely we are not. As previously mentioned, we are prone to fatigue, susceptible to distractions, and often interpret our observations within the context of personal beliefs and biases. We can do better, though, particularly when made aware of these limitations. What seems to be needed are some fine-tuning of our observational skills and a high degree of conscientiousness regarding our limitations as observers. Given training and corrective feedback, humans can very effectively observe and measure research variables. In fact, we can become better observers not only of other people's behavior but of our own behavior as well. Let us take a look at some of the ways in which the process of human observation can be strengthened for purposes of applied research.

Training Human Observers. Human beings are remarkably adaptive creatures, and we can acquire skills with amazing proficiency and speed. Although you may not realize it, as a college student or member of the workforce, you have learned dozens of skills, some of them perhaps quite specialized, to help you accomplish academic and work-related tasks. Observing behavior with skill is no exception. Many professionals, including anthropologists, ethologists, psychologists, and police officers, are trained how to observe other people. They do so for different reasons, but all require top-notch observational skills in order to do their jobs well.

The first order of business in learning to be a good observer is coming to terms with the operational definition that will be employed in the study. Remember, this is an issue that requires a good deal of attention before the study's observational period begins. The actual definition arrived at will be one that best fits the particular setting and the specific question being asked by the researcher. It is absolutely essential that all observers grasp what behaviors do or do not meet the requirements of the operational definition. With the current availability of video recording devices, it is easy to record a sample of the actual behavior of interest before beginning the study. These samples can then be used to train observers and flesh out the nuances of the behavior being studied. Now is the time, prior to actual data collection, to iron out any difficulties and ensure that all observers are on the same page with regard to behavioral observations.

INTERIM SUMMARY

Because observing behavior continuously is demanding and probably not feasible in applied settings, many researchers utilize some version of interval recording to acquire a representative sample of the target behavior. Although automated recording devices are sometimes available, human observers are still relied on frequently to collect data in such settings. Humans can be fallible as observers, but through appropriate training their reliability and validity in collecting data can be increased substantially.

INTEROBSERVER AGREEMENT

Notice that in the previous section we referred to *observers*, indicating that more than one person may be observing and recording the relevant behavior in a study. The rationale behind this practice is fairly intuitive. Because many studies in applied settings may not allow for automated recording and measurement, human observers will be doing the business of data collection. As we have seen, humans are not infallible observers, even when well trained prior to the study. As a means of controlling for error and maintaining the integrity of the observational and measurement process, applied studies frequently employ two—and, on rare occasions, more than two—observers to collect data. Typically, a study employs one primary observer and one secondary observer. The primary observer usually observes during each and every session of a study. The secondary observer usually observes, concurrently but independently of the primary observer, during some subset of the sessions of a study; 20% to 33% of the total number of study sessions is a suggested standard in single-case research studies that use observation recording systems. Data collected by the secondary observer serve essentially as a check against the data collected by the primary observer and permit the researcher to calculate indices of observational reliability or interobserver agreement.

We cannot be lulled into thinking, though, that just because we have two individuals observing behavior the measures they provide will be accurate and worthy of supporting whatever conclusions they may prompt. This means some effort must be made to ensure the reliability of the observations made by our human observers. **Interobserver agreement** represents an objective method of calculating the amount of correspondence between observers' reports, thus indicating a measure of reliability for the collected data. Because human observers are the major source of data in many applied research projects, a considerable dialogue has emerged concerning interobserver agreement and how best to assess it. The issue is a complex one, and no consensus yet exists. We can nevertheless present some of the more frequently used methods for evaluating interobserver agreement and come to appreciate some of the thorny issues that surround this topic.

Interobserver Agreement for Frequency/Rate Measures

One of the simplest ways to evaluate interobserver agreement (also known in the literature as *interobserver reliability* and *interrater reliability*) is by calculating percentage agreement among observers. This essentially amounts to counting all observations made by the observers and identifying the percentage of observations on which the observers agreed. For instance, say that two observers count, during a 12-hour period, how frequently a resident of a nursing home initiates conversations with other residents. The primary observer records 11 such occurrences, and the secondary observer reports having observed 13 occurrences. By simply dividing the smaller number by the larger, and then multiplying by 100%, we obtain a percentage agreement, in this case $11/13 \times 100\% = 85\%$. Although this agreement would seem to be pretty high, the number does not tell us whether the two observers agreed or disagreed on specific instances of the behavior.

Interobserver Agreement for Duration and Latency Measures

Recall that duration represents the amount of time that elapses between the onset and offset of the target behavior. Suppose two separate observers collect measures of exercise duration for a person recovering from a stroke. Prior to calculating agreement, the researcher must ensure that the observers are collecting data for exactly the same time period. It makes no sense to check the reliability of the observers' data if this is not the case. Suppose that for the designated observation period, one observer reports a duration of 37 minutes and 0 seconds, and the second observer reports a duration of 40 minutes and 0 seconds. To calculate agreement, we simply divide the smaller number by the larger number and multiply by 100%. In this case, interobserver agreement would be reported as 93% (37 minutes/40 minutes $\times$ 100% = 92.5%). Calculating agreement for latency, which is the amount of time elapsing between a stimulus and the target behavior, follows the same formula. The shorter time period is divided by the longer time period and multiplied by 100% to render a percentage agreement index.

Interobserver Agreement for Interval Recording and Time Sampling

Calculating agreement for data obtained through interval recording and time sampling methods is a bit more involved because we are counting not simply how often the behavior occurred or how long it takes but rather the percentage of intervals in which our observers agree that the behavior did or did not occur. Figure 3.2 depicts a typical scoring sheet showing the recorded observations of two observers for a sequence of 15 successive intervals. Remember, the length of the interval or how often the behavior occurred during each interval does not matter. A check is placed in the box to indicate that, for that particular interval, the behavior was observed to occur.

Given two observers and a dichotomous recording decision (behavior occurred or did not occur), four outcomes are possible for each interval. Both observers could record the occurrence of the behavior, in which case there will be a check in both of the corresponding interval boxes (see interval boxes 1–5, 8, and 12–14 in Figure 3.2). This first outcome represents an agreement between the primary and the secondary observer. It also is possible, of course, that both observers record a nonoccurrence, in which case both boxes will be left blank or marked with an "X" (see interval boxes 6, 9, and 11). This outcome also represents an agreement. In addition, the primary observer could record an occurrence while the secondary observer records a nonoccurrence (a disagreement). Finally, the primary observer could record a nonoccurrence while the secondary observer records an occurrence (also a disagreement—see interval boxes 7, 10, and 15 for examples of disagreements). We can quantify interobserver agreement for these data by calculating the overall percentage of agreement across intervals.

Two of the preceding interobserver outcomes are relatively straightforward. If both observers record an instance of behavior for the same interval, we say that agreement has occurred. If one observer records an instance of behavior and the other does not, we score this as a disagreement. The more complicated outcome is one for which neither observer scores an instance of behavior (interval boxes 6, 9, and 11). Although you might be tempted to view this as an agreement, there are conflicting views on this matter. If the behavior being observed is very subtle or tends to occur at very low rates, or if the interval is very brief, then occurrences of the behavior could go unnoticed by both observers. For this reason, our confidence in agreements of nonoccurrence is suspect relative to agreements of occurrence. Consequently, some authorities suggest that researchers should report three indices of interobserver agreement: (1) one for occurrences only when behavior is observed in 30% or fewer intervals; (2) one for nonoccurrences only when behavior is scored in 70% or more intervals; and (3) all boxes, that is, occurrences and nonoccurrences combined (Cooper, Heron, & Heward, 2007). Each of these measures of interobserver agreement can be reported in published studies, and readers can interpret these reported levels of agreement and make their own decisions about the reliability of the measurement system. Let us take a look at how the data in Figure 3.2 would be calculated as interobserver agreement percentages using each of these three methods.

Occurrences Only. This method of calculating agreement uses only those interval boxes in which at least one, but possibly both, of the observers (primary and/or secondary) placed a check, indicating an occurrence of the behavior. This means that boxes 6, 9, and 11 are omitted from the calculation because neither observer recorded an occurrence. Thus, the calculation for *occurrences only* becomes the following: agreements on occurrence/agreements on occurrence + disagreements on occurrence × 100% = % agreement on *occurrence only* or 9/12 × 100% = 0.75(100%) = 75% agreement on *occurrence only*.

Nonoccurrences Only. There are six interval boxes in Figure 3.2 in which a nonoccurrence was recorded by one or both of the observers: boxes 6, 7, 9, 10, 11, and 15. This means that the calculation of interobserver agreement can utilize only these six boxes. Of these six intervals, both primary and secondary observers recorded nonoccurrences in three boxes (6, 9, and 11), and these represent agreements. Calculation of interobserver agreement for nonoccurrences only reduces to agreements on nonoccurrence/agreements on nonoccurrence + disagreements on nonoccurrence = % agreement on *nonoccurrence only*, or 3/6 × 100% = 0.50(50%) = 50% agreement on *nonoccurrence only*.

Occurrences and Nonoccurrences. This measure of interobserver agreement utilizes all interval boxes, regardless of outcome (recorded occurrences or nonoccurrences). For the data in Figure 3.2, the 15 interval boxes result in the following calculation of interobserver agreement agreements on occurrences and nonoccurrences/agreements + disagreements on occurrences and nonoccurrences = % agreement on occurrences and nonoccurrences = 12/15 × 100% = 0.8(100%) = 80%.

Clearly, the method of calculating interobserver agreement has significant implications, not only for these hypothetical data but for actual data reported in the literature. In the current example, calculations ranged from 50% to 80% agreement, a disparity that seems to justify recommendations that researchers report both calculated agreement percentages and their methods of calculation. This practice allows readers of the study to interpret the reported levels of agreement and make their own decisions about the reliability of the measurement system.

Perhaps the bigger question to be addressed, however, is just what makes for acceptable levels of interobserver agreement when human observers provide the primary data for a study. This is not an easy question to answer because there is no magical level of interobserver agreement that defines a good study, although clearly researchers strive for high levels of reliability. Generally speaking, sources in the literature suggest that 80% constitutes a general guideline for minimally acceptable interobserver agreement, although even this level of reliability may be

	Successive intervals														
	1	2	3	4	5	6	7	8	9	10	11	12	13	14	15
Primary observer	√	√	√	√	√	X	√	√	X	X	X	√	√	√	√
Secondary observer	√	√	√	√	√	X	X	√	X	√	X	√	√	√	X

√ = target behavior was observed to occur in interval (occurrence)

X = target behavior was not observed to occur in interval (nonoccurrence)

Figure 3.2   Calculating interobserver agreement for interval recording

insufficient when the behavior of interest is well defined and commonly studied (Miller, 1997). Other factors, such as the observational setting, complexity of operational definition, and whether multiple behaviors are being observed simultaneously, may influence the level of agreement that would be acceptable in a specific study. Interobserver agreement levels that fall below acceptable standards suggest that it might be a good idea to revisit the operational definition or to retrain the observers.

It is not unusual for interobserver agreement to fluctuate during the course of a study, particularly studies that entail long periods or phases of observation and data collection. The tendency for an observer to provide inaccurate measures of behavior over time is referred to as **observer drift**. This phenomenon may be due to fatigue, boredom, or simply forgetting to apply or haphazardly applying the operational definition. Whatever the cause, observer drift needs to be attended to in order to maintain measurement integrity. This can be done by retraining observers on the operational definition and conducting periodic reliability checks on observations. Observers who are aware that their observations will be monitored tend to be less susceptible to observer drift and provide more reliable data (Kent, O'Leary, Dretz, & Diament, 1979).

Reactivity

The social nature of human behavior has consequences as well for subjects whose behavior is being observed for research purposes. Although it is sometimes possible to observe behavior unobtrusively, without the subject or client being aware of the observation, this is frequently not the case in behavioral and health science research. More often, subjects and clients are fully aware not only that their behavior is being observed but also of the purposes for which it is being observed. To understand why this may be important, all you have to do is imagine how your own behavior differs depending on whether you think someone is or is not watching you. A case in point is the encounter with the uncooperative vending machine. We have all had the frustrating experience of putting our money into a machine, making our selection, and standing helplessly by as the machine fails to deliver our requested food or drink. This is, of course, where things get interesting. People can become marvelously creative problem solvers under this condition, and their behavior often runs the gamut from pressing every button on the machine to reaching their arms as far up into the machine as they can to attempting to coax their selection out of the machine by slapping, rocking, and otherwise assaulting the mechanical monster. Naturally, the degree of frustration actually vented on the machine is largely determined by whether there is an audience. Vandalism, after all, is an act punishable by law.

When people behave in a different-from-usual manner in response to being observed by others, we say that **reactivity** has occurred. The problem with reactivity is that the behaviors observed may represent not the person's usual pattern of behavior but rather an idiosyncratic response to being observed. Any parent who has ever visited an elementary classroom to observe his or her child understands the impact that his or her presence has, at least initially, on the children. A strange adult in the classroom is a very conspicuous change in the classroom environment, and some disruption of the daily routine is to be expected. Fortunately, reactivity tends to diminish with repeated observation (Haynes & Horn, 1982). Eventually, the children will habituate, or get used to, the parent's being present and will settle down into their daily schedule. For the most part, reactivity is problematic only during the initial portion of an observation period. The threat that reactivity poses is that our measures of behavior will paint an artificial picture of the target behavior. For this reason, it is often a good idea to allow initial observation to continue long enough to establish whether reactivity has occurred. If it has, continuing observation and measurement will allow the behavior to return to its natural state, and this is essential if the data being collected are to be used in drawing meaningful inferences.

INTERIM SUMMARY

Before collecting the primary data for a study, researchers must assess the reliability of the behavioral measures reported by human observers. Interobserver agreement, reported as a percentage measure, can be calculated for various dimensions of behavior, including response frequency/rate, duration, latency, and occurrence or nonoccurrence. Establishing sufficient levels of interobserver agreement should occur during training of observers and before formal data collection begins for the study. Finally, individuals being observed may behave in an atypical manner in the beginning stages of observation, a phenomenon known as *reactivity*. Reactivity is usually short lived, and researchers should allow for its effects to diminish before beginning data collection. In the next chapter, we will begin considering the unique strategies used to both monitor and graphically present the repeated measures data that are so instrumental to single-case research methodology.

KEY TERMS GLOSSARY

Observation The act of hearing, seeing, feeling, or otherwise coming into contact with some stimulus in the environment.

Operational definition Definition of a research variable based on operations used to measure the variable.

Response rate A dimension of behavior consisting of number of responses occurring during a period of time.

Duration A dimension of behavior consisting of time from onset to offset of the behavior.

Latency A dimension of behavior consisting of time between an antecedent stimulus and the onset of a behavior.

Intensity A dimension of behavior consisting of magnitude or strength.

Environmental by-products A dimension of behavior consisting of a lasting or permanent impact on the environment produced by the behavior.

Interval recording A method of observation in which a specified time period is subdivided into shorter blocks and observation occurs systematically for each block.

Time sampling An interval recording strategy in which observation and non-observation intervals are alternated over a prolonged period of time.

Reliability A measurement strategy or tool that renders consistent and accurate measures of a variable.

Interobserver agreement An objective method of calculating the amount of correspondence between observers' reports.

Observer drift The tendency for an observer to provide inaccurate measures of behavior over time.

Reactivity Unnatural behavior that people adopt in response to being observed by others.

SUPPLEMENTS

Review Questions

1. How would you go about operationally defining the variable "self-esteem"? Why might your operational definition differ from that of another person studying this concept?

2. A researcher is interested in how often a preadolescent utters the term *dude* during a phone conversation with a friend. What dimension of behavior is the researcher probably going to measure and why?

3. Suppose you were measuring how long it takes people to begin accelerating from a stopped position at an intersection when the light turns. Which temporal dimension of behavior are you measuring in this case?

4. A behavioral psychologist is measuring self-stimulatory behavior in a 4-year-old autistic child. The psychologist distributes her observations across a 2-hour period, alternating between 5-minute observation and 5-minute nonobservation intervals. Each observational interval is scored for the presence or absence of self-stimulatory behavior. Which kind of observational strategy is the psychologist using?

5. What is the purpose of calculating interobserver agreement? What role might videotaping play in strengthening interobserver reliability?

6. Suppose the owners of a new puppy are trying to reduce the frequency of the dog's barking because they live in an apartment. Before beginning their training program, they wish to establish just how often the dog barks. The two owners both count the number of times the dog barks during a predetermined 1-hour period. One observes 26 instances of barking; the other observes 30. How would these two dog owners calculate interobserver agreement for their observations? What method of calculation would you use? What is the calculated value of interobserver agreement for these data?

7. How do reactivity and observer drift serve to reduce the reliability of behavioral observation?

SUGGESTED READINGS/HELPFUL WEB SITES

www.noldus.com/site/nav100000
This is the Web site of Noldus Information Technology, a company in the Netherlands that specializes in creating technology for behavioral research. Among their products is the Observer XT program, which allows for sophisticated analyses of ongoing behavior. The program integrates videotape with software that categorizes and quantifies various dimensions of behavior, even permitting correlating behavioral episodes with physiological indicators.

Dixon, M. R. (2003). Creating a portable data-collection system with Microsoft Embedded Visual Tools for the Pocket PC. *Journal of Applied Behavior Analysis, 36,* 271–284.

This article reviews the use of an easily accessed and utilized computer program for assisting researchers in the data collection phase of a single-case study. The author describes some of the computer programs available historically to researchers, their limitations, and advantages of Microsoft's Embedded Visual Tools program for contemporary behavioral researchers.

Chapter 4

DIMENSIONS OF SINGLE-CASE RESEARCH DESIGN AND DATA DISPLAY

As we saw in Chapter 2, single-case research has a rather long history in the behavioral sciences. Despite having been largely overshadowed for much of the past century by the large-group-hypothesis testing designs introduced by Fisher, single-case designs have emerged as an important alternative, particularly for researchers who conduct empirical studies of clinical interventions in the field. No longer is the single-case strategy relegated to basic studies of operant conditioning (Sidman, 1960) or psychophysics within the relatively artificial environs of the laboratory. Increasingly, clinical researchers are taking advantage of the natural flexibility of single-case designs to assess the effectiveness of psychological and physical interventions in applied settings (Borckardt, Nash, Murphy, Moore, Shaw, & O'Neil, 2008; Elder, 1997; Kuentzel, Henderson, Zambo, Stine, & Schuster, 2003; Nuehring & Pascone, 1986; Robey, Schultz, Crawford, & Sinner, 1999; Sterling & McNally, 1992). Thus, the single-case method finds itself today being applied to a much larger universe of natural phenomena than could have been envisioned by some of its earlier practitioners. Nevertheless, the method is characterized by a unique set of philosophical assumptions and strategic practices that set it apart from the Fisherian tradition. In this chapter, we explore these philosophical and strategic features of single-case research as well as the methods used by researchers for displaying single-case data.

AN IDIOGRAPHIC APPROACH TO BEHAVIOR

The most fundamental feature of single-case research design is an exclusive focus on the behavior of the individual organism. Research in this tradition is often referred to as **idiographic**, because the entire research enterprise, from conceptualization to observation and measurement, is directed toward drawing conclusions at the level of the individual case. This approach contrasts with a **nomothetic** perspective, which involves studying many cases for the purpose of ascertaining generalizable principles or laws. As we have already seen, the nomothetic approach is exemplified in the large group designs that have dominated research in the behavioral sciences for many years.

The distinction between idiographic and nomothetic approaches takes on special significance for scientists conducting research in applied settings. For example, a psychologist implementing a behavior analysis program for an autistic child engaged in self-injurious behavior would be expected to have a considerable interest in the effectiveness of the program. Although the psychologist might be curious as to whether the program would prove helpful to other clients exhibiting such behavior, this would not be the central question addressed by the study. The primary question is undoubtedly an idiographic one: Does the program as implemented bring about a clinically relevant reduction in the self-injurious behavior of *this particular client*? If it does, then the program will be considered successful, even if the same program fails to impact the same type of behavior in other clients. In fact, this kind of variability in treatment outcome is common. The same surgical technique, for instance, does not always prove successful, even for patients whose diagnoses are identical. Nor do chemical interventions, including standard antibiotics, produce the same outcome in all patients.

Inductive and Deductive Research

Of course, none of this implies that single-case researchers are entirely disinterested in the generality of a particular experimental or treatment effect. Obviously, a busy psychologist, nurse, or occupational therapist would be very appreciative of an intervention that proved useful to large numbers of clients presenting similar symptoms. In fact, it is nearly inevitable that once an effect is demonstrated for one research participant or client, the question will arise as to whether the effect will generalize to others. For the single-case researcher, answering this question requires a follow-up replication study, in which all elements of the research design are repeated systematically with another participant or client. Through a series of additional replications, the generality of the particular finding can be established, ultimately leading to the identification of a general principle, or law. Moving from specific cases to general principles represents an **inductive** research strategy and remains a hallmark of single-case research design. In contrast, **deductive** strategies involve moving from general principles to specific cases. The large-group research tradition established by Fisher is, in fact, often called the *hypothetico-deductive method*, in part because the process of drawing inferences begins with a general principle, from which specific, testable hypotheses can be generated. Support for this generic principle is usually obtained through large-scale group designs, and it may then be used to make more specific predictions about individual cases.

It may strike you that both inductive and deductive approaches to science have the same ultimate objective. All scientific endeavors strive to make sense of the world, and this is best done when general, widely applicable principles can be identified. The laws of gravity, after all, would be of little use if they changed daily or if they were applicable in only isolated regions on earth. Similarly, we would have little use for principles of behavior or physiological functioning that were in need of substantial revision with every new client. A treatment regimen that proves effective for only one client will naturally be appreciated by that client, but it will have limited utility to the clinician if it is not more widely effective. The question, then, of generality is important to scientists working in applied settings. Both inductive and deductive strategies converge on the issue of generality, but in doing so they rely on different kinds of data (individual vs. group), and thus they draw inferences in different directions.

As we have seen, the single-case approach is decidedly idiographic in nature and supports an inductive method of drawing inferences. This philosophy is particularly "user friendly" to clinicians conducting research in applied settings because the concern in such cases is ordinarily with the effectiveness of a treatment regimen for a particular client and not establishment of a general principle or confirmation of a theory. All data collection, analysis, and decision making are understood to pertain only to the specific case under study. In a sense, applied research entails a conscientious effort to integrate scientific logic and professional practice. The general philosophy of this position was well articulated by Stricker and Trierweiler (1995) in their construct of the "local clinical scientist":

> The local clinical scientist brings the attitudes and knowledge base of the scientist to bear on the problems that must be addressed by the clinician in the consulting room. The problems of inadequate generalizability are reduced by a recognition of the value of local observations and local solutions to problems. (p. 995)

Idiographic and nomothetic perspectives on behavior should not be viewed as competing or mutually exclusive conceptual stances. Remember that all research represents an effort to reduce uncertainty about some natural phenomenon. The kinds of questions asked by scientists approaching their subject matter from an idiographic perspective are often informed by data and theory generated by nomothetic research. A case in point is the concept of reinforcement in behavioral psychology. Psychologists refer to *reinforcers* as response-contingent stimuli that increase the frequency of the behavior that produces them. This definition is explicitly functional, meaning that reinforcers are identified solely on the basis of their ability to strengthen behavior, regardless of whether we would expect them to or whether we understand how they do so. Thus, at the conceptual level, reinforcement is viewed as a fairly generic process, believed to have relevance to all biological creatures.

Although the concept of reinforcement is considered a general principle of behavior, the actual study of reinforcement as a process becomes a much more specific enterprise. In many laboratory-based studies of operant conditioning, reinforcers include important biological resources, such as food and water. If an experimental animal is deprived of the reinforcer prior to the experiment, then that stimulus will tend to be effective in increasing almost any behavior on which it is made contingent. Because food and water are so vital to the survival of all animals, it hardly surprises us that they can be effective reinforcers in operant experiments.

In the applied human setting, however, the use of reinforcement principles becomes very idiosyncratic. Suppose you were a behavioral psychologist charged with enhancing the social skills of a shy and withdrawn adolescent. Your first order of business would be to conduct a proper assessment to identify possible reinforcers that might be effective in altering the child's behavior. Because depriving a human client of basic necessities such as food and water is an unethical practice, these particular stimuli would not be available to you to be used as reinforcers. However, by talking with the child or simply observing the child's natural behavior, you could probably obtain useful information about potential reinforcers for that client. Perhaps you would observe that the child likes to play video games, read books, go on hikes, shoot pool, and listen to country music. For this particular child, these represent preferred activities that might function as effective reinforcers; consequently, you might develop a program that allows the child to obtain a preferred activity by first engaging in some appropriate social behavior.

On the other hand, you would not necessarily expect these same activities to be preferred by other children for whom you might be developing an intervention. To construct a behavioral program for another child, you would need to do a separate assessment because events that act as reinforcers for one person may not function in the same way for another. Social attention is a good example. For many of us, there is nothing more powerful or self-validating than to have others, such as parents, teachers, or coworkers, draw attention to or praise our achievements. Thus, for most people, positive social attention and commendations are quite effective reinforcing consequences. For some people, however, particularly socially withdrawn individuals, social attention is actually an aversive stimulus and would probably be ineffective if used as a reinforcer. This simply highlights the importance of conducting an idiographic assessment of possible reinforcers before constructing a program to alter behavior.

Notice that in the preceding example we are not claiming that the concept of reinforcement would not be expected to apply across many clients. In fact, reinforcement remains one of the most powerful and well-documented behavior principles in psychology, and its general applicability is for the most part uncontested. Reinforcement, as a nomothetic principle or law of behavior, enjoys rather rare status within the behavioral sciences. This fact, however, is of little use to the applied clinician who intends to use the principle idiographically to alter the behavior of a specific client. The specific stimuli that function as reinforcers differ from one person to the next, and a stimulus that reinforces behavior at one time may not reinforce it at another. Reading may be an effective reinforcer if one has not had the opportunity to read for some time, but if one has been reading uninterrupted for hours, the reinforcing capacity of reading may diminish. This is true simply because reinforcement, though a general principle, operates idiographically, or, as Stricker and Trierweiler (1995) would say, at the "local" level.

Replication in Single-Case Research

An important part of the logic of science is the establishment of important findings through experimental replication. The purpose of replication is straightforward. Scientists, like everybody else, are capable of making mistakes. When an especially important scientific finding is published, we want to be sure that it is reliable, particularly if large amounts of money are going to be invested in further research or technological development generated by the finding. But we all lose when a scientific finding receives substantial acclaim or attention, only to be proved incorrect by subsequent research. This is the reason that potentially significant findings are usually followed up immediately by attempts at replication, in which the procedural details of the experiment are repeated in order to discover whether the results remain the same. Only when a finding can be replicated over and over does it become an established part of the corpus of scientific knowledge. It is this continual process of experiment and replication that gives scientific knowledge its cumulative or progressive nature.

In single-case research, replication takes on added importance, especially in applied settings, where independent variables usually take the form of clinical treatments. In such circumstances, replications actually serve two functions, one of which is idiographic, the other nomothetic.

Intrasubject Replication. When an independent variable is manipulated in a single-case study, repeated measurement of the dependent variable allows the researcher to detect any change in behavior brought about by the independent variable. Remember, though, that an essential part of drawing conclusions from experiments is eliminating other possible explanations for the results. We cannot identify a causal relationship between the independent and dependent variables if some other extraneous variable intervened. If some other variable, unbeknownst to the researcher, happened to coincide with the independent variable, then the researcher could falsely identify the independent variable as the reason for the change in the dependent variable. In many applied studies, this amounts to declaring the treatment to have an effect when in fact it may not. We wish, quite obviously, to guard against such conclusions and the potentially dire implications they may provoke.

One method of ensuring that the change in behavior (dependent variable) observed in a study is, in fact, due to the independent variable (treatment) is to replicate the manipulation of the independent variable with the same subject. This ordinarily amounts to withdrawing or removing the treatment, allowing behavior to return to its pretreatment or baseline level, and then once again introducing the treatment. Because all of this is done at the level of the individual subject or client, we call this process **intrasubject replication**.

Suppose, for example, that a parent consults with a psychologist about a child who has developed the habit of crying, whining, and throwing tantrums each night at bedtime. The psychologist hypothesizes that the parent's tendency to comfort the child when this behavior emerges is actually reinforcing the problem behavior. As a result, the psychologist recommends that the parent no longer respond to the problem behavior at all, thus placing it on an extinction schedule. If the tantrum behavior diminishes or ceases altogether during the extinction phase, we would be tempted to attribute this behavior change to the extinction strategy. There are, however, other possibilities. Perhaps the child simply tired of the nightly tirades, or developed some precocious empathy for his or her frazzled parents. To evaluate whether the behavior change was due to the extinction procedure or some other variable, the parent could once again respond to inappropriate bedtime behavior with attention and comforting. Should the tantrum behavior return, the parent could implement extinction once again. This second application represents a replication of the first extinction phase. Should tantrum behavior reduce or extinguish once again during this phase, we would be unlikely to attribute it to an extraneous variable. It is simply improbable that some such variable just happened to coincide twice with the extinction component. In general, each successive replication of an independent variable's effect increases the researcher's confidence that behavior change was due to the manipulated variable, not some extraneous factor. Thus, intrasubject replications represent an idiographic strategy for strengthening causal conclusions concerning the independent and dependent variables, thereby enhancing the internal validity of a study.

Intersubject Replication. Single-case researchers utilize **intersubject replication** as an inductive strategy to establish the generality or applicability of a manipulation or treatment beyond one subject or to other kinds of behavioral phenomena. For instance, having demonstrated that extinction of tantrum behavior in a child could be brought about by removing parental attention, we might want to know whether the same effect could be produced with a separate child. Successful replication of the treatment with several different children would demonstrate that the conclusions drawn from the first study seem to be applicable or generalizable to others, thus suggesting the **external validity** of the original findings.

Because they bear important consequences for the generality of particular findings, intersubject replications play an especially critical role in both basic and applied science. Results that are known to generalize, or apply across a wide variety of subjects, settings, or behaviors, clearly are likely to be taken quite seriously. Indeed, the more circumstances across which a particular principle seems to hold, the more status it will probably enjoy, either as a basic scientific principle or as an applied intervention. To discover, for instance, that withdrawal of parental attention successfully leads to the extinction of tantrum behavior in a particular child is certainly noteworthy. However, to demonstrate this principle across several children shows us that this relationship is not entirely idiosyncratic. Obviously, the more domains across which the finding can be shown to generalize, the more powerful the principle would appear to be. We might want to know, for example, whether a similar intervention might work in a classroom setting. We could also determine whether other kinds of behavior, besides tantrums, could be extinguished by simply removing attention. Would the same be true of adults as well? Notice that in each case we are asking whether a particular independent–dependent variable relationship will continue to hold up when applied to different types of subjects, behaviors, or settings than originally studied.

The use of intrasubject and intersubject replication often parallels the distinction between basic and applied research. As we have already seen, a clinical researcher evaluating a specific treatment in an applied setting is primarily interested in whether that intervention is effective for a particular client. Questions about treatment generality may simply not emerge. On the other hand, the question of whether the same treatment would be equally effective for a different kind of client population, or in a different institutional setting, is an inquiry on a larger scale. Some scientists believe that research of the latter sort is much needed in the behavioral and health sciences and that the esteem afforded applied interventions will prove to be proportionate to the amount of data attesting to their generalizability. This is a rather tall order, though, given that many applied researchers have neither the time nor the interest in establishing the conditions under which specific treatments will or will not prove effective. Research of this kind must usually be conducted programmatically, using a series of well-planned experiments intended to answer specific questions about generality. Johnston and Pennypacker (1993a) referred to this kind of research as *thematic* and argued that researchers pursuing generality must necessarily adopt a different kind of agenda than do most applied researchers: "In thematic research, when there is a conflict between experimental and service goals, the scales are tipped in favor of science so that the resulting interpretations may be unambiguous" (p. 179).

Tracking Behavior in Real Time

Most behavioral research from a nomothetic perspective places a major emphasis on collecting information from a large sample of research participants. Because time constraints place restrictions on how long the data collection phase of a study can take and because observations are being made of many participants (perhaps in the hundreds), it becomes impractical to make several observations of each participant over time. Thus, group designs often restrict themselves to one or two observations of behavior for each participant. In the case of experimental designs utilizing both experimental and control groups, this may amount to a single measure of behavior in each research participant after manipulation of the independent variable, as in a posttest-only control group design (Leary, 2004). Thus, behavior in large group studies is usually measured only once.

Behavior as a Continuous Subject Matter

Single-case researchers have long argued that observational and measurement strategies that treat behavior as a discrete subject matter fail to do justice to a phenomenon that is actually extended in time. For many scientists, **behavior** represents an ongoing, adaptive interplay between an organism and its environment; by its very nature, behavior as a subject matter resists efforts at discrete categorization. This point should not be underestimated, nor should it be viewed as merely esoteric, intellectual nit-picking. The position taken by single-case researchers is in fact quite consistent with commonsense perceptions of behavior. You need only consider examples from your own life to see why this is so. It is difficult to conceptualize even mundane instances of behavior without taking their temporal qualities into account. Even relatively unsophisticated behaviors, such as tying your shoes, cooking a meal, holding a phone conversation, or writing a letter, involve sometimes lengthy sequences of responses and fine adjustments to ongoing environmental feedback.

In fact, understanding behavior is often inconceivable without taking environmental feedback into account. Riding a bicycle is a particularly good example. Keeping a bicycle upright while riding involves moment-to-moment sensory feedback about body posture and shifts in one's center of gravity, and this information must be integrated with the ongoing activity of the arms (steering) and legs (pedaling). Suppose you were going to try to teach a child to ride a bike and your first order of business was to discover how far along the child was in acquiring this skill. Assume that two kinds of information were available to you prior to the first lesson: (1) a still photograph of the child and (2) a videotape of the child, both depicting the child attempting to ride the bike. Which kind of information would you prefer? Naturally, the answer to this question is pretty transparent. The still photograph represents a very impoverished and unrepresentative portrayal of the behavior of interest, whereas the videotape offers a rich database from which to draw conclusions about how best to help the child learn to ride. In the same vein, single-case research endorses the logic that observation and measurement of behavior should, whenever possible, be continuous, not discrete; that is, our research design should be developed in such a way as to accommodate the natural dimensions of the subject matter.

Behavior Change as Focus of Applied Research

An emphasis on behavioral continuity is especially apparent in applied research, primarily because this kind of research ordinarily concerns itself with some aspect of behavior change. Regardless of differences in training and credentials, mental health workers, nurses, and occupational and physical therapists all serve as behavior change agents. The interventions utilized by these professionals all entail helping clients address behavioral deficits or excesses that have implications for adaptive functioning. The psychologist providing relaxation training to a client paralyzed by social anxiety, the nurse teaching a diabetic patient how to assess his or her own blood sugar levels, the physical therapist developing an exercise regimen for an accident victim are all trying to bring about functional changes in the behavioral repertoires of their respective clients. Evaluating whether such efforts are effective requires a measurement strategy that is sensitive to changes in relevant dimensions of behavior, and such measurement presumes an ability to track the behavior over time.

Of course, the logic of continuous measurement extends to many nonclinical domains as well. Many human interactions have behavior change as their primary objective, although this fact is not always readily acknowledged. Both parenting and teaching, for instance, involve explicit attempts to alter behavioral repertoires. Learning to read, for instance, involves mastering incremental skills, from letter recognition and pronunciation to word and sentence recognition. The ability to read fluently does not emerge instantaneously at any point, and it would be an odd claim to say that a child was not able to read on Wednesday but was able to do so on Thursday! Adequate assessment of a program designed to teach reading would require frequent, if not continuous, monitoring simply because the phenomenon itself unfolds incrementally over time.

INTERIM SUMMARY

Single-case research focuses on behavioral development within the individual, and this idiographic approach differs from the nomothetic approach typical of traditional group research. The primary vehicle for drawing conclusions is experimental replication. Intrasubject replication allows for rigorous conclusions at the level of the individual subject, and intersubject replication allows single-case research to be extended inductively to the more general case. Behavior change is the major emphasis in applied research, and single-case research is well adapted to studying behavior change because of its commitment to continuous observation and measurement of behavior over time.

INDEPENDENT AND DEPENDENT VARIABLES IN SINGLE-CASE RESEARCH

Single-case research design represents an experimental approach to the study of behavior. We have already seen that an experiment is a study in which the researcher controls or manipulates an independent variable while also controlling the effects of extraneous variables. When these two objectives can be achieved, alternative explanations can be ruled out, and the researcher is in a position to draw cause-and-effect conclusions about the variables in the study. Notice that this is the fundamental logic of experimentation, regardless of whether we are considering single-case or more traditional group designs. Moreover, the ability to manipulate the independent variable and rule out alternative explanations is also what distinguishes a single-case experiment from a case study. The latter involves no control over variables, usually because the relevant variables have already occurred for natural reasons. The resemblance between single-case designs and case studies is primarily due to the focus on the individual, not the procedural or design strategies or the kinds of inferences that each type of study supports.

Types of Independent Variables

The range of independent variables manipulated in single-case research is enormous, particularly if one surveys research endeavors across such varied disciplines as psychology, nursing, physical therapy, and occupational therapy. The nature of the independent variable will depend on a number of factors, one being whether the study addresses a basic or an applied issue. For instance, an operant psychologist studying the effects of reinforcer magnitude on lever-pressing in rats might vary the number of food pellets (one vs. three) delivered contingent on responding on two separate levers. The research is probably being conducted to answer a specific question about reinforcement, or perhaps to evaluate a specific theory of reinforcement, not necessarily to solve a problem concerning rodent behavior in the wild.

On the other hand, a therapist providing a specific cognitive intervention for a stroke patient is not only manipulating a different kind of independent variable but is also doing so to bring about meaningful changes in the patient's functional behavior. In fact, in most clinical studies the independent variable is some kind of therapeutic or educational program, perhaps made up of several phases or components. A cognitive intervention for a stroke patient, for example, may include such specific tasks as learning rehearsal strategies, self-monitoring of behavior, and imagery enhancement. This *cognitive intervention*, as an independent variable, is a qualitatively and quantitatively more complex variable than is *reinforcer magnitude*, as used in the laboratory study just described.

This point is important because the scientific strength of any study, whether in the laboratory or the field, depends on the precision with which variables are conceptualized, manipulated, and measured. In applied settings, interventions must consist of thoroughly defined, concretely articulated activities, and the actual delivery of the intervention must be consistent with its verbal description. Indeed, one of the major sources of controversy surrounding therapy outcome research is the problem of defining and standardizing treatment methods (McGlinchey & Dobson, 2003; Nezu & Nezu, 2005; Schlosser, 2002). If one researcher's cognitive restructuring intervention is different from another therapist's cognitive restructuring therapy, then the two studies, even if otherwise well controlled, will yield uninterpretable results, at least with respect to this ambiguously defined independent variable. Moreover, the cumulative nature of science requires that experiments be replicated to establish the reliability or generality of any particular finding. This proves difficult when an independent variable, particularly in the form of a clinical intervention, is either poorly operationalized or is delivered in a manner that bears no relationship to its verbal description. Fortunately, the issue of *treatment integrity* has received a good deal of recent attention, and a resounding alarm has been sounded by several scientists (Carr, Bailey, Carr, & Coggin, 1996; Gresham, 1996; Gresham, Gansle, Noell, Cohen, & Rosenblum, 1993; Moncher & Prinz, 1991; Perepletchikova & Kazdin, 2005; Peterson, Homer, & Wonderlich, 1982). Treatment regimens, however complex, are the independent variables of applied research and are thus likely to be interpreted as causes of any observed improvements in clinical behavior. Consequently, the proper identification and consistent manipulation of such interventions are essential to establishing both the scientific and applied validity of any particular research study.

Types of Dependent Variables

The range of variables that serve as dependent measures in behavioral and health science research is truly immense, as one would expect from a collection of such diverse disciplines as psychology, nursing, and physical and occupational therapy. Although defined and measured in different ways, variables in this kind of research usually represent behaviors having important adaptive or functional repercussions for the subjects or participants. The acquisition of simple self-care activities (proper hygiene or getting dressed), though taken for granted by most of us, may reflect an important milestone for a child with developmental disabilities. A home care patient may be required to learn how to monitor and operate an intra-venous drip as a part of an ongoing medical regimen. A victim of an industrial accident, having lost a dominant limb, may have to train the nondominant limb to do the work of the lost limb. The following are some of the kinds of dependent variables encountered in applied behavioral and health care settings:

- Words read per minute by a person with visual impairment (Buning & Hanzlik, 1993)
- Weight distribution of an affected limb in a patient suffering from a form of paralysis known as *hemiplegia* (Wu, Huang, Lin, & Chen, 1996)
- Walking speed in meters per second in chronic stroke patients (Kollen, Rietberg, Kwakkel, & Emmelot, 2000)
- Number of observation intervals containing tics in children exhibiting different kinds of motor tics (Woods, Miltenberger, & Lumley, 1996)
- Caffeine intake in milligrams (Foxx & Rubinoff, 1979)
- Frequency of on-topic and off-topic conversational statements by nursing home residents with dementia (Hoerster, Hickey, & Bourgeois, 2001)
- Number of prompted signs given per minute in infants being taught American Sign Language (Thompson, McKerchar, & Dancho, 2004)
- Number of correct football moves (e.g., tackles) as a result of feedback via posted performance charts (Ward & Carnes, 2002)
- Correct pronunciation of Mandarin Chinese characters by college students (Wu & Miller, 2007)

Of course, it is difficult to assess the adaptive nature of a behavior unless it can be observed for a time course sufficient to exhibit change. This is the primary justification for the continuous, or at least repeated, measurement of dependent variables that characterizes single-case research. Many behaviors, especially those undergoing treatment, exhibit gradual change over time, not abrupt, discrete shifts. We would not, for example, expect an accident victim to transfer a complex manual function from an amputated dominant limb to a nondominant limb in a few days. In fact, a successful response to therapy in such a case may not be noticeable for weeks or even months. Thus, a single measure of the behavior after treatment may tell us very little about the effects of treatment and absolutely nothing about the process itself. Repeated measurement provides not only an "after" treatment picture but also a more refined and informative "during" treatment picture.

Importance of Multiple Measures of Dependent Variables

The treatment of dependent variables in single-case research follows logically from the manner in which the subject matter itself is conceptualized. If, as we have argued, behavior represents a continuous interplay between an organism and its environment, then our measures of behavior must reflect this fact. It makes little sense to observe and measure a phenomenon one time only, in a discrete manner, if one is primarily interested in how the phenomenon changes or unfolds over a period of time. Because behavior exhibits this basic characteristic and because most behavioral and health care research, especially in applied settings, is conducted for the purpose of assessing changes in behavior, then continuous measurement emerges as a necessary strategy. Thus, instead of obtaining a single measure of the dependent variable of interest, single-case researchers utilize observation and measurement tactics that allow for multiple measures of the dependent variable over a period of time.

The process of measuring the dependent variable is frequently not entirely unique to single-case designs. Group researchers do, on occasion, conduct *repeated measures designs* in which subjects in all groups (experimental and control) are observed more than once after manipulation of the independent variable. Nevertheless, the number of dependent variable measures that can be taken when dealing with large numbers of subjects is likely to be constrained by practical considerations. For this reason, one seldom encounters a group study in which the dependent variable was measured more than two or three times following independent-variable manipulation. Single-case designs, on the other hand, ordinarily involve many more measures of the dependent variable. Indeed, the ideal strategy would be to continuously measure behavior throughout the entirety of the study. This is of course not always possible, particularly in applied settings, but the logic of single-case research quite clearly places a premium on collecting repeated measures of behavior.

The single-case reliance on multiple measures of the dependent variable extends not only to postintervention phases but also to behavioral measurement prior to the intervention. This feature also distinguishes single-case designs from group designs that utilize some degree of repeated measures strategy. The purpose of obtaining multiple measures of the dependent variable prior to independent variable implementation is to establish a benchmark against which each subject's behavior during treatment can be evaluated. This benchmark is referred to as a **baseline**, and it represents a critical strategic feature of single-case designs. In essence, the subject's level and pattern of behavior during the baseline, or nontreatment, phase of the study serve as a comparison phase for that same subject's behavior during treatment. In this way, the subject in this type of study serves in both the control and experimental conditions, thus providing the same kind of rationale for a comparison seen in group designs that use separate control and experimental groups.

INTERIM SUMMARY

Single-case research represents an experimental approach to studying behavior in which independent variables, often in the form of clinical treatments, are directly controlled by the researcher. Dependent variables usually consist of behaviors deemed clinically or socially relevant to the subject, as identified by the relevant health science discipline (e.g., psychology, nursing, physical therapy). A key feature of single-case research is the repeated observation and measurement of the dependent variable both prior to and during or after the independent variable or intervention condition. Such repeated observation and measurement are viewed as necessary to tracking and effectively interpreting behavior change in individual subjects or clients.

DATA PRESENTATION IN SINGLE-CASE RESEARCH

In many ways, data serve the same function in single-case research as they do in traditional group designs. In applied health care settings, behavioral and/or medical data collected from subjects are used to draw conclusions about the relative effectiveness of a clinical intervention. As in group designs, data collected under different independent-variable conditions are compared, and such comparisons form the basis of conclusions drawn by the researcher. However, unlike group designs, single-case research designs involve no aggregating or summing of data across multiple research subjects, and the resulting data analysis usually does not consist of evaluating group means through tests of statistical significance. Data collected from individual subjects over prolonged periods of time are importantly different from single, discrete measures summed across many subjects; consequently, the collection, presentation, and analysis of single-case data differ markedly from the conventions of group designs.

We have made reference on occasion to the fact that single-case research tends to resemble more the methodological practices of the natural sciences than those of the behavioral and social sciences. This fact is evident as well in the manner in which single-case researchers present data collected during the course of a study. Because single-case researchers have no group data to present, the presentation of means or other measures of central tendency are not as paramount as in group designs. However, single-case researchers do routinely report central tendency measures, particularly the mean, as one descriptive statistic, to help illuminate an individual subject's performance within particular phases of a study, for example, the mean number of vocalizations during baseline and the mean number of vocalizations during intervention. What the single-case researcher has, on the other hand, are large amounts of data collected from an individual subject or participant, representing appropriate dimensions of the behavior over time and in response to various experimental conditions. Data are presented to describe individual performance for reasons that have already been detailed, most notably the fact that aggregating data across subjects usually misrepresents or obscures the behavior of individuals, and professionals providing health care are, almost without exception, interested in the responses of individuals to clinical interventions.

THE REAL TIME OR TIME-SERIES GRAPH

The prevalent vehicle and long-standing convention for presenting single-case data are the *real-time graph*, also referred to as a *time-series* or *trend graph*, and sometimes simply as a *line graph*. Tufte (2001) reported that 75% of all graphs published in journal articles and magazines are time series graphs, and Henry (1995) noted that such graphs were used to portray political and economic trends, such as importing and exporting, as early as the 1700s. Given the ingenuity of the researcher, the amount and type of information that can be conveyed in a time-series graph is actually quite astounding, as attested to by Figure 4.1, a graph depicting New York City's weather for the year 1980.

Graphing Conventions

Researchers benefit from practices of data presentation and analysis characterized by some degree of standardization, and although no such universal regulations govern graphing, some effort has been made to bring consistency to this process. Among the researchers whose efforts frequently result in graphed data, applied behavior analysts have exhibited an especially steadfast devotion to depicting behavior change in single-case data. Indeed, the *Journal of Applied*

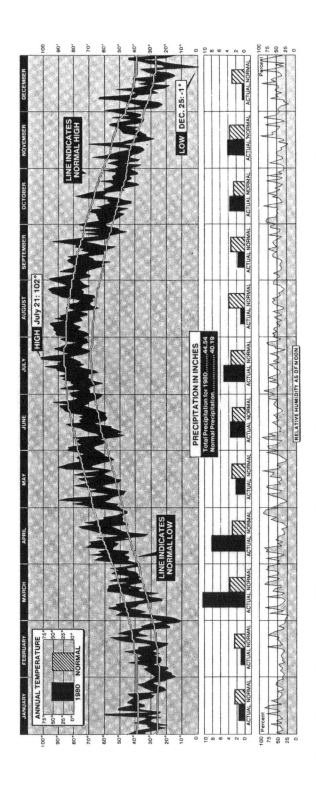

Figure 4.1 Time-series graph of New York's weather for 1980

Source: Tufte, E. R. (2001). *The Visual Display of Quantitative Information*, 2nd ed. Cheshire, CT: Graphics Press. Reprinted with permission.

Behavior Analysis (JABA) has been the primary outlet for research in this field since 1968, and it may be unique in the behavioral sciences in its commitment to publishing single-case data generated in applied settings. Although representing various dimensions of behavior observed and recorded under differing conditions, all graphs published in *JABA* are expected to meet the following guidelines:

- Individual data points represent the relevant dimension of behavior (rate, percentage correct, etc.) for the subject across all experimental conditions.
- Condition changes (nontreatment/baseline to treatment) are denoted by a vertical dotted line.
- The zero level on the *y*-axis (denoting the dependent variable) is raised above the horizontal line to allow for less confusing visual assessment.
- Data representing different experimental conditions are labeled with a descriptor centered above the data.
- A break in the *y*-axis is used to indicate that the axis scale is not continuous.
- Subject information (e.g., pseudonyms) is placed in a box in the graph's lower right-hand corner.
- All relevant information is placed within the boundaries of the graph.

These graphing conventions ensure that some degree of uniformity exists in data presented in *JABA*, even though the data may represent very different kinds of behaviors, measured in different dimensions, and across similarly varying independent variable conditions. The flexibility of time-series graphs allows for an accommodation of an extraordinarily wide assortment of dependent variables measured under varying independent variable conditions and, perhaps most important, from very disparate applied fields, such as psychology, nursing, and physical and occupational therapy.

Such graphs have become an indispensable tool for contemporary single-case researchers. An example of a real-time or time-series graph depicting the behavior of a single person is depicted in Figure 4.2. The data in the graph represent how often a client, John Doe, washes his hands each day over a 2-week period. John experiences a debilitating behavior problem known as obsessive–compulsive disorder, characterized by an obsessive fear of contamination. This fear leads John to wash his hands compulsively, with more frequency than is desirable, even to the point of washing away the natural oils produced by healthy skin, eventually leading to dry, chapped hands, covered with ulcerations. We will use the data from John Doe throughout this chapter to illustrate not only graphing conventions but also how a behavior therapist would go about evaluating the effects of a clinical intervention for this client.

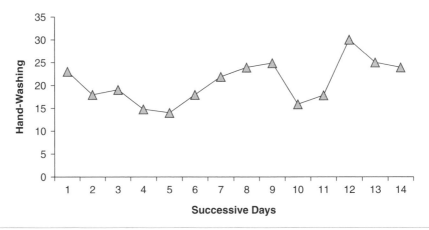

Figure 4.2   John Doe's hand-washing behavior

You'll notice that the graph in Figure 4.2 shares many features with other graphs you may encounter in textbooks, magazines, newspapers, and other sources. Two lines running perpendicular to one another meet or intersect at a point called the *origin* (lower left-hand corner). These lines, ordinarily referred to as *axes*, are labeled to represent the relevant quantitative and/or qualitative variables of the study. Although deviations from this convention are sometimes warranted, such graphs are ordinarily depicted in an aspect ratio of 1:2, meaning the horizontal axis—that is, the *x*-axis—tends to be twice as long as the vertical axis, the *y*-axis. In the behavioral and health sciences, graphs are usually presented to depict some aspect of the subject's behavior, recorded repeatedly over time, both prior to and during the clinical intervention or independent-variable manipulation. Ordinarily, the dimension of behavior (e.g., response rate, percentage correct responses, intensity) is represented on the vertical axis, and some dimension of time is represented on the horizontal axis. Of course, the passage of time is not itself a variable influencing behavior, but any intervention must necessarily occur over time, and only by representing behavior in this manner can we entertain questions about behavior change in relation to an intervention or independent variable. Also, the horizontal axis and the particular dimension of time that it depicts further illustrate the importance of repeated, or continuous, measurement which is a hallmark of single-case research. Repeated measures across time allow for a much more fine-tuned tracking and assessment of behavior change than discrete measures for groups, often collected at one or two points in time, giving single-case data collection and presentation a descriptive power unprecedented in conventional behavioral research.

Importance of Scale Decisions

As is always the case with graphing conventions, researchers must make important decisions about how to represent both independent and dependent variables on the graph. Perhaps the most important decision is the choice of how variables will be scaled on each axis. If it is true that a picture is worth a thousand words, then single-case researchers are in the business of "talking" with graphs. Thus, the researcher has the responsibility of presenting data in a manner that accurately portrays the behavior of interest and increases the likelihood of proper conclusions concerning the effectiveness of the intervention.

Figures 4.3 and 4.4 demonstrate how graphing conventions may result in misleading interpretations. The data representing John Doe's hand-washing rate are identical but presented on graphs using different scales on the vertical axis. Despite the identical nature of the data, Figure 4.3 would seem to provoke the conclusion that John's hand washing is fairly stable, exhibiting little variability from day to day. Figure 4.4, however, seems to suggest a good deal more variability in this behavior. It is important to be aware of how scale axes will affect interpretation, but at the same time, there are no hard-and-fast rules concerning which scale to use for a particular graph. Clearly, the scale needs to be able to depict the full range of the dependent variable. At the same time, the scale should be sensitive enough to render an accurate picture of trends and variability in the behavior. In the present example, Figure 4.3 uses a y-axis that exceeds the highest frequency of hand washing observed by nearly three times, so that most of the data are "squeezed" into the lower third of the graph. Consequently, this graph wastes

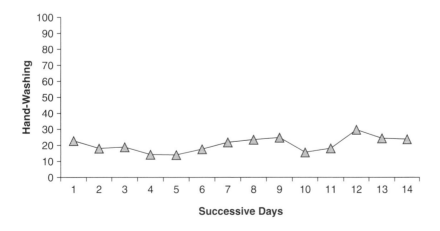

Figure 4.3   John Doe's hand-washing behavior

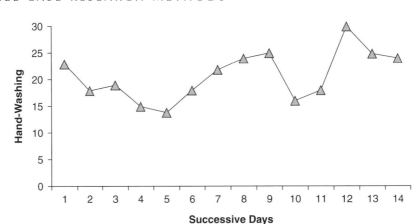

Figure 4.4   John Doe's hand-washing behavior

space and probably underrepresents the degree of variability occurring in John's hand washing over the 2-week period. The y-axis in graph 4.4, on the other hand, both utilizes space more effectively and demonstrates the considerable day-to-day variability in the dependent variable.

Of course, there is more information to be gleaned from the y-axis of a graph than just the measurement scale. The text found running alongside the axis is important because it identifies not only the behavior or dependent variable that was of interest to the researcher but also the relevant dimensions along which this variable was measured. In fact, the nature of the dependent variable and its measurable dimensions is often the most distinguishing factor about a study and what separates one study from the next, both within and across research disciplines.

In most published accounts of clinical interventions, single-case graphs are a bit busier than those depicted in Figures 4.3 and 4.4. This is because the function of such graphs is to show the effects of the intervention on the relevant target behavior. To show the effects of the intervention, some kind of comparison of behavior both prior to and during or after the intervention is necessary. An example of how this is done can be seen in Figure 4.5, which depicts our client with obsessive–compulsive disorder (John Doe) once again. The major difference between Figure 4.5 and the earlier figures (4.3 and 4.4), however, is that now we have an opportunity to compare John's frequency of hand washing prior to and during treatment. We will assume, for current purposes, that John has received some version of cognitive–behavior therapy, a fairly standard intervention for obsessive–compulsive disorder.

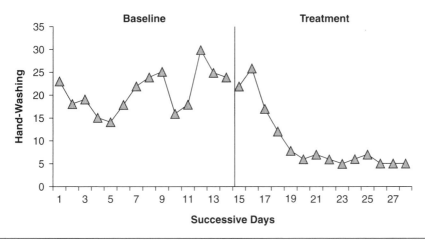

Figure 4.5　John Doe's hand washing before and after treatment

Figure 4.5 depicts John's hand-washing episodes both prior to the clinical intervention (cognitive–behavior therapy) and during the intervention. These two phases of the study (before and during intervention) are separated on the graph by a vertical line, and each phase is also identified by text at the top of the graph. The data represented on the left side of the graph are referred to as *baseline* data, because they represent the level of the target behavior before any clinical intervention has been delivered. It is the comparison of these data in the baseline phase with the data subsequently presented on the right side of the vertical line—that is, data in the treatment or intervention phase—that allows us to draw conclusions about the effects of the intervention. This baseline–treatment comparison is logically similar to the control group–experimental group comparison with which you are probably already familiar in group studies. In single-case research, each subject serves as its (or his or her) own control, with behavior being measured both prior to and after introducing the independent variable (clinical intervention).

The data in Figure 4.5 provide the critical information needed for the researcher to draw conclusions about the effects of the independent variable (intervention) on the dependent variable (target behavior) in a single-case study. However, the details of the research design and the criteria for drawing decisions about intervention effectiveness are themselves rather complex issues. We discuss the different kinds of research designs available to single-case researchers, as well as the decision criteria for evaluating intervention effectiveness, in subsequent chapters.

THE STANDARD CELERATION CHART

The real-time or time-series graph is a convenient and flexible device for depicting continuous behavioral data. Such graphs are able to accommodate dependent variables across numerous behavioral and health science disciplines and measured along varying dimensions. However, displaying data in this way requires considerable nuance when the measured dependent variable varies across a sizable number of values. For instance, we might be interested in assessing the rate at which a client experiences undesirable brief facial movements, or tics. Because such movements may occur quite frequently under conditions of anxiety but with very little frequency under less anxious conditions, measures of this dependent variable might vary from dozens of times a minute to only a few occurrences an hour. In fact, the sheer variability of this behavior might lead the researcher to question the appropriate response rate cycle in which to measure the behavior: minutes or hours. Thus in depicting the behavior graphically, the researcher must decide on a scale axis that both accommodates the substantial range of the behavior while also being sensitive enough to demonstrate small amounts of variability that may be of some clinical importance.

Fortunately, data that evidence substantial variability even more than exhibited in Figures 4.3 and 4.4 can be adequately portrayed using the Standard Celeration Chart (see Figure 4.6). Ogden Lindsley and colleagues developed this graphing format in the 1950s and 1960s, primarily within the context of educational research. Lindsley had been a graduate student of B. F. Skinner's during the 1950s and consequently had developed an appreciation for collecting and interpreting data at the level of the individual subject. Lindsley was, in fact, among the first researchers to employ laboratory-based principles of behavior in an applied setting. His pioneering efforts to utilize fundamental conditioning principles to change behavioral symptoms in institutionalized psychiatric patients (Lindsley, 1956, 1960) were early contributions to the development of behavior therapy and behavior modification (Kazdin, 1982a).

By the 1960s, Lindsley had become interested in the application of behavioral interventions to educational practice. His background in experimental methodology and the study of operant behavior led Lindsley to question not only the instructional methods that characterized American schools at the time but also the methods for evaluating their relative effectiveness. Lindsley argued, not surprisingly, given his scientific training, that assessment of learning had to take place at the level of the individual student and that the development of objective and standard measures of learning was a necessary first step in this process. Lindsley and his colleagues suggested that the rate at which an academic behavior occurs (e.g., number of words read per minute) represents not only a universal dimension of

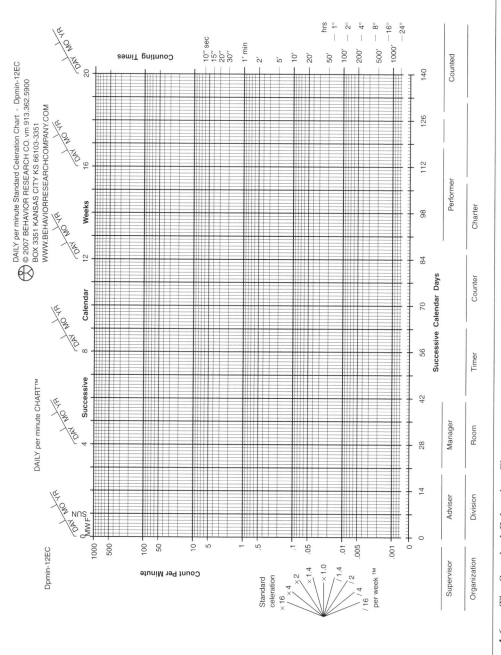

Figure 4.6 The Standard Celeration Chart

behavior but also a highly sensitive metric of skill development. This may have seemed an odd idea at the time because many educators then, and even now, tended to favor percentage of correct responses as the best indication of academic progress. One problem with percentage correct as a dependent measure is that once a skill has reached a certain level of proficiency, a percentage measure can no longer depict continued progress. For example, two children who both answer 10 out of 10 math problems correctly would be considered equivalent in amount of learning, because the percentage of correct responses, 100%, is the same for both students. However, one child may be able to answer these 10 math problems correctly in less than 1 minute, whereas the other child may require 3 minutes to achieve this same percentage level of correct responding. A percentage-correct measure fails to depict the differences in *fluency* (correct responses per unit of time) that characterize the two students' performances (Binder, 1996). Consequently, Lindsley and his colleagues chose response rate as their primary dimension for measuring behavior change in academic settings. As we saw in chapter 3, rate is an important dimension of many kinds of behavior; indeed, the objective of many clinical or applied interventions is to bring about marked increases or decreases in the frequency of a target behavior.

Over the course of several years, Lindsley and his colleagues experimented on various graphing strategies for depicting academic learning. Having observed that academic progress often occurs rapidly (at least under optimal instructional conditions) and that many types of behavior change occur proportionally, not arithmetically, these researchers opted against using a standard equal interval or add–subtract graph to depict learning; instead, they spent several years developing a graph that would more properly display the proportional or multiplicative changes characteristic of behavioral processes. The result of these efforts is the *Standard Celeration Chart*, an example of which is shown in Figure 4.6.

Although the chart shares many properties of any Cartesian graph, including x- and y-axes, the Standard Celeration Chart utilizes a logarithmic progression rather than an arithmetic progression to depict behavior change on the y-axis. Notice that in Figure 4.6 tick marks on the y-axis represent multiples of 10, ranging from .001 to 1,000. Distances between multiples (e.g., 1 to 10, 10 to 100, 100 to 1,000) are equal, indicating proportionally equivalent changes in the dependent variable. On such a graph, a behavior that increases from once per minute to 10 times per minute would demonstrate the same change in slope as would a behavior changing from 10 times a minute to 100 times a minute. On a more conventional equal-interval or add–subtract graph a change from 1 to 10 responses per minute will pale in comparison to a change from 10 to 100 responses per minute. Even though both increases represent the same ratio, or proportion, of behavior change, an equal-interval graph produces a considerable distortion that may lead researchers to misinterpret the amount of behavior change. Moreover, it would be challenging to represent a range of behavior change from once per minute to 100 times per minute on an equal-interval graph without severely "squeezing" the y-axis in such a way as to deflate visually the apparent variability in the behavior.

Although there are other characteristics of the Standard Celeration Chart that recommend its use to applied professionals, its strongest feature is the extent to which it allows for standardized depiction of behavior change in individual subjects. The chart allows researchers and clinicians to monitor subjects' progress on a continuous basis and to follow changes in trend, such as target behaviors that accelerate and decelerate, hence the name Standard Celeration Chart. The Standard Celeration Chart has become a vital component of educational assessment among a growing number of teachers who utilize the principles of precision teaching developed by Ogden Lindsley and his students in the 1960s and 1970s. Relying heavily on the basic behavior principles studied by behavior analysts for many decades, precision teaching represents a decidedly science-based instructional strategy characterized by objective measurement, continuous behavioral monitoring, and development and modification of instructional practices informed by empirical data. A major source of data in precision teaching are the Standard Celeration Charts maintained by both teachers and students alike in precision teaching classrooms. In response to the question "What does our Standard Celeration Chart do?" Ogden Lindsley offered the following answer:

> It simplifies things. It simplifies charting so that six year olds can learn it and teach it to others. It simplifies chart reading, making it so fast that we can share charts at 2 minutes each. It simplifies chart checking so much that you can check for x2 learning on 60 charts posted on a ten foot stretch of wall as you walk past without slowing your pace. It simplifies understanding of all growth and decay. (See http://www.celeration.org/faqs)

The Standard Celeration Chart has for many years been enthusiastically endorsed and used by precision teaching educators, but it has not been widely adopted by most researchers and clinicians in the applied health sciences, or by most schoolteachers. This reluctance may be due to many people's lack of familiarity with measuring proportional changes in dependent variables and the corresponding logarithmic scale used by the Standard Celeration Chart. Interested readers are encouraged to contact the Standard Celeration Society (http://www .celeration.org) to learn more about the history of the chart's development, charting tips, and the many applications of the chart to studies of behavior change.

INTERIM SUMMARY

The typical manner of presenting single-case data for purposes of interpretation is as continuous behavior on a time-series or real-time graph. This form of display takes full advantage of the continuous nature of single-case data collection and allows for meaningful interpretation of behavior change in response to independent-variable manipulation. Interpretation of behavior change is influenced by a number of graphing strategies, perhaps most important being the scale dimension chosen to depict the dependent variable. In an effort to standardize both display and interpretation of single-case data, Ogden Lindsley and his colleagues developed the Standard Celeration Chart, which uses a logarithmic (multiplicative) rather than traditional additive scale for plotting behavior on the y-axis. This multiplicative scale not only allows for a standardized method of depicting proportional change in behavior but also makes it possible to portray behaviors that may show excessive variability over time. In the next chapter, we begin discussing the specific kinds of design strategies used by single-case researchers to evaluate data collected during actual applied studies.

KEY TERMS GLOSSARY

Idiographic research Research that utilizes observation and measurement at the level of the individual subject with no intention of establishing general laws.

Nomothetic research Research that collects and aggregates data across subjects for the purpose of establishing general laws.

Inductive strategy Research in which general principles are derived from specific observations.

Deductive strategy Research in which specific observations or hypotheses are derived from general principles or theories.

Intrasubject replication Research in which replications of experimental conditions occur at the level of the individual subject.

Intersubject replication Research in which replications of experimental conditions occur across two or more subjects.

External validity The extent to which the results of a particular study are applicable or generalizable to other populations or settings.

Behavior An adaptive, ongoing interplay between an organism and its immediate environment.

Baseline A period of observation of the target behavior in its natural state prior to manipulation of the independent variable or intervention.

SUPPLEMENTS

Review Questions

1. What is the difference between an idiographic and a nomothetic approach to studying behavior? Which one of these approaches is endorsed by single-subject researchers, and why?

2. What is the difference between intrasubject and intersubject replication? Which kind of replication study would be conducted if a researcher were interested in discovering generally applicable principles of behavior?

3. Suppose a physical therapist is conducting an intervention study in which a power-walking regimen is used to try and build leg strength in a patient recovering from leg surgery. In this study, what are the independent and dependent variables, respectively?

4. What is a time-series graph, and how does it help exhibit the continuous nature of behavioral data? Also, on which axis is time usually represented on such a graph?

5. What is the primary difference between conventional time-series graphs and the Standard Celeration Chart? Why did Lindsley and his colleagues recommend use of the Standard Celeration Chart?

SUGGESTED READINGS/HELPFUL WEB SITES

Tufte, E. R. (2001). *The visual display of quantitative information* (2nd ed.). Cheshire, CT: Graphics Press.

Edward Tufte has been called the "Galileo" of graphic presentation. In several elegant books, including this one, Tufte has described the powerful and flexible use of graphics to portray evidence, as well as the common mistakes made by scientists and others in the presentation of data. Tufte's books are both extremely attractive and fascinating explorations of the use of imagery in conveying information.

http://www.edwardtufte.com
This is Edward Tufte's Web site. You can purchase any of Tufte's highly acclaimed books on graphic display, read articles by Tufte about display strategies, including the problems with PowerPoint, and even ask Tufte questions about display issues.

http://www.celeration.org
This is the Web site of the Standard Celeration Society, which publishes the Standard Celeration Chart and data gathered by scientists and educators using the chart. There are links to articles describing the history of the Standard Celeration Chart, its advantages over equal-interval charts for behavioral research, and examples of the chart used in applied settings, especially by precision teachers.

http://seab.envmed.rochester.edu/jaba/
This is the Web site for the *Journal of Applied Behavior Analysis*, a scientific journal devoted to research involving basic behavioral interventions in applied settings, including schools, workplaces, and the home. *Journal of Applied Behavior Analysis* researchers are devoted to the single-case method of data collection, analysis, and display. The journal is an especially good resource for individuals who want to learn how to display single-case data in graphic form.

Chapter 5

SINGLE-CASE EXPERIMENTAL DESIGNS
The Withdrawal Design

Lakeesha, a 12-year-old African American girl beginning the seventh grade, had been diagnosed with a possible pervasive developmental disorder when she was 4. Most recently, she had been given the diagnosis of Asperger's disorder on the basis of her symptoms. Specifically, Lakeesha has difficulties interacting with her peers, exhibiting reduced eye contact, "odd" facial expressions and gestures, a lack of social or emotional reciprocity, and failure to develop appropriate peer relationships. Typically, Lakeesha can be found by herself in the school library rather than interacting with the other students. Although her verbal skills are good, she dislikes writing, and she rarely seems to understand the jokes of the other students. Because of her gullibility, she is frequently the brunt of jokes by some of the more popular children in the school. This is intensified by Lakeesha's intense focus on geometry proofs. For the past year, Lakeesha has been fascinated by geometry proofs, and she spends hours each day completing all of the proofs she can find in geometry texts. Prior to her interest in geometry, she was fascinated by origami in the fifth grade, making and displaying more than 3,000 origami creations. In the fourth grade, Lakeesha had been focused on animal tracks and had spent hours each day in the local woods finding and drawing animal tracks. This pattern of intense focus had been documented from the time that Lakeesha was 2. Despite these difficulties, Lakeesha has been a fairly good student, typically earning As in honors math and science and Bs in her other subjects.

Prior to beginning seventh grade, Lakeesha attended a local elementary school, where she had been since kindergarten. Although the other children made fun of Lakeesha and were aware of her oddities, Lakeesha was fairly comfortable with the routine and seemed to be fine. However, as a seventh grader, Lakeesha entered a junior high with students from five local elementary schools. This transition has not been very successful. Lakeesha's grades have fallen, and she has begun to develop aggressive outbursts when she is frustrated. As might be expected with this age group, Lakeesha's oddities have also led to increased social rejection. This is especially frustrating to Lakeesha; she has stated that she would like to have a friend but does not know how to "get one."

WITHDRAWAL DESIGNS: THE ABA MODEL

So far in this book we have discussed several features of single-case research, particularly with respect to how this type of design differs from the more traditional group designs that have dominated the research scene in the behavioral and health sciences for several decades. In addition to understanding the unique features and advantages of single-case design, researchers must also be familiar with the various design options that are available to pursue single-case research. As with any other research design, single-case strategies must be flexible enough to apply to a variety of settings while being sensitive to the special restrictions that may characterize any particular research environment. In this chapter, we describe one of the basic kinds of designs available to single-case researchers: **withdrawal** (also referred to as *reversal* or *ABA*) **designs**. In addition, we consider features of the research setting or behavioral phenomena that may render one design more appropriate than the other. Finally, we will see how two professionals in the health care setting would use a withdrawal design to address the problems presented in the case of Lakeesha described at the beginning of this chapter.

The classic single-case research design is referred to as a *withdrawal design* because it involves presentation and then subsequent removal of an independent variable, or, in applied settings, a clinical intervention. The design is also referred to as an *ABA* or *reversal design* because of the sequence of experimental conditions from nontreatment (A), to treatment (B), and back to a nontreatment phase (A). This design sequence represents a simple yet powerful means of assessing the effects of the independent variable on behavior, and it has played a significant role in both basic and applied behavioral research. The logic of the withdrawal design follows closely the experimental practices of the natural sciences, particularly with respect to the drawing of causal inference. It is important, in fact, to consider in detail the nature of this logic because it informs all single-case designs in one way or another.

The Baseline (A) Phase

All scientific research begins with observation, and in the behavioral and health sciences observation is normally directed toward some activity on the part of a subject. Assuming that operational definitions are in order and that details of the observational strategy have been worked out, formal observation and collection of data can begin. The first order of business is to establish what the behavior looks like prior to manipulation of the independent variable or implementation of the intervention program. Remember that in single-case research, the subject or participant will be serving as his or her own control, and this requires that we be in a position to make reasonable comparisons. Thus, as mentioned earlier, the beginning phase in such a study is something like the *before* condition in a *before–after* clinical trial.

This initial phase of the research study, during which observation and data collection occur in the absence of any manipulated variable, is referred to as the **baseline phase**. Our goal as researchers is to ensure that we are obtaining a representative picture of what the behavior of interest looks like in its natural state, or at least as natural as the behavior can be under the somewhat unusual circumstances of observation. Keep in mind that in many studies reactivity is to be expected, and the wise researcher will collect data during this phase long enough to account for this atypical behavior. During the baseline phase, relevant dimensions of behavior (rate, duration, latency, etc.) will be recorded systematically and repeatedly for each subject. These measures will be depicted graphically and will serve as the baseline or comparison against which to judge behavior change during the manipulation or intervention phase of the study.

Steady State (Stability). Like any other natural phenomenon, behavior exhibits considerable variability, both between subjects and within a single subject over time. The logic of single-case research eliminates this first source of variability because all data collection is conducted at the level of the individual and because data are not aggregated across subjects. Within-subject variability, however, is not eliminated but is in fact a major focus of the repeated-measures aspect of this research design. Because many measures of the relevant dependent variable will be taken during all phases of the study, the researcher has the opportunity to directly and continuously assess the degree and pattern of behavioral variability throughout the study.

When observed continuously over time, any phenomenon can be expected to fluctuate or show small deviations from a central value, and behavior is no exception to this rule. We cannot expect that any specific target behavior, when measured repeatedly under the baseline condition, will be entirely stable or show no variability. Looking back again at Figure 4.2, we can see that the number of times that John Doe washes his hands changes some from day to day. If this were not the case, then the line in the graph would be completely flat, depicting the same frequency of hand washing every day. This would be unusual, not only for hand washing but for virtually any human behavior. Nevertheless, the amount of variability in the behavior is fairly minimal, and, more important, there appears to be no substantial trend toward more or less hand washing throughout the observation period. In other words, we are inclined to conclude that John Doe's hand washing appears fairly stable, not increasing or decreasing significantly throughout the baseline phase. This stability, or absence of upward or downward trend, in the data is referred to as a **steady state**, and it serves a critical function as a benchmark against which to compare behavior in the subsequent treatment phase of the study.

Notice that a steady state does not imply a lack of variability in the data, only that there is no discernible trend upward or downward. Achieving a steady state during the baseline phase of a study is crucial if the researcher wishes to be in a position to draw reasonable conclusions about the effects of an intervention. If behavior is moving upward or downward during baseline, when no treatment or independent variable is being presented, then the researcher's ability to interpret the effects of treatment is seriously compromised. A continuing trend in the behavior during treatment may have no relationship to the treatment itself but reflect instead the impact of some variable present even prior to the intervention.

Because steady-state responding will serve as the control phase of the experiment, its establishment assumes tremendous importance in all single-case studies. Among the practical concerns that researchers face in this regard is the length of time during which baseline observations should be made and, correspondingly, the amount of data that contribute to a steady state. This issue often pits the demands of scientific rigor against the ethical and practical concerns of the clinical practitioner. From a scientific vantage point, the more data collected, the more confidence one can place in their representativeness as well as the conclusions they provoke (Barlow & Hersen, 1984). Small samples of behavior may not reveal the full range of responding that might be characteristic of a particular subject, especially with respect to the kinds of cycles or fluctuations that are common in many behaviors and physiological processes.

Figure 5.1 illustrates the principle of **behavioral cyclicity** and its consequences for measurement. The figure depicts Jane Doe's exercise regimen (riding a stationary exercise bike), in minutes per day, over the course of more than 3 weeks. Notice that, despite considerable variability, the pattern of exercise for Jane is actually quite orderly. Throughout the observation period, 5 days of relatively longer exercise periods (20–35 minutes) alternate with 2 days of shorter exercise periods (10 minutes or less). This pattern may represent changes in Jane's personal schedule that correspond to the work week and to days off during the weekend.

Continuing the observation period through this 3.5-week period allows the researcher to see the full sweep of this behavior cycle. On the other hand, if the researcher had collected baseline data only for the first 5 days of observation and then moved on to the intervention condition, a very different picture would have emerged. The researcher might have drawn the conclusion that the behavior was stable, thus justifying application of an independent variable or intervention. Any change in behavior during the subsequent phase would likely be attributed, though erroneously, to the intervention. In this case, this inference would be wrong because the change in behavior simply represented a natural fluctuation or cycle that happened to correspond accidentally with a manipulated variable. By collecting more baseline data, the researcher would have become aware of this cycle, and incorrect inferences about the effects of the intervention would have been less likely.

The natural behavior cycle portrayed in Figure 5.1 is not at all uncommon. Many behavioral processes, including mood states, attention span, eating and sleeping, leisure activities, and a host of others, exhibit patterns, either for fundamental physiological reasons or in response to environmental variables that also fluctuate. Fortunately, cycles in behavior pose no serious problem for the researcher, as long as the baseline condition is carried out long enough to allow the full cycle to be expressed. Notice, too, that the considerable variability in responding represented in Figure 5.1 has no bearing on judgments about steady-state behavior. As long as no trend in the behavior in an upward or downward direction is apparent, then the behavior can be viewed as stable, and further experimental conditions can be instituted. This point is especially important to the applied researcher because the degree of variability observed in natural settings is

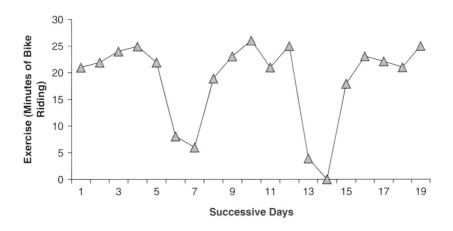

Figure 5.1   Jane Doe's exercise

likely to exceed that obtained under controlled laboratory conditions. One cannot, for example, be expected to control those factors, such as work responsibilities, family issues, and others, that might contribute to the variability in exercise seen for Jane Doe in Figure 5.1. The variability evident in the graph is acceptable so long as it represents the full cycle characteristic of this behavior and so long as it does not contain evidence of an upward or downward trend.

Of course, in an applied setting, scientific validity often must take a back seat to practicality. A professional clinician may not have the luxury of observing behavior and taking baseline measures over a prolonged period of time, such as several weeks. Constraints on time may emerge either from the clinician's heavy caseload or from policies or regulations specific to the institution or setting in which the intervention is being conducted. In addition, ethical issues sometimes prohibit long baseline observation periods. If the behavior being targeted is extremely disruptive or potentially dangerous to oneself or to others (e.g., self-injurious behavior in autistic children), drawn-out baseline observation periods cannot easily be justified. (Remember that baseline represents a period during which no treatment or therapy is being instituted.) Consequently, applied researchers seldom have the opportunity to continue baseline observation as long as would be considered optimal by the laboratory scientist. Efforts to quantify optimal baseline length are admirable but must be viewed within the context of the practical and ethical considerations characterizing any applied setting. The trade-offs between scientific rigor and clinical accountability are substantive in applied settings, and we revisit this issue throughout this book.

Independent-Variable Manipulation or Intervention (B) Phase

Once baseline observation has been carried out sufficiently to allow for a steady state to emerge (when ethically and logistically possible), manipulation of the independent variable or intervention is in order. This phase of the study is of course the crucial part of the experiment; indeed, it is the reason the study was designed in the first place. We wish either to know what impact an independent variable has on the behavior of interest or, in an applied study, whether some treatment or intervention produces a clinically useful effect.

Treatment Integrity

In Chapter 4, we dealt at length with the importance of identifying and specifying the dimensions of the target behavior or dependent variable. It is similarly imperative that researchers describe adequately the independent variable, which in most applied studies is a clinical intervention. The difficulty of this task depends on the complexity of the intervention. In one setting this might amount to nothing more than a relatively simple pharmacological regimen. In another setting, however, intervention may entail a collection of therapeutic components, as in the administration of a token economy in a psychiatric facility.

Researchers use the phrase **treatment integrity** to describe the extent to which an independent variable (or intervention) is delivered in a way consistent with its intent or operationalization. For instance, a child care worker may be utilizing a time-out procedure to alter the disruptive behavior of a preschool-age child. To establish the effectiveness of the intervention, a researcher would need to specify the components of the procedure (there are several varieties of "time out" as used in such settings) and ensure that the procedure was being implemented consistently as specified by the treatment protocol. Periodic deviations from the specified program prove troublesome for the scientist trying to draw inferences from the study. If the treatment plan is not followed as written and no change in the dependent variable is observed, no viable conclusion is possible. The treatment may appear to have been ineffective because it was not implemented properly. On the other hand, if an improperly administered intervention is followed by improvement in behavior, questions will remain as to why the treatment was effective or which component was responsible for the behavior change.

Regardless of the dimensions of any specific intervention, researchers are obligated to describe how the intervention has been operationalized as well as the specific procedures for carrying it out. The former requirement is necessary for purposes of replication. If the intervention is insufficiently described and potentially important clinical features omitted, attempts at replicating the study may prove unsuccessful. Such an outcome may lead to abandoning an otherwise effective treatment. In addition to specifying the details of the intervention, researchers must be vigilant in ensuring that the intervention is carried out as specified. This requirement, though often overlooked, is a challenge to meet, particularly when the intervention will be delivered by someone other than the researcher. In many applied interventions this is the case, as clients, teachers, parents, and perhaps even coworkers assume some responsibility for administering the intervention. This may require not only substantial amounts of time and effort devoted to training the administrators of the intervention but also occasional checks on whether the intervention is being delivered consistently and as specified (Neef, 1995; Schlosser, 2002). Carr, Bailey, Carr, and Coggin (1996) addressed this issue in a study of a client with Tourette's syndrome who had been trained to self-administer an intervention, which included self-monitoring of tics and competing response practice. The researchers report that the study results were not interpretable because the client had not properly instituted the intervention.

Unfortunately, the issue of treatment integrity has received less attention on the part of researchers than has the issue of dependent-variable operationalization and measurement (Gresham, 1997; Gresham, Gansle, & Noell, 1993; McDonell et al., 2007; Perepletchikova & Kazdin, 2005). Several literature reviews suggest that although published studies in the behavioral and health sciences invariably describe their rationale for defining and measuring target behaviors (dependent variables), most researchers fail to describe any process for ensuring treatment integrity. Peterson, Homer, and Wonderlich (1982), for example, reported that the issue of treatment integrity was essentially ignored in about 80% of more than 500 articles appearing in a major behavioral psychology journal, the *Journal of Applied Behavior Analysis,* from 1968 through 1980. Other, more recent reviews have reached similar conclusions (Gresham, Gansle, Noell, Cohen, & Rosenblum, 1993; McDougall, Skouge, Farrell, & Hoff, 2006; Moncher & Prinz, 1991), suggesting that the topic of treatment integrity deserves additional attention at the hands of both researchers and clinicians.

Once the intervention or independent variable has been instituted, data from this condition can be graphed alongside the baseline measures, thus serving a comparative purpose. Hypothetical treatment data for John Doe, our now-familiar obsessive–compulsive hand washer, are depicted in Figure 5.2. We will assume that this client was exposed to a typical treatment, such as a form of cognitive–behavioral therapy. Although we will not describe the details of this treatment, keep in mind that in the interest of treatment integrity, such a detailed description would be expected in the case of an actual study being carried out for publication. The client's rate of hand washing during the treatment condition is represented in the right-hand panel of Figure 5.2. Notice that the graph is split into two halves separated by a vertical line. This division is a standard method of presenting data from single-case studies that allows the reader to directly compare the level of the target behavior both prior to and during the treatment. In this hypothetical example, it is fairly easy to discern a substantial reduction in hand washing for John Doe during the treatment phase of the study.

Return to Baseline (A) Phase

The essence of the withdrawal design is the return to baseline, or nontreatment condition, after a treatment phase. The rationale for this reversal is quite straightforward. If we want to be certain that the behavior change that occurred during treatment was in fact due to the treatment and not to some other variable, then withdrawing the treatment should return behavior to its nontreatment, baseline levels. In other words, the reversal phase is a check on the effect of treatment on the target behavior. It would be improbable that behavior change would occur

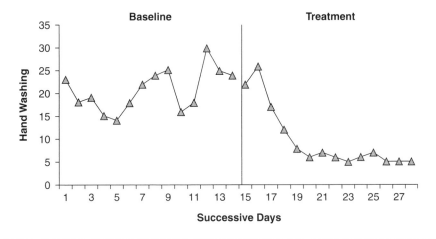

Figure 5.2   John Doe's hand washing

simply by coincidence at the same time that treatment was presented and then again with its removal. In essence, each change in an experimental condition in single-case studies represents an opportunity for drawing causal inferences. The ABA or withdrawal design allows for two such inferences, one with the initial presentation of treatment and the other when treatment is removed.

Figure 5.3 depicts the hand-washing data for John Doe across all three conditions: initial baseline, treatment, and subsequent baseline (withdrawal). There would seem to be little ambiguity about the results of the intervention. John's hand washing reduces substantially during treatment, only to recover to its original level when treatment is removed. Drawing inferences in science depends largely on being able to eliminate potential alternative explanations for a given phenomenon. Research conducted by applied scientists and practitioners clearly has as its goal the identification of effective clinical interventions. Thus when a treatment or intervention is applied and changes in behavior are observed, the scientific objective of the study is to ensure that the resulting behavior change was not due to something other than the treatment. Ensuring that the change was due only to the treatment establishes the study's **internal validity**. In single-case research, the primary rationale for returning to baseline is to establish that behavior change occurring during treatment was in fact due to the treatment, not to some other variable that may have coincidentally occurred simultaneous with the treatment.

For example, perhaps John Doe's treatment for his hand washing was implemented the same week that he formally retired from a 30-year career. Although not

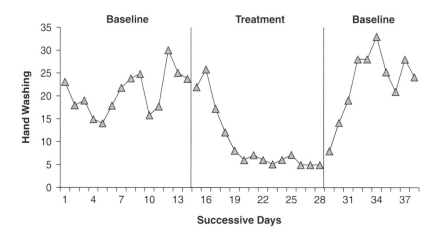

Figure 5.3 John Doe's hand washing

likely, it is certainly possible that the reduction in John Doe's hand washing was brought about by a reduction in stress due to retirement, not anything having to do with the treatment. If this is the case, hand washing should remain at low levels even when treatment is removed during the subsequent return to baseline (the second A phase in the ABA design). If, however, hand washing shows a corresponding increase during the second baseline, as is the case in Figure 5.3, we can be more confident that the reduction during treatment was due to the intervention, not some extraneous variable. When the researcher can rule out an extraneous variable as a potential explanation for behavior change, our confidence is increased in the effectiveness of the independent variable or intervention.

Examples of withdrawal designs being used to evaluate clinical interventions are quite common in the health care literature. For example, Figure 5.4 depicts actual data from a study in which both visual stimulation and auditory stimulation were limited during mealtime for two children who had suffered traumatic brain injury (Hartnedy & Mozzoni, 2000). Clients with brain injuries often have difficulty processing environmental stimulation, and such stimulation can distract clients from engaging in important rehabilitative activities. In this study, auditory and visual stimuli, primarily in the form of social interaction, were presented and withdrawn in an ABA fashion, and the amount of food eaten by each child during the meal functioned as the primary dependent variable. The baseline phases of the study are denoted by B1, B2, B3, and so on, and the treatment phases (reduced stimulation) are denoted by T1, T2, T3, and so on. In this study, four baseline conditions, characterized by normal social conditions, were alternated with treatment conditions in which amount of social stimulation was substantially decreased. As can be seen in Figure 5.4, the dependent variable, amount of meal eaten, increased during periods of treatment relative to baseline conditions. The frequent alternation of baseline and treatment conditions for both children allows for strong inference about the effects of the independent variable because of the numerous replications made possible by this experimental design.

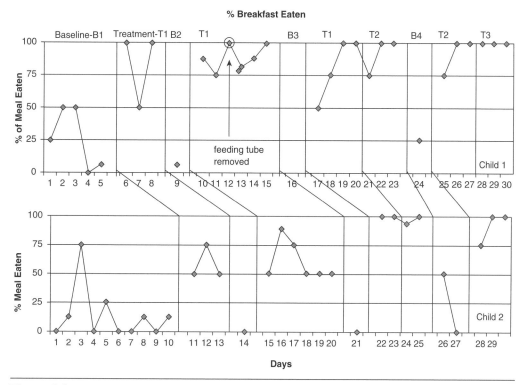

Figure 5.4 Percent of breakfast eaten for children 1 and 2

Source: From "Managing environmental stimulation during meal time: Eating problems in children with traumatic brain injury," Hartnedy, S. & Mozzoni, M. P. 2000 © John Wiley & Sons Limited. Reproduced with permission.

A withdrawal design was also used by Cleland, Hunt, and Palmer (2004) in a study of the effects of neural mobilization on range of motion and pain in a 29-year-old female patient suffering from lower-extremity neurogenic pain. Reported pain was measured using the visual analog scale, in which respondents make a mark on a 10-centimeter line (with 0 indicating no pain and 10 indicating maximum pain) indicating their subjective level of pain. Figure 5.5 depicts the woman's pain ratings during two baseline phases (A1 and A2) as well as during two treatment phases (B1 and B2). During treatment, the patient, lying on her left

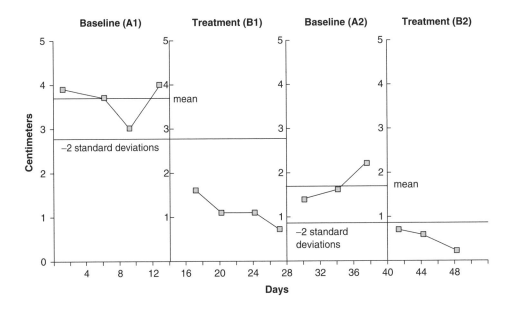

Figure 5.5a   Plotted data for the visual analog scale using the two-standard deviation band method of data analysis

side, was guided by the therapist through both hip and knee flexion exercises. Range of motion was measured using a standard goniometer. Figure 5.5a depicts the results for subjective pain and Figure 5.5b depicts the results for range of motion for both baseline periods and treatment periods. In addition to evaluating the overall level and trend in subjective pain and range of motion during baseline and treatment conditions, the researchers utilized the 2–standard deviation band method to assess the statistical significance of the treatment effect. Details of this method are described in a later chapter of this book.

Yuen (1993) conducted a study in which a cortically blind female patient traced patterns on pine boards during 15-minute work sessions. The treatment involved use of a template to enhance the patient's ability to draw within the borders of the pine boards. A withdrawal design containing two baseline and two treatment conditions was utilized, and separate observers recorded the patient's productivity in the drawing task. Figure 5.6 depicts the drawing data for the patient under both baseline and treatment conditions. The results indicate an average 28% increase in productivity under the treatment conditions relative to baseline productivity rates.

Meza, Powell, and Covington (1998) demonstrated the effects of maternal breast milk odor on the feeding behavior of a preterm (31 weeks gestational age) female infant using a withdrawal design. Preterm infants frequently do not show the sucking reflex typical of full-term babies, and consequently they are often fed

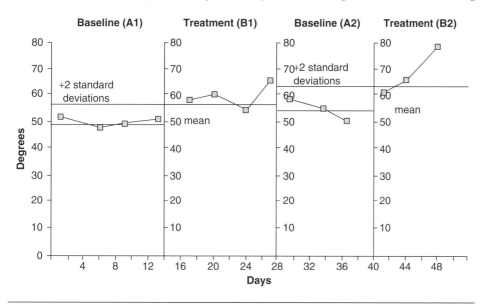

Figure 5.5b   Plotted data for passive hip range of motion during the straight-leg raise using the two-standard deviation band method of data analysis

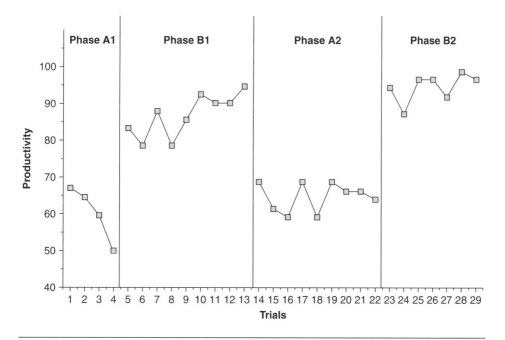

Figure 5.6   Drawing productivity across study phases

through a tube inserted into the nostril and extending to the stomach, a process known as *gavage feeding*. Occupational therapy often focuses on enhancing *non-nutritive sucking*, a term that refers to sucking on pacifiers, nipples, or other objects that do not directly provide nourishment. Strengthening this response is an important developmental milestone, leading eventually to more effective nutritive feeding. Frequency and force of non-nutritive sucking was measured during baseline periods, in which no maternal breast milk odor was present, and during treatment conditions in which a sterile gauze pad soaked with maternal breast milk was held under the infant's nose. The results indicated that frequency and force of sucking increased under treatment (maternal breast milk odor) conditions relative to baseline conditions.

Wu, Huang, Lin, and Chen (1996) utilized a withdrawal design to assess the effects of physical activity on standing posture of three adult patients with *hemiplegia*, a paralysis on one side of the body, often resulting from traumatic brain injury. The patients' ability to stand symmetrically, bearing equal weight on both legs, was measured by the Balance Master System, which determines a patient's center of gravity while he or she is standing on the instrument's forceplate. Intervention involved two physical activities, pushing and pulling a block sander while standing in front of a table, and throwing bean bags at a target, also while standing. All of the patients experienced a sequence of baseline and treatment conditions in an ABAB series. As can be seen in Figure 5.7, patients distributed more weight to the affected limb during treatment conditions, thus attaining closer approximations to symmetrical posture. The dotted line seen in each treatment condition is a *celeration line,* used to predict the dependent variable (in this case, center of gravity) under conditions of no treatment. The deviations of the actual treatment data from what are predicted by the celeration line indicate that the dependent variable was influenced by the treatment. Use of the celeration line in interpreting results from single-case studies is discussed in more detail in a later chapter.

INTERIM SUMMARY

The withdrawal, or ABA, design is a common single-case design utilizing the logic of intrasubject replications to evaluate the effectiveness of an independent variable or clinical intervention. An initial baseline phase (A) establishes the natural occurrence of the target behavior prior to intervention. The baseline phase is used to achieve a steady state, indicating no significant upward or downward trend in the target behavior. The intervention phase (B) is then implemented, and changes in the target behavior are interpretable against the benchmark of baseline responding. Finally, a return to baseline allows the researcher to establish

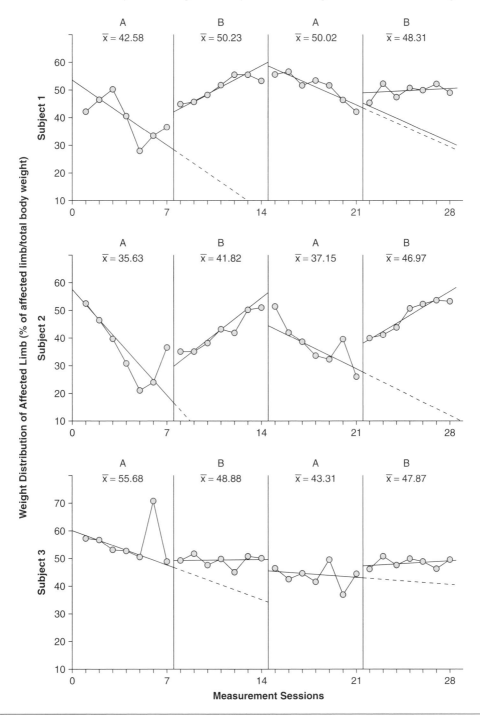

Figure 5.7   Weight distribution by subject across study phases

Source: From Wu, S., Huang, H C., & Chen, M. (1996). Reprinted with permission from the *American Journal of Occupational Therapy.*

whether changes corresponding to intervention resulted from the treatment or from extraneous variables unrelated to treatment.

THE CASE OF LAKEESHA

The case of Lakeesha, presented at the beginning of this chapter, highlighted the dilemma of a child diagnosed with Asperger's disorder. Lakeesha is in regular seventh-grade classes but, because of her disorder, has begun to experience more frustration, leading to several difficulties. If not corrected, these difficulties—frustration leading to aggressive outbursts and the problems she has in making friends—may result in Lakeesha's being unable to remain in her current classroom and increases the probability that she will develop additional psychological difficulties, including major depression.

Asperger's disorder, named after Hans Asperger, who first described the syndrome in 1944, is typically described as a milder variant of autistic disorder. Both Asperger's disorder and autistic disorder (autism) are listed as subgroups of a larger diagnostic category, called either *autistic spectrum disorders*, mostly in European countries, or *pervasive developmental disorders* in the United States. Individuals with Asperger's disorder are characterized by severe impairments in social interaction and the development of restricted and repetitive patterns of behavior, interests, and activities. Unlike autistic individuals, those with Asperger's disorder do not exhibit any impairments in cognitive development, adaptive functioning outside of social interactions, or early delays in language development, although more subtle aspects of social communication, chiefly nonverbal communication, may be impacted, such as the normal give-and-take in conversations.

Because of the difficulties with social interaction encountered by persons with Asperger's disorder, significant social impairment often increases as those individuals approach adolescence. Some of these individuals may learn to use their strengths (particularly rote memorization) to successfully navigate social situations. Other individuals, such as Lakeesha, may experience significant frustration in social situations, leading to aggressive outbursts, depression, or anxiety.

Although Asperger's disorder was originally identified in 1944, it was not until 1994 that this disorder was added to the fourth edition of the *Diagnostic and Statistical Manual of Mental Disorders* (American Psychiatric Association, 1994). Recognition of Asperger's disorder by professionals and parents has increased dramatically in the past few years. Today, many patients with Asperger's are turning to a multidisciplinary treatment team—a group of specialists from diverse disciplines working together with one common goal: managing Asperger's better. Such a treatment team might include physicians, clinical psychologists, psychiatrists, school psychologists, occupational therapists, and speech therapists.

It is likely that Lakeesha will benefit from the services of all of the professionals involved in such a multidisciplinary treatment team. For purposes of our understanding of withdrawal designs, we will focus on how two of these experts—school psychologists and occupational therapists—might be able to assist Lakeesha and document the success of their treatment approach with a withdrawal design.

From a School Psychologist's Perspective

Estimates of Asperger's disorder have ranged as high as 20 to 25 per 10,000. That means that school officials can expect to encounter several children with the disorder. This is especially true of mainstream academic settings, where most children with Asperger's disorder will be found.

With Asperger's disorder, academic progress in the early grades is typically an area of relative strength; for example, rote reading and calculation skills may be strong, whereas pencil skills may be considerably weaker. The teacher may become aware of the child's "obsessive" areas of interest because they may often intrude into the classroom setting. Although most children with Asperger's disorder will show at least some social interest in other children, they are likely to show weak friend-making and friend-keeping skills. During the elementary school years, problems may range in magnitude from mild and easily managed to severe and intractable, depending on factors such as the child's intelligence level, appropriateness of management at school and parenting at home, temperamental style of the child, and the presence or absence of complicating factors such as hyperactivity/ attentional problems, anxiety, and learning problems.

As a child with Asperger's disorder moves into middle school, the most challenging areas continue to be those related to socialization and behavioral adjustment. It is interesting that children with Asperger's disorder may be both helped and disadvantaged by being placed in a mainstream setting. Unfortunately, if the child is bright and does not act too "strange," teachers and other children may easily overlook the problems associated with Asperger's disorder or may misattribute these difficulties to emotional or motivational problems. In settings less familiar or structured, such as the cafeteria, physical education class, walking between classes, or the playground, a child with Asperger's disorder may get into escalating conflicts or power struggles with teachers or students who may not be familiar with his or her developmental style of interacting. This may lead to more serious behavioral flare-ups. As with Lakeesha, the pressure builds, with few external clues, until she then reacts in a dramatically inappropriate manner.

In middle school, where the pressures for conformity are greatest and tolerance for differences least, children with Asperger's disorder may be ostracized, misunderstood, or teased and persecuted. Wanting to make friends and fit in but unable to, they may withdraw even more, or their behavior may become increasingly problematic in the form of outbursts or refusal to cooperate with teachers. Some degree of depression is not uncommon as a complicating feature. If there are no significant learning disabilities, academic performance may remain strong, particularly in areas of interest; often, however, there will be ongoing subtle tendencies to misinterpret information, particularly abstract or figurative/idiomatic language.

Building more appropriate social interactions and helping the child fit in better socially will continue to be a major area of concern for children with Asperger's disorder, as it is for Lakeesha in the current case. Formal, didactic social-skills training can take place both in the classroom and in more individualized settings. Approaches that have been most successful utilize direct modeling and role-playing at a concrete level, such as in the Skillstreaming curriculum (Goldstein, Glick, & Gibbs, 1998). By rehearsing and practicing how to handle various social situations, the child learns to generalize the skills to naturalistic settings. It is often useful to use a dyad approach in which the child is paired with another student to carry out such structured encounters. The use of such a "buddy system" has been found to be very useful, especially because these children tend to relate best one to one. Careful selection of a peer buddy without Asperger's disorder for the child can be a tool to help build social skills, encourage friendships, and reduce stigmatization. Care should be taken, particularly in the upper grades, to protect the child from teasing both in and out of the classroom, because this is one of the greatest sources of anxiety for older children with Asperger's disorder.

In the case of Lakeesha, the school psychologist worked with Lakeesha's core teachers (teachers in English, social studies, math, and science) to select a peer buddy. The identified peer buddy shared many of Lakeesha's interests in math and computers. With the approval of the peer buddy's parents, the peer buddy was provided information about Asperger's disorder, and five skills were identified: (1) sharing ideas, (2) complimenting others, (3) offering help or encouragement, (4) recommending changes nicely, and (5) exercising self-control (Vernon, Schumaker, & Deshler, 1996). Lakeesha worked with the school psychologist to memorize each of these skills and to role-play the appropriate use of these skills. The peer buddy was asked to reinforce Lakeesha by simply smiling at her or telling her she was doing a great job when she engaged in one of these five skills.

Prior to initiating the program, Lakeesha's behavior was tracked during a 4-week baseline period. Figure 5.8 depicts the baseline data for one of these relevant dependent variables, number of conversations, which Lakeesha initiated with others. Each data point depicts accumulated initiated conversations for a period of a week. As can be seen in the figure, Lakeesha initiated no conversations with others during this baseline period. Although not depicted in the figure, Lakeesha demonstrated no instances of voluntarily interacting with other students, and she experienced three incidents of yelling at her fellow students or the teacher. After the baseline period, the peer buddy provided reinforcement and encouragement of appropriate social skills during lunch, walking between classes, and, when appropriate, during classes.

Unfortunately, after 6 weeks of treatment, the peer buddy moved to another school district unexpectedly. This led to a 6-week gap during which the treatment—peer reinforcement of appropriate social behaviors—was not implemented. This gap represented a naturally occurring withdrawal of treatment, as can be seen in the middle right panel of Figure 5.8. Although this is not an ideal situation because the provider of the treatment changed, this type of design allows for a clear understanding of the effectiveness of the program. After this withdrawal period, a second peer buddy was identified and trained and began providing reinforcement and encouragement.

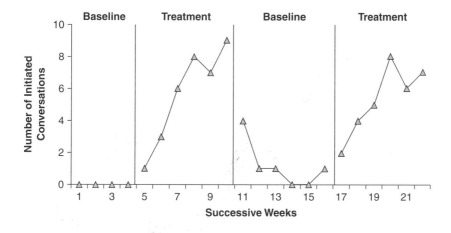

Figure 5.8   Lakeesha's social behavior

Figure 5.8 shows that Lakeesha's appropriate social behavior (e.g., initiation of conversations) was nearly absent during baseline, increased to more appropriate levels during the peer buddy intervention, and then decreased once again during the natural withdrawal produced by the peer buddy's relocation. A reintroduction of the intervention with the newly trained peer buddy led to increases once again in social behavior. In this particular case, the withdrawal of treatment (third panel) served to replicate the data observed during the initial baseline period, while the reintroduction of treatment (last panel) served as a replication of the original treatment. At this point, the psychologist would probably conclude that continuation of the treatment is strongly supported by scientific, clinical, and ethical considerations.

FROM AN OCCUPATIONAL THERAPIST'S PERSPECTIVE

Occupational therapy is primarily focused on improving functioning at home, at school, and in the community. Occupational therapists use developmental tests, parent interviews, and structured observations of activities of daily living to evaluate children and adolescents with Asperger's disorder. To adapt specific tasks to the child, occupational therapists may also perform an *activity analysis* (Porr & Rainville, 1999). The most common interventions utilized by occupational therapists are sensory processing support, social skills training, and behavior management. Occupational therapy includes a wide variety of interventions depending on the needs and level of functioning of the individual. Increasing participation in community activities is a major focus of treatment planning. For individuals diagnosed with Asperger's disorder, more solitary activities, such as swimming programs, horseback riding lessons, and drawing classes, have been found to be more successful than traditional youth programs at churches and group sports teams. Because deficits in reciprocal social skills are the hallmark of individuals with Asperger's disorder, engaging in community activities can be enormously challenging. Interventions with adolescents such as Lakeesha must emphasize preparation for success as workers and community members and should identify environments that will best support it.

It became evident that Lakeesha's increasing frustration and resulting depression were related to her inability to understand nonverbal cues or interact appropriately with others. These difficulties were impacting not only her school performance and school relationships but also her leisure activities. With the school psychologist engaged in addressing Lakeesha's school behaviors, the occupational therapist began working on Lakeesha's interaction with others in leisure activities.

Prior to the occupational therapist's intervention, Lakeesha's only extracurricular activities involved her church. Lakeesha and her family attended church services on Wednesday and Sunday and were involved in several other church-related activities. An analysis of these activities clearly indicated that Lakeesha demonstrated no problems with the structured services on Wednesdays and Sundays; however, the youth group meetings were another story. Lakeesha was ostracized by the other members of the youth group and had experienced an increasing number of behavioral outbursts, including yelling and hitting. The leader of the youth group had asked Lakeesha's mother to not send Lakeesha to the youth group meetings again until her behavior improved. Allowing Lakeesha to choose another activity, such as swimming or horseback riding, was not an option acceptable to her parents. Lakeesha's mother and father were both insistent that Lakeesha be active in her youth group. As a result, the occupational therapist focused on reducing the incidence of the behavioral outbursts.

Prior to instituting any intervention, the occupational therapist met with the leader of the youth group. After Lakeesha's difficulties were explained to him, the youth leader said he was willing to work with the occupational therapist in an effort to allow Lakeesha to improve her behavior in the group. For the first 2 weeks, the occupational therapist simply observed Lakeesha's behavior during the group meetings. On each occasion, Lakeesha began yelling when asked to engage in a task she was reluctant to attempt. Also on each occasion, her outburst led to her not having to complete the task. Believing that Lakeesha's outbursts had been negatively reinforced by removal of an undesirable academic task, the occupational therapist worked with the youth leader to modify his reaction to Lakeesha. For the next six youth group meetings, when Lakeesha began yelling, she was asked to leave the room and sit in the hall. Once she had quieted, Lakeesha was asked to return to the room and complete the activity originally requested. Over the course of the 6 weeks, the number of outbursts decreased (see Figure 5.9). Because of this improvement, after the sixth youth group meeting, the youth leader requested that Lakeesha no longer be required to complete the activity upon returning to the room. He reported that he believed this took too much time and that Lakeesha was doing so much better that he was not sure she needed this part of the treatment.

Over the course of the next six youth group meetings, the youth leader continued to make Lakeesha sit in the hall when she began yelling. However, when she returned to the room, she was not required to complete the original activity. This decision was made in part because of the difficulty and time involved in getting

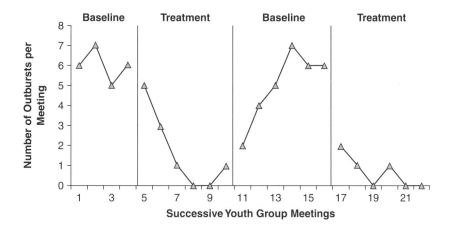

Figure 5.9   Lakeesha's outbursts

Lakeesha to complete assignments and because the occupational therapist wanted to be sure that Lakeesha's outbursts were in fact due to the desire to successfully escape unwanted tasks. In many clinical populations, particularly people with developmental disabilities, including autism-spectrum disorders and mental retardation, escape from aversive or undesirable tasks is a common motivation, or reinforcer, for aggressive, self-injurious, or other inappropriate behavior (Hanley, Iwata, & McCord, 2003; Iwata, Dorsey, Slifer, Bauman, & Richman, 1994; Iwata, Pace, et al., 1994). Consistent with the occupational therapist's hypothesis about Lakeesha's behavior, removing the requirement of completing assignments led to a dramatic increase in the number of outbursts. In essence, this condition involved a withdrawal of the intervention and a return to the conditions that were in place during the original baseline observation. Quite understandably, the occupational therapist and group leader made a joint decision to institute once again the removal and task completion requirement characterized by the original treatment protocol for the remaining nine weeks of the youth group.

Limitations of the Withdrawal Design

The withdrawal design and its strategy of implementing and then removing independent variables or clinical interventions allow for strong causal conclusions; consequently, the design has enjoyed a storied history in the behavioral sciences. Nevertheless, this strategy possesses certain limitations to go along with its strengths as a research design. There are in fact occasions when conducting a withdrawal design would be inappropriate on either logistical or ethical grounds, and under these circumstances single-case researchers should probably opt for another design.

For example, behavioral changes resulting from systematic interventions often become quite enduring, even *after* removal of the treatment. This means that returning to baseline conditions does not always result in a return of behavior to its preintervention level. Indeed, we might expect this to be the case with John Doe's hand-washing treatment. If in fact the treatment is successful in reducing or eliminating his anxiety about contagion and if this reduction in anxiety continues even after formal treatment has been terminated, we would not expect his hand-washing rate to return to its original baseline level. Such permanent changes in behavior are both common and desirable, regardless of the specific behavior being targeted for change. For instance, a cognitive–behavior therapist may be helping a client to change negative attributions the client makes about co-workers' behavior. Using take-home assignments, the client practices reevaluating the possible causes of co-workers' actions, and eventually comes to view their behavior less negatively. Once this reevaluation has been mastered, the client naturally reconsiders coworkers' behaviors without the prompting of the therapist. Thus, this cognitive strategy, once learned, occurs fairly automatically for the client. As it turns out, even such mundane everyday behaviors as dressing ourselves, cooking meals, reading, balancing a checkbook, and numerous others become permanent fixtures of our repertoires once they have been learned.

The problem of enduring behavior change following treatment termination is of course primarily problematic only to the scientist. If behavior does not return to original baseline levels, some question will remain as to whether a causal relationship has been demonstrated between the treatment and the target behavior. On the other hand, the issue is likely to be viewed differently by the clinician, who considers the maintenance of behavior change following treatment as a defining feature of the intervention's effectiveness. After all, any therapeutic program entails as a primary objective the independent or autonomous functioning of the client after treatment termination; that is, long-term treatment maintenance is an altogether desirable outcome in clinical practice. Numerous studies have been conducted for the purpose of identifying the variables that impact long-term maintenance of treatment gains so that these factors can be intentionally programmed into the intervention (Horner, Dunlap, & Koegel, 1988; Landrum & Lloyd, 1992; Stokes & Baer, 1977; Stokes & Osnes, 1989).

The withdrawal strategy may also be inadvisable when removing a potentially effective treatment poses ethical implications. Particularly when targeted behavior has profound consequences for either the client or others, as is the case with aggression or self-injurious behavior, removing treatment for purposes of assessing its effectiveness may be unacceptable. Under these circumstances, most researchers would use an alternative design strategy, particularly the multiple-baseline designs, which do not require removing treatment (see Chapter 6, this volume). If a withdrawal design was used, the researchers would likely conclude the study with a second intervention phase, which would result in an ABAB design. Doing so allows for an additional replication, which adds strength to the scientific conclusions the study will support. The fact that the ABAB design terminates with a treatment phase might help, in some cases, diminish, although not altogether remove, the ethical concern about removing treatment.

Another strategy for dealing with the ethical dilemma of not delivering treatment is to alter the sequence of phases in a withdrawal design. In other words, it is possible to move from an immediate treatment condition to a subsequent, perhaps shortened, baseline condition, making the design effectively a BAB design. The general logic of the withdrawal design remains intact, but the sensitive question of beginning with a prolonged baseline, during which time the target behavior is occurring without treatment, is eliminated. For example, Pace and

Toyer (2000) conducted a study in which a multivitamin supplement was given to a 9-year-old girl diagnosed with severe mental retardation and with *pica*, which involves eating nonfood substances. In the present case, the girl was observed to eat string, cloth, and synthetic fibers. Because at the study's onset the girl was already taking a physician-prescribed multivitamin (a common medical treatment for pica), this condition served as the original period of observation. Removal of the supplement constituted the second phase of the study and served as a baseline condition. Finally, the multivitamin was reintroduced in the final treatment phase, thus creating a BAB single-case design. During all observation periods, actual ingestion of nonfood substances was physically disallowed; if the child moved a nonfood object toward her mouth, the behavior was scored as an instance of pica, but the object was taken away before it could be ingested. Instances of pica were reduced under the multivitamin condition, indicating the usefulness of this particular medical intervention for this client. The study also demonstrates how, in applied settings, the decision criteria of science must frequently take a back seat to ethical and clinical considerations.

Despite its advantages, then, the withdrawal design possesses limitations as well. How severe these limitations are for any particular study must be ascertained by the researcher. Fortunately, when the withdrawal design is considered inappropriate on either logistical or ethical grounds, alternative single-case strategies exist for evaluating the effects of an intervention. We describe these design alternatives in subsequent chapters.

INTERIM SUMMARY

The case of Lakeesha demonstrates how a single-case researcher would evaluate the effects of a multidisciplinary treatment delivered by a psychologist and by an occupational therapist. Although the dependent variables of interest may differ between the disciplines, the withdrawal or ABA research design is well equipped to offer a rigorous assessment of the effects of the differing interventions. The primary shortcomings of the withdrawal design are its inability to account for maintained behavior change in the absence of ongoing treatment and the ethical difficulties associated with withdrawing potentially effective treatments.

KEY TERMS GLOSSARY

Withdrawal design A single-subject design in which baseline phases (A) are alternated with treatment phases (B); also referred to as *reversal* and *ABA* design.

Baseline phase Observation phase during the study when the target behavior is measured in its natural state, unaffected by the intervention or independent variable.

Steady state A condition in which a measured behavior or dependent variable exhibits relative stability over time, with little to no upward or downward trend.

Behavioral cyclicity Normal, systematic upward and downward cycles or trends, often seen in behavior even under baseline conditions prior to manipulation of variables.

Treatment integrity The extent to which an independent variable or intervention is delivered in a manner consistent with its operationalization.

Internal validity The extent to which changes in the dependent variable can be inferred to be due to manipulation of the independent variable in a study.

SUPPLEMENTS

Review Questions

1. In the case of Lakeesha, why is a multidisciplinary treatment approach endorsed? Also, what are the relevant dependent variables being measured in this hypothetical study?

2. In group designs, researchers usually end up comparing the mean of a treatment group with the mean of a control group. What kind of comparison is being made in a single-subject research design?

3. What role does the baseline phase serve in a single-subject design? How is the interpretation of baseline data influenced by whether the behavior demonstrates stability (a steady state)?

4. What is treatment integrity, and how would you ensure that it was maintained in the intervention delivered by the occupational therapist and youth leader in the case of Lakeesha?

5. If Lakeesha's outbursts had remained at low levels during the withdrawal phase of the study (see third panel of Figure 5.9), how would you interpret this result? In what way is this finding somewhat perplexing to the scientist but pleasing to the clinician?

SUGGESTED READINGS/HELPFUL WEB SITES

http://www.ninds.nih.gov/disorders/pdd/pdd.htm
This Web site offers information and links to other Web sites dealing with pervasive developmental disorders, including autism and Asperger's disorder. Lakeesha, the female student introduced in this chapter, has been diagnosed as having a pervasive developmental disorder.

Carr, J. E., & Burkholder, E. O. (1998). Creating single-subject design graphs with Microsoft Excel™. *Journal of Applied Behavior Analysis, 31,* 245–251.

This article describes in step-by-step fashion how to construct a single-case graph using a spreadsheet program (Microsoft Excel) that is probably somewhat familiar to many readers.

Chapter 6

MULTIPLE-BASELINE DESIGNS

Juan is a 27-year-old man of mixed Latino and African American descent. For the past 5 years, he has lived in a series of group homes and apartments for men diagnosed with schizophrenia and bipolar disorder. Juan, an only child, was diagnosed with disorganized schizophrenia midway through his senior year in high school following a 7-month period of deterioration during which his behavior became increasingly inappropriate both at school and at home. Prior to his deterioration, Juan had always been considered somewhat odd by the other children because of his unusual ideas and physical and social awkwardness. Juan had been a low-average student, earning mostly Cs and a few Ds in his courses. He played saxophone in the band and was friends with two other students who were also in the band. After school, Juan worked as a bagger in a small grocery store owned by his parents. Juan's teachers contacted his parents when Juan began wearing unusual combinations of clothing, such as wearing a pair of shorts over his jeans, and failing to bathe on a regular basis. His speech also became more unusual, with his responses littered with rhymes, such as "Let's go to the store, in the door" and made-up words, such as "Don't touch the nikto." His affect also changed and became more inappropriate, with giggling during serious discussions and facial grimacing. Juan's parents brought him to the hospital after he was found playing with his feces in the school bathroom. When the teachers attempted to remove him from the bathroom, Juan shouted at them to leave him alone and not to touch his "masterpieces."

Initial treatment for Juan was followed by an attempt to return him to his home. This led to another episode of disruptive behavior, resulting in his readmission to the hospital. Eventually, Juan was placed in a group home, where he received consistent monitoring and was able to spend a few hours each day working as a dishwasher in a local restaurant. Juan has been in a series of group homes and apartments over the past 5 years. He is typically asked to leave his group home or apartment when his behavior becomes so inappropriate that the staff or other residents can no longer tolerate him. Juan reports that using his medication "just depends on whether the sun hiccups," leading to an inconsistent and potentially dangerous pattern of medication usage. At this point, Juan has been readmitted to the hospital to stabilize his medicine before he is placed in another group home or apartment.

Dylan and Daryl are identical 29-year-old twins of Caucasian and African American descent. Their childhood and teen years were described as "fairly normal" by their parents, because the boys had a small group of friends and adequate school performance. Both boys showed an early interest in religion and had planned to enter the ministry. However, during their first year at college, Dylan experienced a psychotic break. First, Dylan began skipping his classes to spend more time researching the Knights Templar and the Holy Grail. He believed that the Holy Grail was hidden on campus and that messages were carved into bricks on the campus buildings. Dylan was removed from school after failing the first semester and over the break was hospitalized with a diagnosis of paranoid schizophrenia. He was placed on antipsychotic medications to address his delusions and showed a reduction in his symptoms. However, on returning to college, he discontinued his medication and experienced a relapse. Since the initial relapse, Dylan has experienced four subsequent relapses separated by stays in group homes and apartments. In contrast, Daryl completed his first year of college successfully. During the second year, however, he experienced a psychotic break quite similar in nature to Dylan's. Daryl began spending more and more time locked in his dorm room and refused to eat in the dorm cafeteria. Daryl reported that he had tasted an odd metallic flavor in his food and was convinced that the cafeteria workers were trying to poison him. As weeks passed, he became more unkempt, quit sleeping, and refused to eat any food he had not prepared himself. By the end of the fall semester, it was clear that Daryl was also experiencing paranoid schizophrenia, and his parents admitted him to a psychiatric facility. As in the case of his twin, antipsychotic medications reduced his symptoms, and he was able to return to his college studies. Daryl finished his undergraduate degree in social work, but during his first job he discontinued his medication, leading to a relapse. Hospitalization and medication once again reduced his symptoms, but not as significantly as after the first episode. In the intervening years, Daryl has experienced two subsequent relapses, both related to his decision to discontinue his medication. Before his most recent relapse, Daryl was living in the same apartment facility as his twin, Dylan.

LOGIC OF THE MULTIPLE-BASELINE DESIGN

In Chapter 5, we described the classic withdrawal research design, a powerful and storied strategy for evaluating behavior change in individual subjects in response to manipulated variables and applied interventions. Because of its strong reliance on intrasubject replication, the withdrawal design allows one to make strong inferences about behavior change, and this may explain the design's exalted status, both in basic laboratory studies and in applied settings. However, such designs become problematic when changes in behavior become permanent and unlikely to return to preintervention or baseline levels, or when removal of a clinical treatment may be ethically questionable. Fortunately, researchers need not despair when deciding against the use of a withdrawal design for ethical or logistical reasons. Confident conclusions about treatment effectiveness can be achieved through the use of **multiple-baseline designs**, in which a single transition from baseline to treatment (AB) is instituted at different times across multiple clients, behaviors, or settings (situations or conditions). Remember that the essential logic of all single-subject designs rests on the ability to replicate the effects of an independent variable or clinical intervention. This replication is simply achieved in a different manner in multiple-baseline designs from that in a withdrawal design.

Multiple Baseline Across Subjects (Clients)

You may recall John Doe from earlier chapters. A corporate executive suffering from obsessive–compulsive disorder, John spends a great deal of time each day washing his hands thoroughly because of a fear of contamination. Suppose that the psychologist working with John wishes to implement a behavioral therapy program for John but is not sure he wants to utilize a withdrawal strategy. This decision might be made either on ethical grounds or because the psychologist believes that once John's behavior changes, treatment removal is unlikely to result in a return of hand washing to its baseline level. The latter scenario is probably most likely in this particular case. It is, after all, the goal of behavior therapy to permanently alter some aspect of a client's functioning, and this is brought about through relatively well-researched and established principles of learning. As you can well appreciate, many skills, once learned, tend to persist in a person's repertoire, often for a lifetime. You possess numerous behavioral skills, such as dressing yourself, reading, cooking, driving, and many others, that you learned probably years ago but continue to rely on daily. In fact, you may not recall with much clarity when and how you learned these skills, but you would be dramatically aware of suddenly losing any one of these capabilities.

The goal of exposing a client to behavior therapy interventions is to produce an important and reliable change in the target behavior that will maintain itself beyond the formal parameters of treatment. One would not expect that these behavioral gains would disappear once treatment was removed. Subsequent to behavior therapy for hand washing, we would anticipate that John Doe may never return to the excessively high rate of hand washing that preceded treatment. Nevertheless, the psychologist working with John Doe wishes to ensure that any reduction in John Doe's hand washing is the result of the behavioral treatment and not some other uncontrolled variable. Thus, he decides to conduct and evaluate an intervention using a multiple-baseline design. To do this, the psychologist decides to provide the behavioral intervention at different times for John Doe and for two other clients also diagnosed with obsessive–compulsive disorder, Sue and Dave. The study begins with the collection of baseline data from all three clients, as depicted in Figure 6.1. Notice, though, that the baseline phases are of unequal lengths across clients and that the intervention is consequently begun at different times for each client. This staggered or unequal baseline period is what gives the design its name. Indeed, multiple-baseline designs are often referred to as *staggered baseline designs.*

Notice in Figure 6.1 that each client receives the clinical intervention at a different time and that only one phase change, from baseline to treatment, occurs during the study for each client. There is no return to baseline after treatment. Thus, the multiple-baseline design represents a simple AB design, but it is replicated more than once to establish the reliability of the effect. The internal validity of such a design is ensured by the multiple replications of the intervention delivered across subjects, settings, or behaviors.

The design used by the psychologist in the present example is referred to as a **multiple-baseline across subjects (clients) design**. Each transition from baseline to treatment is an opportunity to observe the effects of the treatment, and making this transition at different times allows the researcher to rule out alternative explanations for any behavior change that occurs during treatment. If the phase change from baseline to treatment were instituted at the same time for all three clients, changes in behavior during treatment might prove difficult to interpret. Perhaps some extraneous event happened to coincide with the implementation of treatment and this variable had a comparable influence on all three clients' behavior. However, the likelihood that this variable (e.g., some historical event that impacts the target behavior) happened to occur simultaneously with treatment at different times for each client is extraordinarily low. This is one of the strengths of the multiple-baseline design. If each client's behavior (hand washing or other compulsive behaviors, in this case) remains stable during baseline, changing only with the transition to treatment, then we can be quite confident that the change resulted from the treatment, not from some uncontrolled variable. Thus, the multiple-baseline design, by allowing for several baseline-to-treatment phase changes at different points in time, is a powerful single-subject alternative to the withdrawal design.

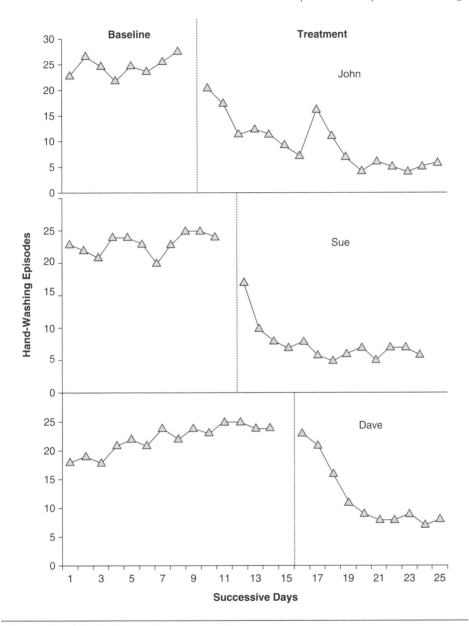

Figure 6.1   Multiple-baseline across subjects

Baseline data play the same comparative role in multiple-baseline designs as they do in withdrawal designs. Consequently, researchers place importance on ensuring a stable or steady-state baseline for each participant in the study. Substantial variability in behavior during baseline, or a trend in the same direction as the intended goal of intervention, proves problematic to the business of drawing conclusions. Such changes do occur on occasion, however, and the likelihood of this happening increases when the study is conducted in institutional settings in which clients have the opportunity to interact. When this is the case, the client receiving intervention first (John Doe, in our case) may undergo a change in behavior that influences in some way the behavior of the other clients, even though the others remain in the baseline condition. This may represent a social learning or modeling effect, and it is not altogether unusual in such settings. Obviously, the researcher would need to be aware of this possibility because it poses consequences for scientific decision making. On the one hand, strong causal inferences are difficult to support when changes in target behaviors occur prior to intervention, meaning that this kind of occurrence could challenge the internal validity of the study. On the other hand, a social modeling effect that might lead to positive changes in the behavior of clients not yet targeted for intervention is a pretty desirable clinical outcome. Such an effect may reduce the need for delivering the intervention individually to every client and takes advantage of the normal kinds of peer influences inherent in social settings. As we have seen before, an applied researcher encountering behavior change in clients who have not yet received intervention but who have interacted with other clients who have, is in the awkward position of having to interpret behavioral data that are both clinically desirable and scientifically ambiguous.

While we are in the process of describing an instance in which the real-world exigencies of clinical treatment have a way of trumping the requirements of scientific rigor and control, another aspect of data presentation seen in Figure 6.1 is in order. In the multiple-baseline study described, the same clinical treatment is being administered to three separate clients suffering from obsessive–compulsive cleanliness, with the intervention being delivered at different times for each client. If you look at Figure 6.1, you will notice that it appears that each measure of the target behavior during baseline occurs at the same time for all three clients, at least during the early stages of the baseline phase, prior to the intervention being delivered to John Doe. In actuality, it is not always the case in practice that subjects are being monitored and their behavior recorded and measured at precisely the same time. Watson and Workman (1981) first made the distinction between **concurrent multiple-baseline designs**, in which simultaneous measurement does occur for all clients, and **nonconcurrent multiple-baseline designs**, when data collection does not occur simultaneously for clients. In the latter case, although clients are monitored and their behavior measured for differing baseline phase lengths, it is not the case that all clients begin the baseline period at precisely the same time. In fact, it is possible that all of the data for one client are collected, both during baseline and treatment phases, before any data are collected for the remaining clients. Such decisions are often driven by professional and logistic considerations, not pure scientific logic.

Because concurrent measurement controls better for threats to internal validity, such multiple-baseline designs support somewhat stronger inferences than do nonconcurrent designs. Unfortunately, published accounts of multiple-baseline studies seldom clarify whether data collection occurred concurrently or nonconcurrently, and the manner in which data have historically been graphed in multiple-baseline designs does not allow for such a distinction to be made (Carr, 2005). Glancing again at Figure 6.1, you would probably assume that all three clients (John, Sue, and Dave) underwent baseline measurement initially at the same time and that the first several data points represent measures taken from each client at the same time on the same day. This is an artifact of the conventional manner of plotting data on a multiple-baseline graph, and it may unwittingly lead the reader to conclude that the study utilized a concurrent multiple-baseline design. As suggested earlier, this may very well not be the case in an applied study carried out on clients who have separate lives, family responsibilities, work schedules, and so on. Several authors have argued the merits of nonconcurrent multiple-baseline designs, particularly within applied settings where simultaneous baseline measures may not be feasible (Carr, 2005; Harvey, May, & Kennedy, 2004). However, because of the different inferential strength of concurrent and nonconcurrent designs, these authors recommend that in published reports researchers make clear, in both their description of research design and their method of data presentation whether the design represented a concurrent or nonconcurrent multiple-baseline design. We provide an example of how this can be done graphically in the case study description at the end of this chapter.

The multiple-baseline across subjects design is a very common one in clinical settings, particularly in cases where several clients in the same environment exhibit similar medical or behavioral symptoms. By replicating a treatment regimen across several clients, researchers or clinicians can quickly assess treatment effectiveness without worrying about the logistic or ethical concerns attendant to a withdrawal design. Himle, Miltenberger, Flessner, and Gatheridge (2004) used a multiple-baseline design to evaluate the effects of a behavioral skills training program on the gun-play of eight preschool children. Through verbal instruction, modeling of appropriate behavior, rehearsal, and verbal praise for appropriate behavior, the children were taught the following sequence in response to finding a firearm: do not touch the firearm, leave the room immediately, and go tell an adult. During both baseline and intervention phases, target behaviors were scored on a scale that ranged from 0 to 3, depending on how many of the behaviors in this sequence were performed. A score of 0 indicated that none of the behaviors occurred, and a score of 3 indicated that all three behaviors in the sequence were performed. Children who did not demonstrate the appropriate safety skills (scoring 3 on the target behavior measure) were given additional training until they met the criterion. Finally, a generalization test was done in the children's homes to assess whether the response sequence would occur in more natural environments outside of the original training environment (a room at the child's school).

Figure 6.2 shows the rating scores (0–3) for eight children for baseline, treatment, and additional (*in situ*) training. The figure is instructive because it allows the reader to extract considerable detailed information about the training sequence experienced by each child as well as the results of this intervention. Most of the children, for example, did not perform the trained response sequence consistently during the initial intervention. These children were given additional booster sessions during training, as indicated by the downward arrows on the graph. Also, several of the children required additional (*in situ*) training in which the adult provided corrective feedback and modeled the appropriate behavior. This phase of the study is indicated by the second vertical dotted line for 5 of the 8 children. Finally, generalization tests conducted in the child's home are indicated by closed triangle markers (data points) on the graph, distinguishing these observations from the majority of data collected at the school (closed circles). Clearly, most of the children required additional training on the response sequence to meet the criterion of 3 on the rating score. Figure 6.2 demonstrates the flexibility of single-case graphs in depicting the unique features that often characterize applied interventions. The graph is relatively easy to read and interpret, yet it contains a wealth of specific information regarding not only the details of the treatment phase but also the idiosyncratic responses of the children in both the classroom (training) environment and their home environment.

Apple, Billingsley, and Schwartz (2005) used videotape modeling to help train high-functioning autistic children to offer compliments to one another during social interaction. Autistic individuals often exhibit substantial social deficits, including proper turn-taking, interpersonal sensitivity, and initiating of conversations and/or other social exchanges. The researchers videotaped several segments in which well-liked classroom peers engaged in social exchanges characterized by different kinds of compliment-giving initiations. Each child was exposed to a baseline period of observation, followed by exposure to the videotaped modeling condition. Because the children were not observed to initiate compliments following videotape exposure, a second intervention condition was instituted, in which videotape modeling was again presented but followed by adult reinforcement for initiating compliments in subsequent interactions with peers. Figure 6.3 depicts the number of

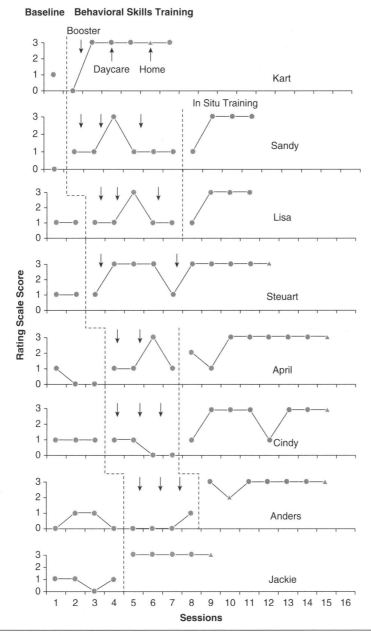

Figure 6.2 Each child's rating scale score during assessments conducted in baseline, behavioral skills training, and *in situ* training (if required) is depicted. The circles represent assessments conducted at the child's preschool, and triangles represent in-home assessments. Downward arrows in the BST condition represent training booster sessions.

Source: From Himle, M. B., Miltenberger, R. G., Flessner, C., & Gatheridge, B. (2004). Reprinted with permission of the Society for the Experimental Analysis of Behavior, Inc.

compliments during 15-minute observation periods for two children both during baseline and subsequent intervention periods. As can be seen, intervention consisted of several phases in which videotape modeling was delivered alone or in combination with reinforcement, followed by a withdrawal of reinforcement in a final phase. Clearly, both children initiated compliments only under the reinforcement condition.

Social competence in autistic children was also the focus of a study conducted by Ingersoll, Dvortcsak, Whalen, and Sikora (2005). Three children with autism-spectrum disorder were exposed to a developmental, social-pragmatic (DSP) language intervention to enhance their rate of spontaneous speech. DSP interventions conceptualize all language as occurring in social contexts, and the interventions focus on enhancing several forms of communication, including turn-taking, initiation of social exchange, and speech episodes. Specific intervention strategies usually include adult prompting of speech, manipulating aspects of the environment to provoke attempts at interaction and speech, and delivery of natural consequences for all forms of communication, including speech. In the present study, spontaneous expressive language in three children was observed during baseline conditions and subsequently during DSP treatment. In addition, spontaneous expressive language was observed and recorded during generalization sessions in the presence of each child's parents. As a result of treatment, all three children emitted more spontaneous speech during treatment relative to the baseline phase, with higher speech rates observed in the presence of the therapist during DSP treatment than during the generalization sessions with parents.

INTERIM SUMMARY

All multiple-baseline designs involve the replication of an AB phase change delivered in a staggered fashion over time. The multiple-baseline across subjects design involves delivering the intervention across two or more clients at different points in time. Each replication of the intervention allows one to draw an inference about the internal validity of the intervention because the staggered nature of the replications eliminates alternative explanations for behavior change. In addition, the multiple-baseline across subjects design contributes to the external validity of an intervention by way of its numerous intersubject replications.

MULTIPLE-BASELINE VARIATIONS

In the multiple-baseline across subjects design, the internal validity of the design is assessed through intersubject replication. In addition, you may recall from

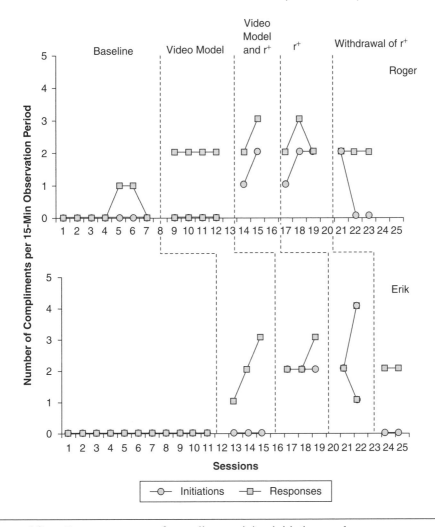

Figure 6.3   Frequency count of compliment-giving initiations and responses per observation period for the participants in Experiment 1

Source: From Apple, A. L., Billingsley, F., & Schwartz, I. S., *Journal of Positive Behavior Interventions* 7(1), 33–46. Reprinted with permission.

Chapter 4 that intersubject replication is also an important process in establishing the external generality of a research finding. Demonstrating the effects of an intervention across more than one client helps to ensure the general utility of the treatment, a matter that may be of some importance to other clinicians. Because of the relative ease with which interventions can be delivered to individual clients, single-case designs actually excel at establishing external validity through intersubject replication. Large-group designs, on the other hand, are inherently more cumbersome to replicate; thus, such designs tend to approach the external validity of findings through various sampling strategies designed to increase the sample's representativeness rather than through experimental replication.

Multiple Baseline Across Settings/Situations

In many clinical settings, however, the question of importance is whether an intervention will prove to be effective for a given client across several different environments or settings. In this case, the researcher is primarily interested in demonstrating intrasubject replication, and this is ordinarily done using a **multiple-baseline across settings or situations design**. In a *multiple-baseline across settings* design, behavioral interventions are staggered across different settings or environments that might be encountered by a particular subject or client. Ordinarily, the same behavior is being targeted in each of the environments. Brandon, a 9-year-old diagnosed with attention-deficit disorder, has encountered significant difficulties both at home and at school because of impulsive and disruptive behavior. On the advice of a therapist, a behavioral intervention consisting of time-out and differential reinforcement contingencies is implemented both by Brandon's teachers at school and by his parents at home. Instances of poor impulse control or disruption of the class or family result in 5-minute time-out periods, and periods of appropriate behavior result in receipt of tokens that can be exchanged for special privileges, toys, snacks, and so on.

The behavioral intervention program is implemented in staggered fashion across three different environments: (1) the home classroom and (2) playground at school, and (3) at home. Figure 6.4 depicts the results of the program as carried out in these separate settings. The multiple-baseline across settings utilizes the same logic as do other multiple-baseline designs, with several phase changes from baseline to treatment being the key to establishing the behavioral intervention's effectiveness. Implicit in the multiple-baseline across settings design is the recognition that therapeutic gains that occur only in very few settings are of little use. Although Brandon's teachers would no doubt appreciate reductions in impulsive and disruptive behavior at school, his parents would be understandably disappointed if these changes were not also evident at home. Obviously, if the reverse were true, Brandon's teachers would consider the behavioral intervention less than successful. Of course, certain interventions might be appropriate only in specific environments (e.g., retraining a clerical worker in word processing in the workplace), but many behavior classes prove adaptive across a variety of settings. The multiple-baseline across settings design is particularly well suited to interventions whose objective is to bring about changes in behavior in more than one relevant environment.

Keep in mind that all multiple-baseline designs derive their strength from multiple AB (baseline to treatment) phase changes staggered over time. Each AB phase

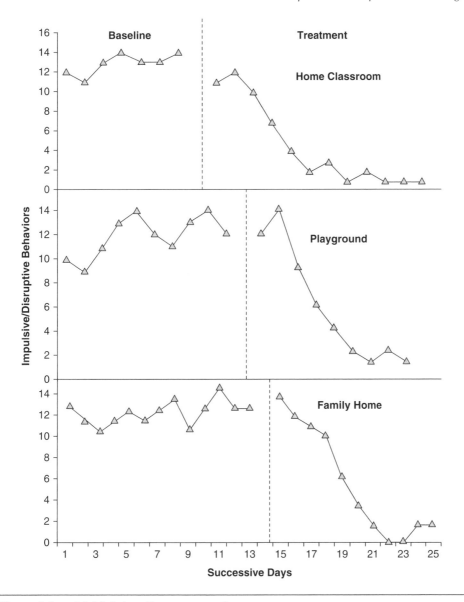

Figure 6.4   Multiple baseline across settings

change beyond the first comprises a replication. Needless to say, the more replications provided within a particular study, the more confident the researcher can be about the effects of the intervention. Most researchers consider two or three separate baseline phases to be the minimum number necessary for strong conclusions because this allows for one or two replications of the original effect (Kazdin, 1994). Clearly, more baseline phases may be desirable in a given study, although the exact number of replications will likely be determined by practical factors inherent to the clinical setting.

In a study of a multicomponent therapy for musculoskeletal pain, Åsenlöf, Denison, and Lindberg (2005) conducted a multiple-baseline across settings design to assess changes in motor behavior, cognition, and perceived disability in two 49-year-old female patients with a history of chronic pain. The treatment was a complex, seven component program, including identification of goals, self-monitoring, skill acquisition, and response maintenance. Dependent measures included self-reported levels of disability due to pain. Because the treatment was a multicomponent intervention, different aspects of the treatment were added sequentially. For one client, treatment was delivered in staggered fashion across the following situations: purchasing food, making beds, driving, and household chores done by the sink. For the second client, the situations included driving, handling of wheelchairs (a job-related skill), and pony-harness racing, the latter being a preferred recreational activity.

Figure 6.5 depicts data for the client who was evaluated across the situations of purchasing food, making beds, driving, and doing household chores by the sink. Although change in the dependent variable was gradual, reductions in self-rated disability were apparent by the end of Phase B (analysis of basic skills) and increasingly so during Phase C (applied skills and generalization). In addition, the study employed a lengthy follow-up period of 1 year. Self-reported disability was measured at 1, 4, 6, and 12 months after treatment. As can be seen in Phase A_2 of the graph, self-reported pain disability was negligible during the follow-up measurements. Some additional discussion of this study is needed because it differs in some respects from conventional use of a multiple-baseline design. As you can see from the graph, the study involved not one phase change from baseline (A) to treatment (B) but two phase changes during treatment, plus a lengthy follow-up period to assess long-term maintenance of treatment gains. Because the treatment involved multiple cognitive and behavioral components, it was delivered in a sequential fashion, with later stages (Phase C) building on skills first developed in the early treatment stage (Phase B). In addition, the follow-up phase (A_2) can be conceptualized as a withdrawal condition, or return to baseline, because formal components of the treatment were not being actively delivered at this time. As a part of the overall treatment, clients had been taught numerous coping skills for managing potential relapse, and Phase A_2, although containing no direct treatment, was used to assess how well the clients managed their pain disability on their own after treatment. Consequently, this design can be viewed as a combination of a multiple-baseline and a withdrawal design because it contains features of both designs. As it turns out, this kind of combination of design features is quite common in applied settings and actually contributes to the flexibility of the general family of single-case designs. We will have an opportunity in later chapters to explore some other ways in which the various design features of single-case research can be modified to more effectively meet the needs of applied researchers.

Kay, Harchik, and Luiselli (2006) conducted a multiple-baseline assessment of an intervention for excessive drooling by an autistic student who attended a public high school. The client, a 17-year-old male, had been diagnosed with both autism and mental retardation. He was capable of most self-care behaviors, possessed some reading ability, and was able to communicate well enough to be placed in a normal classroom. Unfortunately, his drooling problem, present since early childhood, proved disruptive to his academic progress (pooled saliva often damaged paperwork) and socialization (classmates avoided interactions with him and refused to sit near him). Because the client's drooling occurred across several locations, a behavioral intervention, consisting of self-monitoring, verbal prompts to wipe his mouth, and reinforcement for having a dry mouth, was delivered sequentially in three separate environments: (1) the classroom, (2) a community vocational setting, and (3) a cooking class.

As can be seen in Figure 6.6, the intervention was delivered at different times in each location, beginning with the classroom and followed by the community site and cooking class, respectively. A reduction in drooling, as measured by the number of saliva pools, is evident in each successive treatment phase. Because the intervention was initially delivered in the classroom, the two subsequent interventions (in the community and cooking class settings) served as two replications of the first phase change. It is clear that baseline levels of drooling in the community and cooking class settings did not change in response to the intervention being delivered in the classroom; however, when intervention was then delivered successively to the community and cooking class settings, corresponding changes in the target behavior occurred. These two replications following the initial intervention serve as controls to possible threats to internal validity. The staggered, or sequential nature of the phase change from baseline to intervention renders alternative explanations for the behavior change untenable.

Multiple Baseline Across Behaviors

Assessing an intervention through a multiple-baseline design does not require the use of multiple subjects or physical environments or settings, only several opportunities to replicate the intervention. The essential logic of the design is applicable as well

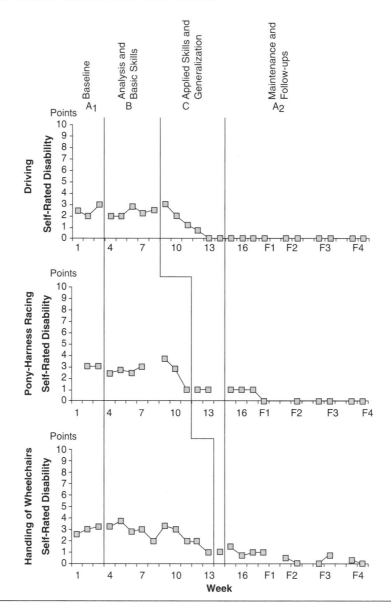

Figure 6.5 Patient 2's self-rated disability related to 3 prioritized behavioral goals (numerical rating scales 0–10, where 0 indicates "no disability"). The goals are presented from top to bottom in the same order as they were targeted in treatment. Weekly average values are displayed for phase A_1 (baseline), phases B and C (intervention), and phase A_2 (i.e., 1-, 4-, 6-, and 12-month follow-up examinations [F1–F-4]). The vertical lines across the graphs, from left to right, show the time of introduction of the different phases of the design.

Source: From Åsenlöf, P., Denison, E., & Lindberg, P. (2005). Reprinted by permission of the American Physical Therapy Association.

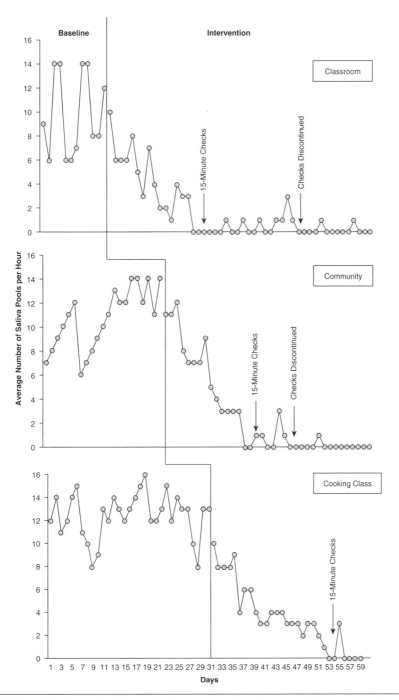

Figure 6.6   Number of saliva pools (average per hour) recorded during baseline and intervention phases

Source: From Kay, S., Harchik, A. E., & Luiselli, J. K. (2006). Reprinted with permission of Pro-Ed.

to different collections of responses or different parts of an individual's behavioral repertoire, as in a **multiple-baseline across behaviors** design. Figure 6.7 depicts a multiple-baseline design for Linda, a patient who, after a snowmobiling accident, has remained largely bedridden and inactive. Linda sustained only minor physical injuries from the accident, but family and friends are concerned that her lack of activity will eventually leave her weak, depressed, and unwilling to resume normal activities. Prior to the accident, Linda was a healthy and very active adult, engaging in numerous outdoor activities. Among the objectives of the intervention is to encourage Linda to engage in different forms of exercise, each strengthening a different group of muscles or enhancing cardiovascular fitness.

Linda's physical therapist decides to monitor three types of exercise prior to implementing the exercise intervention: walking, lifting, and stretching. Walking is targeted because it is a relatively simple behavior in which Linda does engage to some degree (if only to go to the restroom or the kitchen). Lifting, which may consist of simply picking up clothes, books, and other items in the house, is targeted because of its benefits to the muscles of the arms and legs and because many everyday activities require lifting various objects. Finally, stretching is important because muscles that are not used tend to lose their elasticity and become more vulnerable to injury. As with any other single-subject design, the therapist begins by collecting baseline data on each of these separate behaviors. These data are depicted in the first panel of each section of the graph. As you can see, Linda engaged in very little physical activity during the baseline phase. The physical therapist implemented the first intervention phase for the behavior of walking. The other two behaviors continued in baseline without intervention. After a period of several days, the intervention was then applied to the second behavior, lifting. Finally, the intervention was applied several days later to the last behavior, stretching.

In a multiple-baseline across behaviors design, replications of the intervention occur for the same subject or client but across different behaviors or dimensions of behavior. This means, of course, that each targeted behavior must be objectively defined and its dimensions and properties clearly designated for purposes of measurement. Also, as with other multiple-baseline designs, it is not unusual to observe some carryover of the intervention from one behavior to the next, resulting in noticeable trends in behaviors not yet being formally targeted for intervention. You can see in Figure 6.7, for example, that baseline data for lifting seem to be drifting upward near the end of the baseline period. Because this upward trend corresponds to the intervention phase for walking, this increase in lifting may represent a phenomenon known as **behavioral covariation**, in which responses that are functionally similar to target behaviors undergoing treatment exhibit similar changes (Parrish, Cataldo, Kolko, Neef, & Egel, 1986; Sprague & Horner, 1992). For

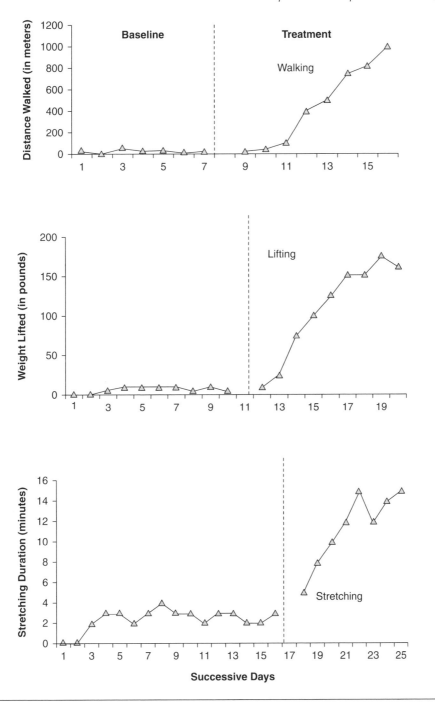

Figure 6.7   Multiple baseline across behaviors

instance, Ludwig and Geller (1991) observed that pizza delivery drivers, whose seat-belt use had been explicitly targeted for change, also were observed to increase their use of turn signals while driving, despite the fact that turn-signal use had not been targeted for change.

When dealing with several different client behaviors, or response dimensions, there is always the possibility that these separate dimensions or behaviors will interact or influence one another in complex ways. These interactions, although posing some difficulty for interpreting the effects of an intervention, can also prove clinically useful. Rosales-Ruiz and Baer (1997) suggested the phrase **behavioral cusp** to refer to changes in behavior that produce unintended, but potentially important, consequences. In the current example, enhancing Linda's ambulatory activity brings her into contact with a much larger and complex environment than she would experience if she remained bedridden. Thus, walking has many attendant consequences, only some of which may be foreseen by therapists in designing specific treatment programs. In the case of Linda, lifting may occur more frequently during the walking intervention because her enhanced mobility brings her into greater contact with physical objects in her environment and the daily routines that normally occur in her environment. Once again, such an occurrence may be somewhat frustrating to the researcher, but it is good news to the clinician. An intervention that brings about change not only in a specified target behavior but also in other, related behaviors—such as other forms of exercise—is in most cases regarded quite positively. At least in the present case, this behavioral cusp leads to a general increase in physical activity for Linda, without the necessity of targeting each behavior for treatment. In many cases, then, behavioral cusps are a desirable, though unplanned, by-product of intervention, even though, in multiple-baseline designs like this one, they may cast some doubt on cause-and-effect conclusions. Bosch and Fuqua (2001) posited that therapists should more proactively consider potential behavioral cusps when developing treatment programs. Smith, McDougall, and Edelen-Smith (2006) liken behavioral cusps to *killer applications* from the business world (e.g., Microsoft Windows obliterating DOS) and noted that behavioral cusps "produce transformational changes—changes that render prior repertoires obsolete" (p. 224).

Shabani, Wilder, and Flood (2001) used a multiple-baseline across behaviors design to evaluate a behavioral intervention for stereotypic rocking in a 12-year-old boy with multiple diagnoses, including autism and mental retardation. The boy, Larry, engaged in frequent and severe rocking motions in both solitary and social circumstances and across a broad array of environmental settings. Because the rocking behavior was observed to occur regardless of whether the boy was standing or sitting at a desk, the researchers delivered the behavioral intervention separately to each of these behaviors. The boy was first taught explicitly to monitor his own behavior and to identify instances of both appropriate (not rocking) and inappropriate (rocking) behavior. Once effective discrimination was taught, a differential reinforcement of other behavior (DRO) procedure was implemented. In a DRO procedure, reinforcers can be obtained by engaging in behaviors other than those that are deemed inappropriate or undesirable. During the DRO procedure, the boy could receive access to preferred stimuli (reinforcers such as snack foods, videos, and Gatorade) if rocking had not occurred for a specified period of time. The length of this DRO requirement was gradually increased until the boy could abstain from rocking for 5 minutes.

Figure 6.8 depicts the results of the intervention for both standing and sitting. The final phase of the intervention involved a *thinning* of the DRO, meaning that the child had to abstain from rocking for longer periods in order to receive access to reinforcers (preferred stimuli). Not only was intervention effective in both the standing and sitting conditions, but the boy was also able to abstain from rocking for longer periods throughout the thinning phase of the study.

A multiple-baseline across behaviors design was also used by Johnson, McDonnell, Holzwarth, and Hunter (2004) to assess the effects of embedded instruction on academic achievement in three children with developmental disability who were enrolled in general education classes. *Embedded instruction* involves the teaching of student-specific academic skills within the context of normally programmed academic units or activities. The particular target skill or skills taught to an individual student are idiosyncratic and based on that student's individualized education program. Johnson et al. (2004) evaluated the use of embedded instruction for three students: two girls (8 and 9 years of age, respectively) and one 7-year-old boy. Because each child's individualized education program indicated different intervention objectives, the embedded instruction occurred across varying academic units and their respective behavioral targets. For instance, Wendy's embedded instruction occurred across three academic units: (1) Plants, (2) Insects and Spiders, and (3) Anatomy. Chuck's embedded instruction entailed identification of sight words chosen from a first-grade reading curriculum, and Brenda, who exhibited very little expressive language, was taught to make specific requests through the use of the Communication Builder, an electronic instrument containing pictorial icons that, when touched, produced a vocal request.

Figures 6.9a, 6.9b, and 6.9c show the results of the embedded-instruction intervention across the relevant academic behaviors for each child. It is clear that the embedded instruction was effective in increasing academic performance in all three children and across each target behavior category. Moreover, the last panel of each figure demonstrates that treatment gains appear to have been maintained beyond intervention, although not all target behaviors were assessed for maintenance for Wendy and Brenda. Finally, Johnson et al. (2004) collected **social validity data** from the

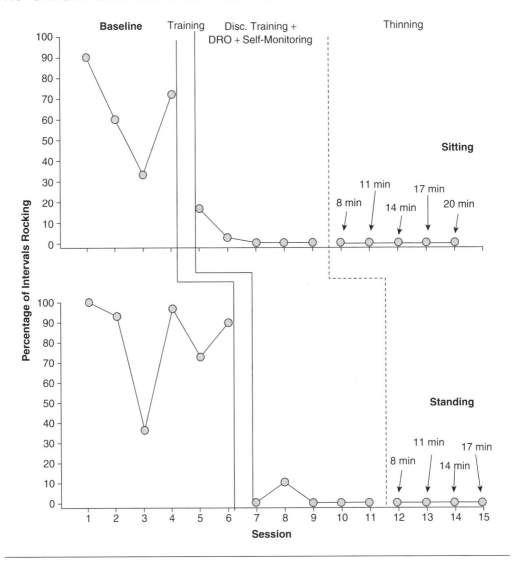

Figure 6.8   Percentage of intervals in which rocking occurred while Larry was sitting and reading a book (top) and standing and talking with the therapist (bottom) across baseline, training, intervention (i.e., discrimination training, DRO, and self-monitoring), and thinning phases

Source: Shabani, D. B., Wilder, D. A., & Flood, W. A. © 2001 John Wiley & Sons Limited. Reproduced with permission.

instructors in the form of a questionnaire that measured perceptions of effectiveness, costliness, and likelihood of implementation of embedded instruction in the future. In general, these ratings suggested that the instructors and paraprofessionals perceived embedded instruction as an effective and appropriate intervention for the

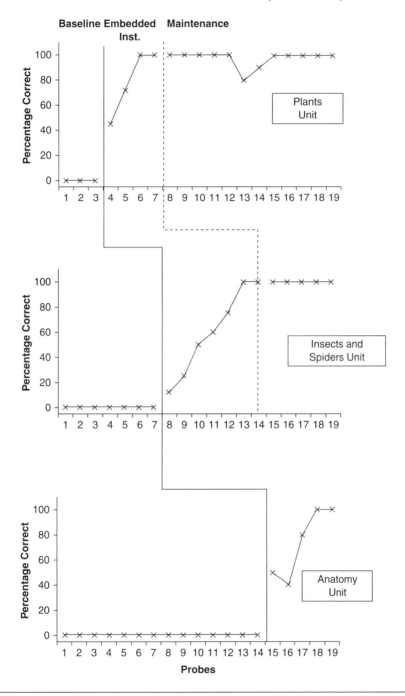

Figure 6.9a Percentage correct during testing probes for Wendy

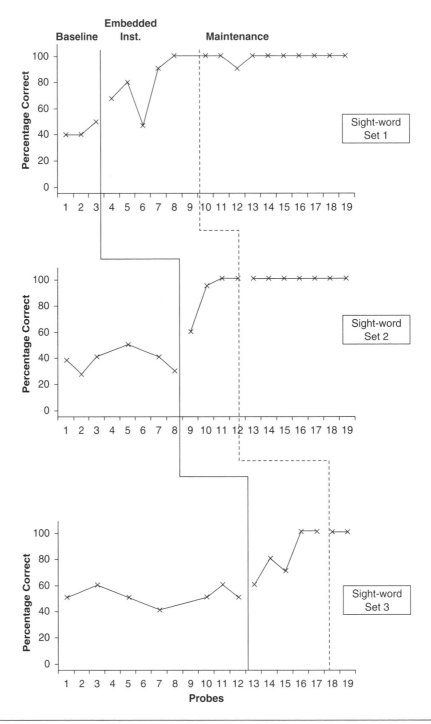

Figure 6.9b   Percentage correct during testing probes for Chuck

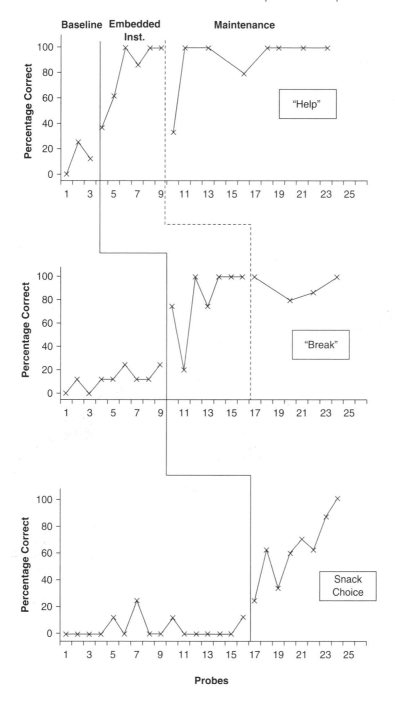

Figure 6.9c   Percentage correct during testing probes for Brenda

Source: Johnson, J. W., McDonnell, J., Holzwarth, V. N., & Hunter, K. (2004). Reprinted with permission of Pro-Ed.

three children. The use of social validation assessment is a particularly admirable aspect of the study. Although such data are seldom reported by researchers, their collection and use have been recommended by applied behavior analysts as an important adjunct to the analysis and interpretation of single-case data (Carr, Austin, Britton, Kellum, & Bailey, 1999; Kennedy, 2002; McDougall, Skouge, Farrell, & Hoff, 2006; Schwartz & Baer, 1991; Wolf, 1978).

Multiple-Probe Designs

The multiple-baseline design is a frequently utilized single-case strategy for applied researchers who wish to evaluate the effectiveness of an intervention likely to produce irreversible changes in behavior, or when withdrawing the intervention would be unethical. However, even the multiple-baseline design, as user friendly as it tends to be for applied researchers, must often be adapted to real-world circumstances that complicate the conventions of scientific measurement. For example, because multiple-baseline designs involve several (usually at least three) separate baselines, with interventions being delivered at staggered intervals, baseline phases tend to become progressively longer over the course of the study. Thus, the practical and ethical concerns regarding long baseline phases, although not unusual in other single-case designs, such as withdrawal designs, become especially relevant in multiple-baseline designs. In many clinical settings it is simply not feasible to obtain numerous measures of the target behavior over prolonged baseline phases.

Another complication that may render conventional baseline measurement irrelevant is that the target behavior may not exist in the client's repertoire. In essence, such a behavior has a zero level of occurrence, and it is consequently meaningless, and perhaps ethically questionable, to submit the client to repeated assessment under such conditions. For example, suppose a parent begins a program to teach a child with a developmental disability important self-care activities, such as tooth brushing. If, prior to the formal intervention, the child has never been observed to brush his or her teeth independently, then this target behavior has zero level of occurrence. Although a prolonged baseline phase of, say, 2 weeks, could be conducted, with daily measures of tooth brushing, the resulting data would be of questionable utility because the behavior has not yet been acquired by the child. Repeated measurements of the target behavior would have no value to the parent and would likely produce only frustration on the part of the child.

Under such circumstances, researchers are likely to opt for an adaptation of the conventional multiple-baseline design called a **multiple-probe design** (Horner & Baer, 1978). In such a study, assessment of baseline levels of the target behavior would likely entail quick probes, rather than repeated, or continuous, monitoring of the behavior. A *probe* is a single, discrete measurement of a target behavior, often conducted at random, or at least not according to any predetermined time, in order to rapidly establish the natural rate of the behavior before intervention. In the case of a behavior that has not yet been established in a client's repertoire or behavior that may show extreme reactivity, one or two simple probes may serve quite adequately as baseline evaluations of the behavior. Thus the intervention can be delivered with less delay, and data obtained during treatment can still be reasonably compared with the levels of behavior obtained through the preintervention probe measures. In addition, researchers sometimes utilize probes to assess the long-term maintenance of behavior change following intervention phases. Once a program has effectively led to consistent tooth brushing in the child in the previously described scenario, discrete probes may occur at monthly intervals in order to assess the program's effectiveness over time. Such probes are rapid and are easily conducted follow-up measures, not continuous or repeated measures, which would likely prove more effort intensive or obtrusive.

Because of the ease with which they can be implemented and their fit to the real world exigencies of clinical practice, multiple-probe designs are commonly employed by applied scientists. Mandel, Bigelow, and Lutzker (1998) used a videotape program to help parents previously reported for child abuse and/or neglect to identify and remove safety hazards in the home. Hazards were identified using the Home Accident Potential Inventory—Revised (HAPI–R) (Tertinger, Greene, & Lutzker, 1984). Because of the sensitive nature of the study and the considerable time (approximately 45 minutes) needed to conduct assessment of the home with the HAPI–R, repeated baseline measurement was considered impractical. Consequently, a limited number of assessments were conducted during baseline (four to seven), and these were separated by intervals of several weeks. In addition, assessment of hazards occurred across different rooms in the house (e.g., kitchen, bathroom, bedroom, living room), and not all rooms were assessed during each home visit by the research assistants. Thus, baseline measurement consisted of probes rather than repeated or continuous monitoring. The intervention consisted of a series of four 10-minute videotapes demonstrating ways to improve safety in the home, and parents were required to watch the tapes in the presence of research assistants. For both families, the number of observed hazards in each room decreased after the videotape treatment. Follow-up probes were taken at 1 and 4 months after the intervention. Because one family experienced increases in safety hazards that approached baseline levels during these probes, a reintroduction of the intervention was conducted.

Padgett, Strickland, and Coles (2006) used a multiple-probe design to evaluate the effects of a virtual reality computer game on fire safety skills of five children with fetal alcohol syndrome. Because none of the children could describe any appropriate behaviors in response to fire prior to the program, prolonged baseline assessment was deemed unnecessary. The virtual reality computer program demonstrated appropriate responses to fire in real-world environments, and all children demonstrated mastery of these steps after completing the program and at a 1-week follow-up assessment. Moreover, the follow-up probe occurred in a natural environment, suggesting that the acquired skills had generalized beyond the initial training environment.

Marshall, Capilouto, and McBride (2007) used a multiple-probe design across participants to evaluate improvement in problem solving among patients with Alzheimer's disease. Problem solving was measured using the Rapid Assessment of Problem Solving Test (Marshall, Karow, Morelli, Iden, & Dixon, 2003), which requires respondents to ask yes/no questions in order to target a picture embedded in an array of distracter pictures. Baseline probe measurement indicated that many of the patients were inefficient in solving this problem, simply guessing at the correct picture. Patients were then taught how to ask yes/no ("constraint") questions in order to identify the correct picture quickly and were taught that this strategy was more successful than simply guessing at the correct picture. After intervention, all patients demonstrated an ability to ask appropriate constraint questions when given word problems that were similar to those used on the Rapid Assessment of Problem Solving Test. In addition, follow-up probes at 2 and 4 weeks indicated that patients maintained the high rates of effective problem solving that resulted from the intervention.

INTERIM SUMMARY

Both the multiple-baseline across settings/situations design and the multiple-baseline across behaviors design allow for replication of an AB phase change within the same subject or client. Thus, these designs involve an intrasubject replication of an intervention and allow one to assess whether a clinical intervention leads to important change in more than one environment or for more than one target behavior. Behavioral covariation can occur in multiple-baseline designs because intervening in one client, behavior, or setting may carry over to nontargeted clients, behaviors, or settings. Although such carryover can prove problematic to drawing causal inferences, its benefits to adaptive functioning may be numerous and in the special case of behavioral cusps can influence in dynamic and transformational ways other aspects of the client's behavioral repertoire. The multiple-probe design represents a special adaptation of the multiple-baseline design, in which brief, discrete measures of the target behavior substitute for the longer, repeated measures ordinarily utilized in single-case designs. These probes are often used to assess baseline levels of behavior when the relevant target behavior is known not to exist in the subject or client's repertoire, thus avoiding the need for unnecessary repeated assessment. Probes are also frequently used to assess long-term maintenance of behavior change following interventions.

THE CASE OF JUAN, DYLAN, AND DARYL

It is likely that no other disorder conjures the label of "madness" more clearly than schizophrenia. This devastating disorder affects approximately 2.2 million American adults, or about 1.1% of the population over the age of 18. Schizophrenia is known as a "thought disorder" that interferes with a person's ability to think clearly, to distinguish reality from fantasy, to make decisions, to manage emotions, and to interact with others. The first signs of schizophrenia typically occur during the teenage years or in one's early 20s. Unfortunately, the younger the person is when the symptoms begin, the worse his or her long-term prognosis. Most people diagnosed with schizophrenia suffer chronically or episodically throughout their lives. Even between episodes of active psychosis, lost opportunities for careers and relationships, stigma, residual or negative symptoms, and medication side effects often impact those who have been diagnosed with schizophrenia. Consistently, reports indicate that 10% of people who suffer from schizophrenia eventually commit suicide (Siris, 2001).

Despite common depictions in the media, a person suffering from schizophrenia does not have a "split personality." A "split personality" is formally diagnosed as *dissociative identity disorder* (American Psychiatric Association, 1994. Schizophrenia encompasses two broad categories of symptoms: (1) *positive symptoms*, which represent excesses of behavior, and (2) *negative symptoms*, which represent deficits in behavior. Positive symptoms include hallucinations (false sensory experiences); delusions (false personal beliefs that are sustained despite evidence to the contrary) that may be bizarre or implausible in nature; disorganized speech and thought characterized by incoherence, tangential speech, neologisms (made-up words), clanging (rhyming), or perseveration; and grossly disorganized behavior that may vary from childlike silliness to agitation to complete catatonia or marked decrease in reactivity to the environment. Negative symptoms may include a decrease or absence of emotional expressiveness, eye contact, and body language; *alogia*, or reduction in speech; and *avolition*, or an inability to initiate and persist in goal-directed activities. Interestingly, the positive symptoms are more amenable to current medications than the negative symptoms.

Although the specific causes of schizophrenia are still unknown, it is clear that both biological and early environmental factors lead to changes in the brains of individuals who exhibit the characteristic symptoms of schizophrenia. Treatment includes medications, increasing the structure of the environment, and reducing the emotional expressiveness, particularly in relation to hostile emotions, of people who interact with these individuals. This three-pronged approach seems to hold the best promise of reducing the positive symptoms and managing the negative symptoms to allow the individual to experience the most functional life possible. Unfortunately, because of medication side effects, disorganized thinking on the part of the individual experiencing schizophrenia, and beliefs that the medications are no longer working, many individuals, such as Juan, Dylan, and Daryl, do not take their medication as prescribed. This leads, as it has for Juan, Dylan, and Daryl, to both medical complications and social effects. To successfully manage cases such as the ones described here, many professionals will be involved, including psychiatrists, psychiatric nurses, clinical psychologists, social workers, and perhaps an occupational therapist. In the present case, we explore Juan's, Dylan's, and Daryl's case from the perspective of a clinical psychologist and a social worker.

A Clinical Psychologist's Perspective

First-generation antipsychotic medications, such as Thorazine and Haldol, which block the action of dopamine, have been found to work best for positive symptoms. Unfortunately, these medications have been found to have adverse side effects. Because of these problems, second-generation antipsychotic medications, such as clozapine (Clozaril), Risperdal, Zyprexa, Seroquel, Geodon, and Abilify were developed beginning in the 1980s. These medications are believed to decrease both positive and negative symptoms and produce fewer adverse side effects.

From the perspective of the individual being asked to take these medications, there are several problems. First, not all patients benefit, and those who do benefit may show only a reduction in symptoms rather than an alleviation of symptoms. Second, these medications are fairly expensive, leading some families to discontinue the medication. In addition, side effects may lead to discontinuation of the medicine altogether. The psychological impact of taking these medications may also be such that patients would rather take their chances without the medication. Finally, in cases such as Juan's, where there is significant disorganized thinking, the symptoms of the disorder lead to poor decision making on the part of the individual. Obviously, when Juan reports that he takes his medication depending on "whether the sun hiccups," it becomes clear that medication adherence is a major issue.

Compliance is of particular importance in psychiatric disorders. It has been estimated that as many as 50% of patients do not take their medications as prescribed.

For those suffering from schizophrenia, this percentage rises as high as 60% to 75% (Misdrahi, Llorca, Lancon, & Bayle, 2002; Weiden & Zygmunt, 1997). For Juan, Dylan, and Daryl, maintaining a consistent pattern of medication usage, as prescribed by their psychiatrist, is critical for their physical health and for reducing the strong positive symptoms of schizophrenia that they experience. With each subsequent relapse, Juan's, Dylan's and Daryl's prognosis for a functional life decreases (Shepherd, Watt, Falloon, & Smeeton, 1989). Without the medication, Juan's symptoms lead to so much disruption that he is deemed an in-appropriate candidate for the group home and ends up back on the street. For Dylan and Daryl, the nature of their delusions makes it difficult for them to function successfully. The current hospitalization, then, has two main goals for each of the men: (1) finding a medication that reduces their symptoms while presenting a minimal number of side effects and (2) helping each man to be more compliant with his medication regimen.

Risperidone, a second-generation antipsychotic drug, was chosen for use with each man. This drug has been shown to be effective in reducing positive symptoms of schizophrenia and for creating few extrapyramidal side effects (Song, 1997). As a result, Juan was started on a regimen of 4 mg of risperidone daily, eventually being stabilized at 6 mg of risperidone daily. Both Dylan and Daryl were able to be stabilized on a regimen of 4 mg of risperidone daily. Once the men were stabilized, the clinical psychologist began work with each man on adherence to the medication regimen after being released from the hospital. When released, Juan will be placed in an apartment for men with psychiatric disorders, at the request of his parents. Dylan's and Daryl's parents have chosen the same facility for their sons. Men living in this apartment complex are visited once a week by a social worker. Given that the social worker will meet with the men once a week, the clinical psychologist and the social worker decided to work together to facilitate compliance. No staff members, other than an apartment manager, live at the apartment complex, making it critical that the men comply with their medication with minimal assistance.

A Social Worker's Perspective

From the perspective of a social worker, the responsibilities associated with a patient diagnosed as schizophrenic may be numerous. First, upon the initial diagnosis, the social worker will need to establish a relationship with the family or significant other to formulate a psychosocial assessment. A social worker may also work with the family to help them understand and cope with their family member's schizophrenia. This may involve addressing the family's denial of the disorder and in handling the possibly severe mourning reaction that is commonly experienced. When a child experiences his or her first psychotic break, the family's reaction may be severe, requiring regular and intense contact with a social worker. Social workers frequently need to work in a crisis mode, addressing the many issues arising as a result of the initial or subsequent hospitalization and the readjustment of family relationships. Finally, social workers may conduct therapy groups to help patients discuss their feelings in relation to discharge and to make plans for aftercare. This may involve going with a patient to a day program or making home visits. Today, most individuals diagnosed with schizophrenia are able to live and work in the community.

For Juan, the repeated hospitalizations and relapses he has experienced have complicated his treatment picture. His parents, who are now in their late 60s, are unwilling to have Juan back in their home. They believe that it is critical for Juan to be able to live in the community on his own so as to be prepared for their eventual deaths. As an only child, Juan has no siblings who might be involved in his care. Likewise, having never married and having lost contact with his high school friends, Juan has few social contacts outside of his part-time job as a dishwasher.

Dylan's and Daryl's parents live in the same city and are only in their 50s, but they have divorced, and neither feels capable of caring for their adult sons. Both parents have professional careers and are gone during the day. Dylan and Daryl have one older sister who lives in another state and is very busy with her own career and family. Daryl's education as a social worker provides the possibility that he will be able to work in the field, which he has done intermittently since graduating from college, if he can maintain his medication. Dylan, however, has few social outlets and prefers to stay in his room or walk by the river.

To achieve the highest level of functioning, each man must adhere to the medical regimen prescribed. Working together, the clinical psychologist and social worker have agreed to monitor and implement a program to assist the men if they become noncompliant upon leaving the hospital environment. During the aftercare planning stages, the clinical psychologist and social worker both stressed to the men the importance of taking their medication on a daily basis, emphasizing that the medications reduce the symptoms of schizophrenia, allowing them to lead more successful and productive lives. As an aid to taking the medication, each man was trained to leave his medications next to his coffeepot and to take the medication each morning. The percentage of prescribed pills actually taken each week was counted by the social worker during her weekly visit. As might be expected, given that the men were not hospitalized on the same day, they were also not released on the same day. Juan was released 4 weeks prior to Dylan, who was released 3 weeks prior to Daryl.

Beginning, then, with Juan, the first 3 weeks following discharge can be viewed as a baseline period. As can be seen in the first panel of Figure 6.10, Juan's

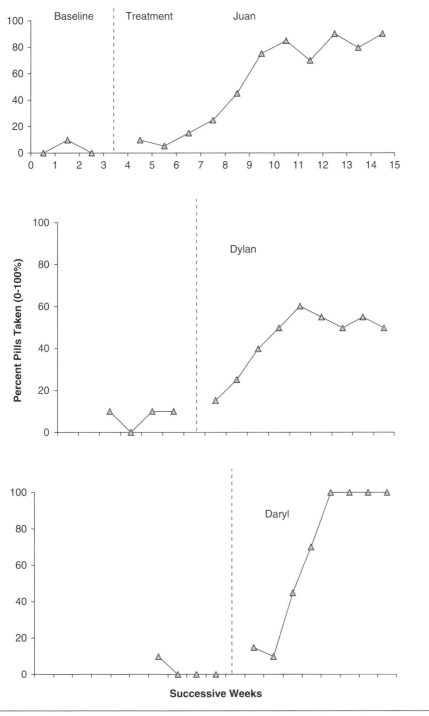

Figure 6.10   Percentage correct during testing probes for Chuck

medical compliance was very low during this baseline period, increasing his chances of a relapse. During the intervention, Juan purchased a pillbox and was then taught to keep his medicine in the pillbox in the same location, that is, next to his coffeepot. The second panel of Figure 6.10 demonstrates that Juan's compliance steadily rose throughout the intervention phase. You will notice that Dylan's baseline data in Figure 6.10 did not begin until Juan's treatment had already begun. This is also true of Daryl's baseline measures, which began only after both Juan and Dylan had begun to receive treatment. Because baseline measures were not taken until the three men were released from the hospital, length of baseline measurement did not increase with each client often the case with multiple-baseline designs. However, because the baseline data were collected at different times and the treatment (medication placement) was also staggered, or delivered at different times for each man, the principal element of the multiple-baseline design remains intact. Thus, the design used in this case study is a nonconcurrent multiple-baseline design, as described earlier in this chapter. This example once again illustrates the common trade-off that occurs between scientific rigor and clinical objectives. The three phase changes at different times add inferential strength to a design despite an inability to collect simultaneous and prolonged baseline measures.

INTERIM SUMMARY

The case of Juan, Dylan, and Daryl illustrates the potential for using a multiple-baseline design to evaluate a clinical intervention delivered to separate clients. Although such interventions may not, for ethical reasons, allow for complete withdrawal of treatment, multiple AB phase changes, conducted at different times and across three separate clients, provide strong evidence for the intervention's effectiveness.

KEY TERMS GLOSSARY

Multiple-baseline designs Single-case designs in which only one phase change from baseline to intervention (AB) occurs but is replicated across either subjects, settings, or behaviors.

Multiple-baseline across subjects (clients) A multiple-baseline design in which several AB phase changes occur in staggered fashion across more than one subject or client.

Concurrent multiple-baseline design A multiple-baseline design in which all baseline measures are taken simultaneously.

Nonconcurrent multiple-baseline design A multiple-baseline design in which separate baseline data are not collected at the same time.

Multiple-baseline across settings or situations A multiple-baseline design in which several AB phase changes occur in staggered fashion across two or more separate settings or situations.

Multiple-baseline across behaviors A multiple-baseline design in which several AB phase changes occur in staggered fashion across two or more distinct target behaviors.

Behavioral covariation Changes in nontargeted behaviors that may be functionally similar to behavior being targeted for intervention.

Behavioral cusp Behaviors that, although not being specifically targeted for change, may have important and very broad consequences in a specific setting or for a specific client.

Social validity data Information, usually obtained from the client or the client's family, friends, or coworkers, that serves to demonstrate the effectiveness of a treatment.

Multiple-probe design An adaptation of the multiple-baseline design in which brief or "probes," or baseline measures, are taken prior to intervention, and sometimes as follow-up measures, because prolonged baseline phases or repeated dependent variable measures are impractical or unethical.

SUPPLEMENTS

Review Questions

1. What is the general rationale for conducting a multiple-baseline design? What is the major difference between this design and a withdrawal design?

2. Why is it difficult to tell from a traditional single-case graph whether a concurrent or nonconcurrent multiple-baseline design was used?

3. Why might researchers in applied settings be more likely to conduct nonconcurrent than concurrent multiple-baseline designs?

4. What is behavioral covariation, and what problems might it produce for drawing causal inferences in a multiple-baseline design?

5. What is meant by the phrase *behavioral cusp*? Describe an example of a behavioral cusp that might be relevant in an applied setting.

6. Why might a researcher use a multiple-probe design? Describe an instance in which this design would be preferred over another variation of the multiple-baseline design.

Suggested Readings/Helpful Web Sites

Rosales-Ruiz, J., & Baer, D. M. (1997). Behavioral cusps: A developmental and pragmatic concept for behavior analysis. *Journal of Applied Behavior Analysis, 30,* 533–544.

This article introduces the important concept of *behavioral cusps*, a term that refers to ways in which specific, targeted behaviors may bring a client into contact with new environments or new consequences. Thus, behavioral cusps have the potential to extend behavioral repertoires beyond the parameters of a specific intervention, making them especially powerful in applied settings.

http://www.nimh.nih.gov/health/topics/schizophrenia/index.shtml
This Web site, offered by the National Institute of Mental Health, provides helpful information about schizophrenia. In addition to descriptions of symptoms, theories of etiology, and treatment options, several links lead to Web sites that detail medications, contemporary research on schizophrenia, and support organizations.

Chapter 7

CHANGING-CRITERION DESIGNS

Ruth, a 45-year-old married, stay-at-home mother of two teenagers, was admitted to the hospital by her personal physician due to problems with her newly diagnosed rheumatoid arthritis (RA). Ruth had been diagnosed with RA 6 months prior to the hospital admission after many years of increasing problems with the use of her hands. Unfortunately, Ruth seems to have a fairly aggressive form of RA and is currently suffering pain, swelling, stiffness in the joints, and fatigue. Of most concern to Ruth is that her hands are so swollen and painful that she can no longer perform her normal tasks in her home, such as cooking for her family and housecleaning. Since her diagnosis, Ruth has become increasingly despondent and has taken to spending most of the day in bed. She reports that she cries all the time, sleeps 14 to 16 hours a day, and does not feel like eating, leading to a weight loss of 12 pounds over the last two weeks. Ruth's husband, a bank vice president, reports that he is concerned about his wife's loss of interest in daily activities, and he is worried that she might be suicidal.

THE LOGIC OF THE CHANGING CRITERION DESIGN

Sometimes health care professionals are fortunate in that the behavior change that they are trying to bring about in a client comes readily and without difficulty. In such cases, changes in rate, duration, or other relevant dimensions of targeted behavior occur almost immediately and to the full extent desired as soon as the intervention begins. Of course, this is often not the case, especially when the desired or target behavior requires considerable skill or has not previously existed at all in the client's repertoire. You may recall Linda (Chap. 6, this volume), the victim of a snowmobiling accident, whose physical therapy entailed various exercise regimens targeting different muscle groups and cardiovascular fitness. Depending on the severity of her accident and on her personal history of exercise before the accident, getting Linda to engage in any kind of physical activity may prove very challenging. In Chapter 6, we described how physical therapy interventions with Linda might be evaluated across several different behaviors utilizing a multiple-baseline design. It is also possible, however, to monitor a gradual increase in Linda's activity level utilizing a different single-case research design, as we discuss in this chapter.

Enhancing physical exercise, and activity in general, is not an objective unique to individuals who have been rendered inactive because of accidents. Indeed, this is a common goal for many people whose lives have been very sedentary for many years. You might be able to relate to this difficulty if you have ever made a New Year's resolution to "get in shape" during the coming year. In fact, millions of Americans every year vow to do so, sometimes purchasing thousands of dollars worth of high-tech exercise equipment to get them started. Unfortunately, the vast majority of these well-intentioned exercise routines are terminated within the first few weeks, to be resurrected, if at all, only the following New Year!

So, what goes wrong? Why are we notoriously bad at sticking with an exercise program for the long haul? The answer is actually quite simple. Behavioral psychologists often make an important distinction between the *immediate* and the *delayed* consequences of behavior. More often than not, immediate consequences are much more powerful in influencing the future likelihood of a behavior, and this is glaringly clear in the case of exercise, dieting, and other health-related behaviors. You might begin your exercise program with all the enthusiasm of Richard Simmons, and, perhaps in part because of your level of commitment, you begin with a fairly vigorous, challenging workout. But if you have been largely inactive for months, or even years, a serious workout will have consequences you were not expecting. Most likely, the next day you may find the trivial act of getting out of bed to be an excruciatingly painful, arduous task, because muscles that you have not used for a long time are now sore and trying to recover from a workout for which they were not prepared. The result? You are through working out for the next few days, perhaps even weeks, because you are too sore. This is the rather sobering fate of many exercise regimens, as well as other efforts to alter our lifestyles. The long-term consequences of proper diet and exercise are clearly positive and include increased energy, enhanced muscle tone and cardiovascular fitness, less body fat, and so on, but these consequences are anything but immediate, and they may pale in comparison to the fatigue or aching muscles produced by exertion.

It is unfortunate that so many self-initiated efforts to modify lifestyle behavior patterns are aborted so quickly because they do not have to unfold like that. By gradually increasing the length and intensity of a workout, much of the stiffness due to vigorous effort can be avoided, and compliance with the regimen can be enhanced. In fact, many behaviors can be successfully changed through methods that encourage small, manageable steps rather than a full-blown "face lift" in the target behavior. Correspondingly, **changing-criterion designs** have been developed especially for evaluating behavior change when the target behavior is not expected to change all at once and when it seems more reasonable to bring about gradual, step-by-step changes. In Linda's case, it may simply be unreasonable to expect long and arduous physical workouts immediately after her accident. In fact, her therapist may find it difficult to motivate Linda to engage in any physical activity at all in the early stages of the therapeutic program. In such a case, the most appropriate intervention would be aimed at bringing Linda's exercise level up very gradually, beginning with perhaps only a few minutes of exercise (say, walking) per day. Only when she is able to exercise consistently for relatively short durations will the therapist recommend incremental increases in amount of exercise time.

Figure 7.1 depicts such a program of exercise development for Linda. The essence of a changing-criterion design is that changes in the target behavior are expected to occur gradually, in small steps. With the help of her therapist, Linda will decide on intermittent goals or criteria that she should be able to meet over the course of several weeks. The therapist will probably employ some kind of reinforcement program to encourage Linda to meet each successive criterion. Once a specific criterion (in this case, a particular number of minutes of exercise) is met on a consistent basis, a new, higher, criterion is set, and to obtain reinforcement the client needs to consistently meet the new criterion. By incrementally increasing the goal or criterion, behavior is moved gradually closer and closer to some desirable terminal level. Perhaps Linda and her therapist are trying to get Linda to exercise for at least 1 hour a day. This goal may be unrealistic early in the program but may be easily realized if successive improvements toward this goal are built into the program. As you can see in Figure 7.1, Linda's amount of exercising (in minutes) steadily increases over time, and she eventually meets the goal of 1 hour of continuous exercise. The changing-criterion design is especially well suited to circumstances in which rapid and large-scale behavior changes are unlikely. Instead of virtually committing a client to failure by expecting too much, changing-criterion designs slowly shape the target behavior toward its ultimate level.

Changing-criterion designs have been used to bring about change in many kinds of behaviors and across a wide array of client populations. They have proved especially valuable in studying the effects of interventions on long-standing, habitual behavior patterns. For instance, Hartmann and Hall (1976) used a reinforcement program to reduce cigarette smoking in a client who smoked an average of nearly 50 cigarettes a day. The client could earn small amounts of money by meeting the requirements of six successive reduction criteria. Each phase change required a

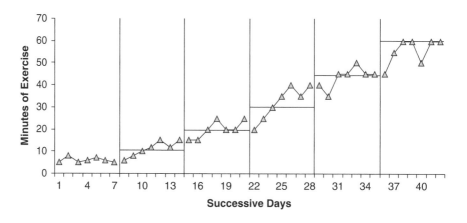

Figure 7.1   Linda's exercise program

reduction of approximately 5% from the previous criterion. The client was able to reduce his cigarette consumption to an average of 35 per day by the end of the experiment. Foxx and Rubinoff (1979) demonstrated similar success reducing the extreme caffeine consumption of three separate clients, using a monetary reinforcement procedure. All three clients began the experiment with average daily consumption of more than 1,000 mg of caffeine (approximately 9 cups of coffee). At the end of the experiment, after four successive criteria shifts, all three clients had reduced their caffeine consumption to less than 600 mg (fewer than 5 cups of coffee). In fact, two clients reduced consumption to less than 400 mg. Moreover, the treatment effect was maintained, as all three clients reported consuming fewer than 5 cups of coffee daily at a 10-month follow-up observation.

Changing-criterion designs are useful not only in monitoring the reduction of behavior over successive phases. Indeed, sometimes the goal of an intervention program is to instill a behavior in the hope that it will become habitual in the individual's repertoire. For example, Bigelow, Huynen, and Lutzker (1993) taught a 9-year-old autistic girl how to get out of her house in response to the verbal prompt "fire." Over successive sessions, the child was placed farther away from her front door, so that eventually she could exit the house successfully from a considerable distance when the prompt was given. DeLuca and Holborn (1992) used a changing-criterion design to gradually enhance exercise in six obese and nonobese young boys. The boys rode stationary bicycles and received feedback in the form of an illuminated light and a bell that rang whenever the requirements of a variable-ratio reinforcement schedule had been met. In a variable-ratio schedule reinforcement is delivered contingent on a varying number of responses occurring; in this case, a variable number of rotations of the exercise bike's wheel. Number of wheel rotations served as the dependent variable, and initially each boy's baseline level of exercise was measured. Then, during the intervention, the boys had to increase their bike riding 15% above the mean performance in the previous condition and throughout several phase changes. After three increases in the reinforcement requirement, a return to baseline was scheduled as a check on the experimental manipulation. All the boys exhibited increased wheel rotations with each successive increase in the requirement, and they demonstrated corresponding decreases during the return to baseline.

The stepwise feature of changing-criterion designs offers special advantages to researchers who are attempting to shape or build novel behavioral repertoires in clients. Cameron, Shapiro, and Ainsleigh (2005) attempted to teach bicycle riding to a 9-year-old boy diagnosed with Asperger's disorder, a developmental syndrome characterized primarily by social awkwardness. The client was uninterested in riding his bicycle, in part because of past attempts to learn that were met with failure, embarrassment, and even pain due to falls. His parents, however, wanted him to learn because of the potential contributions to physical well-being and community engagement. Because of the aversive nature of previous attempts to learn to ride, the client's lack of cooperation proved an initial challenge to the treatment team, and a very brief baseline observation revealed complete absence of the target behavior. Consequently, an eight-step task analysis was conducted, in which the client was first instructed and physically guided through very small, incremental movements related to bicycle riding. In addition, the initial stages of the intervention were delivered by having the client practice on a bike that was mounted on a stationary training pedestal. This allowed the client to master prerequisite skills, such as mounting and pedaling, without having to worry about maintaining balance. Once fundamental bicycle riding skills had been mastered, the bike was removed from its pedestal, and the intervention continued outside, first on a slightly sloping grassy hill, then on the street next to the client's house.

Over successive phase changes, the boy had to demonstrate an increased percentage mastery of one of the steps in the task analysis for a specified duration. For example, during the first intervention phase, he had to mount the bicycle on its pedestal and pedal uninterrupted for 5 minutes. Access to his GameCube video console served as the principal reinforcer for meeting each riding criterion. Time requirements for riding the bicycle increased across phase changes, and additional criteria, including braking, dismounting, and gliding, were added over time as well. The results of this study are shown in Figure 7.2. Because of the small increments that were required to master bicycling, the client was able to meet criteria specified at each phase change without difficulty. By the end of the eight-step task analysis, he was able to ride his bicycle on the road near his house for nearly half a kilometer. A 2-week follow-up revealed that the boy continued to ride his bike for fun, including an 8-km ride with his family for a fundraising event.

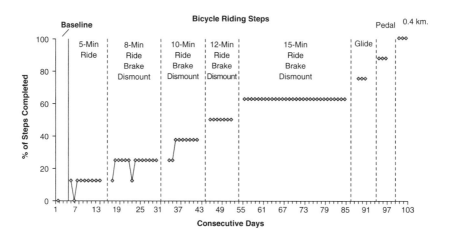

Figure 7.2   The diamonds depict the percentage of the eight-step task analysis that was completed during a session. Condition labels appear between condition lines.

Source: Cameron, M. J., Shapiro, R. L., & Ainsleigh, S. A. (2005). Reprinted with permission of Pro-Ed.

The following studies illustrate the variety of circumstances under which changing-criterion designs may be used. Warnes and Allen (2005), for example, used a changing-criterion design to evaluate the use of biofeedback in treating a 16-year-old girl's paradoxical vocal fold motion (PVFM). PVFM is a condition in which extreme tension of the vocal musculature leads to pain, hoarseness, and even the sensation that one is choking. The researchers used EMG biofeedback to help enhance the client's awareness of the muscle tension because PVFM patients are often unconscious of the tension that leads to later physical symptoms. Muscle tension, sensed via electrodes placed on the exterior of the throat, was measured in microvolts (mV), and the client received visual feedback of this tension on a computer monitor. A moving vertical bar changed from green to red with increased relaxation of the vocal folds. Baseline data revealed that the client exhibited muscle tension corresponding to a reading of 12 mV. During successive biofeedback treatment sessions, changes in the color of the vertical bar occurred only when specified reductions in tension were produced. In general, criteria were changed in 2-mV increments, and the client had to meet each criterion for three consecutive sessions before a new criterion was established.

Data from Warnes and Allen's (2005) study are depicted in Figure 7.3. Muscle tension exhibited a reduction beginning with the second session of biofeedback intervention and met the first criterion of 10 mV during the next three sessions. As can be seen in the second intervention data series, however, the client failed to meet the criterion of 8 mV; consequently, the criterion was actually increased to 9 mV for the next three sessions, a level the client consistently achieved during this condition. Over the next nine treatment sessions, muscle tension criteria were further reduced to 7 mV and 5 mV, respectively. The client successfully met these more stringent criteria. In addition to demonstrating the effectiveness of biofeedback in reducing this client's muscle tension, the researchers collected subjective pain data from her, as well as data on interference of daily activities from her mother. Both of these measures also exhibited improvement as a function of the biofeedback. Finally, the degree of muscle tension observed at the end of the study was shown to be comparable to that exhibited by a small normative group of females who had no history of PVFM, asthma, or other conditions affecting the vocal folds.

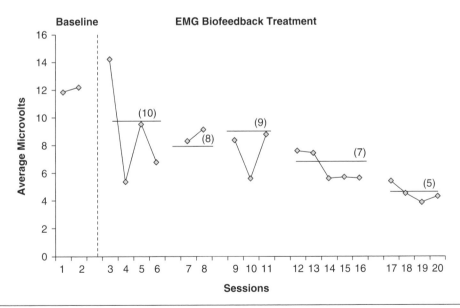

Figure 7.3 Average microvolts per session across baseline and treatment conditions. Horizontal lines and corresponding numbers in parentheses indicate changing criterion levels

Source: From Warnes, E., & Allen, K. D. (2005). Reprinted with permission of the Society for the Experimental Analysis of Behavior, Inc.

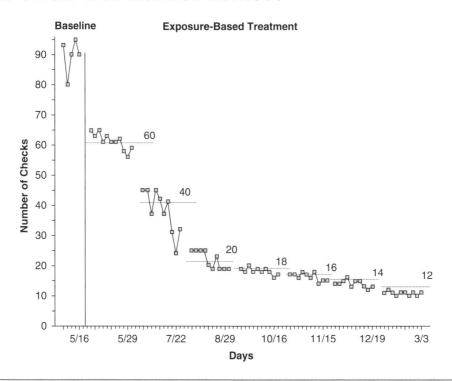

Figure 7.4   Number of blood glucose monitoring checks conducted during the last 10 days at each criterion level. Maximum test strips allotted at each level are indicated by dashed lines and corresponding numbers. The number of checks above the established criterion level reflect the number of additional test strips earned by Amy. Complete data a from testing during the intervention are available from the authors.

Source: From Allen, K. D., & Evans, J. H. (2001). Reprinted with permission of the Society for the Experimental Analysis of Behavior, Inc.

Allen and Evans (2001) utilized a changing-criterion design to assess an exposure-based treatment to reduce excessive blood glucose monitoring in a 15-year-old diabetic girl. Like many people with diabetes, the girl was fearful of developing hypoglycemia, a condition caused by extremely low blood sugar levels. Unfortunately, this fear led her to begin monitoring blood glucose between 80 and 90 times per day, several times the frequency (6–12 times per day) recommended by her physician. This extreme vigilance resulted not only in a financial burden to her parents, who had to buy hundreds of dollars of test strips per week, but also in an elevated blood sugar level of 275 to 300 mg/dl (compared with a recommended range of 75–150 mg/dl). The intervention program entailed having the client's parents gradually reducing access to the strips used to test blood glucose level. As can be seen in Figure 7.4, the parents established 60 test strips as the first criterion, because this was considered a manageable yet substantial reduction from the 80 to 95 strips used during baseline. When the client reached this criterion for 3 successive days, another 20-strip reduction was established as the next criterion. Once a criterion of 20 strips had been met for 3 days, successive criteria were reduced by 2 test strips, until a final criterion of 12 was established. In addition to meeting the 12–test strip criterion, the client's blood glucose had stabilized within the normal range by the study's end, an especially promising, though indirect, benefit of the treatment.

The changing-criterion design, as described by Hartmann and Hall (1976), simply specifies that performance criteria be met in the target behavior with each phase change or change in criterion. As long as the behavior exceeds or stays below this criterion, then the intervention is interpreted as successful, that is, depending on whether the program's goal was to increase or decrease the relevant dimension of the target behavior. For example, in Figure 7.1, we saw that the first criterion set for Linda's exercise regimen was 10 minutes of exercise. This was a level of exercise above what Linda had managed during baseline but nevertheless viewed by her therapist as a reasonable amount of exercise for Linda to achieve. Notice that in the second panel of Figure 7.1, Linda eventually met this requirement, and she exceeded it on 4 successive days. In the traditional use of a changing-criterion design it would not have mattered how much Linda's exercise duration exceeded this first criterion of 10 minutes. Any amount of exercise exceeding 10 minutes, including 12, 15, 20, or 30 minutes, would have met the requirements of the program at this phase.

The Range-Bound Changing-Criterion Design

In some circumstances, it might be desirable for a therapist to specify a range of values around which the target behavior should occur while still meeting the criterion established by the program. For example, the physical therapist working with Linda may want to avoid having Linda exercise so much that she becomes sore or injured, especially early in the program. Recall that this is a common occurrence not only in people recovering from injuries but also in those who have been sedentary or inactive for long periods of time. Thus, Linda's physical therapist may want to restrict her exercise increases to very manageable durations, even as the overall duration requirement increases with time. Such a program could be developed using a slight modification of the changing-criterion design, known as a **range-bound changing-criterion design** (**RBCC**). This design modification was introduced by McDougall (2005) and was in fact applied to an exercise program for an obese man who wanted to gradually increase the amount of time he spent running. The data, as well as the general strategy of the RBCC design, are depicted in Figure 7.5.

As you can see in the first panel of Figure 7.5, the amount of time the client spent running during baseline varied considerably, although the most common occurrence was no running at all. For this reason, a running time of 20 minutes was identified as a reasonable criterion with which to begin the program. In a conventional changing-criterion design any running duration that exceeded 20 minutes would have met the criterion. In a RBCC design, a range of running durations, circumscribed by an upper and lower limit, are created for this first criterion. Although this range will differ from one program to the next, McDougall (2005) chose a 10% range, meaning that the client was to run for any duration lasting between 18 and 22 minutes, because this represents 10% above and 10% below the general criterion of 20 minutes. The purpose of using this range is not only to allow an acceptable degree of variability in the target behavior but also to avoid encouraging excessive increases that may, in the long run, prove problematic or difficult to achieve. This is especially the case with exercise regimens, because too-rapid increases in exercise duration may lead to fatigue, soreness, or frustration in meeting more challenging criteria. In this particular case, amount of running time was increased gradually, from 20 to 100 minutes, with a range of 10% being maintained throughout. As can be seen in Figure 7.5, the client met all criteria, and his running times stayed within the defined range (10%) through all phases of the study.

You may also notice that the fifth phase change (the sixth panel of Figure 7.5) actually involved reverting to an earlier criterion. This strategy boasts both clinical and scientific utility. From a clinical standpoint, relaxing the criteria momentarily allows the client some respite from the increasing challenge of more strict criteria, as well as a suitable reward for having met previous criteria increases. From a scientific standpoint, this return to an earlier criterion allows the therapist to evaluate the internal validity of the intervention. In this case, the client's running time closely tracks the new criterion (60 ± 6 minutes), making it quite unlikely that the target behavior is attributable to some variable besides the therapeutic intervention. Moreover, subsequent increases in the running time criterion produce corresponding increases in actual running time, with variability occurring within the specified 10% range. The specificity of the RBCC design makes the demonstration of strong experimental control possible. The importance of this feature can hardly be overstated, especially when viewed within the context of applied settings (McDougall, Hawkins, Brady, & Jenkins, 2006).

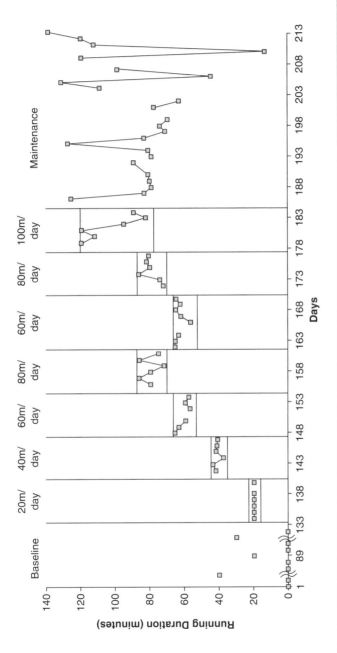

Figure 7.5 Duration in minutes of daily exercise (i.e., running) during baseline, intervention, and maintenance phases. Baseline is truncated to permit display of all data from intervention and maintenance phases. Participant ran on 3 days during 19-week baseline phase. Parallel horizontal lines within the seven intervention phases depict performance criteria that participant established for self to define the range of acceptable performance for each phase. That is, upper horizontal line indicates maximum and lower horizontal line indicates minimum number of minutes. Variability increased during maintenance phase. However, variability was exacerbated by one extreme data point, during session 210, when the participant terminated his daily run after only 13 minutes due to a lightning storm.

Source: From McDougall, D. © 2005 John Wiley & Sons Limited. Reproduced with permission.

171

The Distributed-Criterion Design

McDougall and his colleagues (McDougall, Hawkins, et al., 2006; McDougall & Smith, 2006) have also described the **distributed-criterion design (DC)** as an additional alternative to the conventional changing-criterion design. A DC design would normally be used to evaluate interventions for one target behavior occurring in different environments, or several target behaviors occurring in the same or different environments. The design was specifically created to allow for assessment of programs that require multitasking. The design is actually something of an amalgam of single-case designs because it entails features of a conventional changing-criterion design as well as elements of multiple-baseline and reversal designs. McDougall, Hawkins, et al. (2006) reported an example of a DC design used to evaluate amount of time devoted to manuscript preparation by an academic researcher. Three different manuscripts were being prepared for submission to professional journals, and the manuscripts were in different stages of completion at the beginning of the study. The multiple-baseline element of the design referred to the fact that time was allotted to each manuscript in sequential order, based on how little of the manuscript had been completed at the study's outset. Short-term goals were established for spending specified amounts of time working on each manuscript. Criteria for allotting time to each manuscript were decided on and instituted at different times for each manuscript. These distributed-criteria lines can be seen in Figure 7.6. Also, allotted time requirements were eliminated for a manuscript as it reached a stage of completion; this phase of the study represented the reversal phase of the design. As can be seen in Figure 7.6, allotted time requirements were met during each phase change, and time was differentially allotted to manuscripts as a function of their different stages of completion.

Evaluating the internal validity of an intervention using the DC design is, in many ways, commensurate with the evaluation of the other changing-criterion designs described in this chapter. Indeed, to some extent, establishing the validity of any intervention using single-case designs rests on a single feature: the extent to which phase changes correspond to meaningful changes in the target behavior. As with other single-case designs, changing-criterion designs in which multiple phase changes occur allow for strong causal inference when behavior change corresponds closely to changes in the intervention. Recall that each phase change allows for a comparison of the client's behavior in two different conditions, and this essential logic applies to all single-case designs. Whether that condition change entails withdrawal of a treatment, as in a reversal or ABAB design, application of the intervention at different times or across different subjects, as in a multiple-baseline design, or gradually changing performance requirements, as in a changing-criterion design, each phase change adds to the confidence with which inferences about the intervention may be drawn.

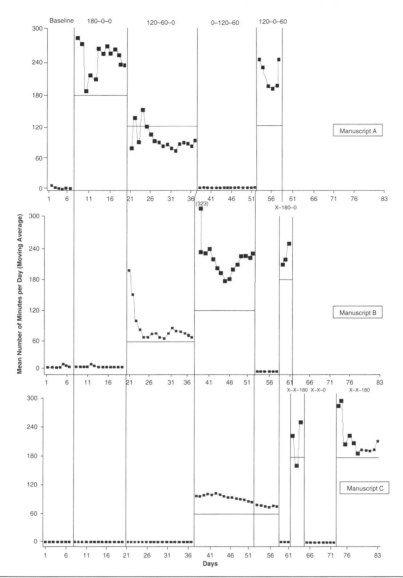

Figure 7.6 Moving average for research productivity (mean number of minutes expended daily) within baseline and intervention phases for Manuscripts A, B, and C. Note. Horizontal lines indicate within-phase productivity criteria (i.e., minimum number of minutes to be expended on manuscript) that participant set for self. Labels for intervention phases appear as numeric sequences (e.g., 120-60-0), with the first numeral indicating the within-phase criterion (mean number of minutes) that the participant established for Manuscript A, the second numeral indicating the within-phase criterion for Manuscript B, and the third numeral indicating the within-phase criterion for Manuscript C. X indicates that a criterion was no longer pertinent because the participant had completed work on that manuscript.

Source: From "The Distributed Criterion Design," by D. McDougall, *Journal of Behavioral Education.* 2006 by Springer-Verlag. Reprinted with permission.

The RBCC design may allow for an even more precise demonstration of internal validity because of the stricter response requirements defined by the preestablished range boundaries. Unlike the traditional changing-criterion design, which accepts considerable variability in responding, in the RBCC design responding must remain within more constrained parameters, so long as the single criterion is met. When this happens and when the criterion boundaries change from phase to phase, strong experimental control over the target behavior is demonstrated. In the case of the DC design, changes in behavior that correspond to criteria changes across environments or target behaviors demonstrate similar experimental control. In short, all changing-criterion designs allow for multiple phase changes, and each phase change represents an opportunity to evaluate the effects of an independent variable or intervention. When changes in the target behavior occur immediately after these phase changes and closely correspond to the established criteria, strong inferences about interventions are possible.

INTERIM SUMMARY

The changing-criterion design is especially useful for assessing interventions that would be expected to produce very gradual change in a target behavior over time. This is, in fact, a frequent tactic in behavioral therapy, occupational therapy, physical therapy, and nursing interventions. After baseline measurement of the target behavior, a series of phase changes occurs in which criteria relevant to the target behavior are adjusted upward or downward, depending on the goals of the program. Because of the frequent phase changes, interpretation of the behavior change is relatively straightforward. Changes that closely track the modified criteria are evidence for the internal validity of the intervention. Because most changing-criterion designs utilize at least three or more phases with corresponding changes in criteria, this strategy allows ample opportunities for drawing causal conclusions. Recently, the RBCC and DC designs have been introduced as modifications of the classic changing-criterion design.

THE CASE OF RUTH

Arthritis is the most common cause of disability in the United States. Rheumatoid Arthritis is one of more than 100 different types of arthritis and is a progressive, symmetrical, and cartilage-destroying condition that can significantly decrease a person's range of motion (ROM). It affects people's lives in many ways, and treating it often requires a multidisciplinary approach. Today, many patients with moderately to severely active RA are turning to a multidisciplinary treatment team—a group of specialists from diverse disciplines working together with one common goal: managing RA better. Such a treatment team might include rheumatologists, nurses and nurse practitioners, occupational therapists, physical therapists, nutritionists, clinical psychologists, and pharmacists.

It is likely that Ruth, the RA patient introduced at the beginning of this chapter, will benefit from the services of all of the professionals involved in such a multidisciplinary treatment team. For purposes of our understanding of changing-criterion designs, we focus on how two of these experts—a clinical psychologist and a physical therapist—might be able to assist Ruth and document the success of their treatment approach with such a design.

A Clinical Psychologist's Perspective

It seems clear from reading Ruth's case that the restrictions placed on her activity by her advancing RA have led to a major depressive episode. To be diagnosed with a major depressive episode, five or more identified symptoms must be present during the same 2-week period and represent a change from previous functioning. In addition, one of the five symptoms must be either depressed mood or a loss of interest or pleasure in everyday activities. By looking at Ruth's reported symptoms, we see that she and her husband report that for the last 6 months Ruth has exhibited a depressed mood, has lost interest in daily activities, has lost 12 pounds because of a loss of interest in eating, is sleeping excessively (hypersomnia), is fatigued, and has been thinking of suicide. Although the fatigue may be more related to the RA than depression, Ruth meets the criteria for a major depressive episode without including this symptom (American Psychiatric Association, 2000).

Major depressive disorder has been found to affect between 13% and 17% of RA sufferers, perhaps because of the increased pain experienced by these patients (Dickens, McGowan, Clark-Carter, & Creed, 2002). This level of depression is two to three times that found in the general population. Functional limitations, such as those experienced by Ruth, also contribute to depression in RA sufferers. Nearly two thirds of adults with RA have some type of functional limitation. Addressing these limitations and reducing pain should clearly be a part of the treatment for persons suffering with RA. In Ruth's case, pain and functional limitations will be addressed directly by the physical therapist. We turn first, however, to the clinical psychologist's efforts to treat Ruth's depression.

Without a doubt, there are many treatment considerations that must be addressed by the psychologist assigned Ruth's case. Might it be possible that Ruth's depression will clear on its own as her RA becomes better controlled? Would an antidepressant be an appropriate choice for reducing the intensity of Ruth's depression? Although antidepressants can be very effective, Ruth is already on several medications for RA, and the psychologist is concerned about the potential for dangerous drug interactions. Moreover, nonpharmaceutical interventions for depression are available, and their effectiveness is well documented by research. In the present example, the psychologist has decided to address Ruth's depressive symptoms with a cognitive–behavioral approach. The actual treatment components will not be addressed here but can be reviewed in Jacobson, Dobson, and Truax (1996).

The first step would be to identify a target behavior. Depression is often referred to as a *syndrome*, meaning that it is characterized by several symptoms cutting across cognitive, affective, and behavioral dimensions. Thus, the psychologist working with Ruth may identify any of a number of behavioral symptoms to observe and measure. Although many target behaviors could possibly be chosen, we can easily use a self-reported count of positive thoughts as our dependent variable. Focusing on thoughts is a typical component of cognitive–behavioral approaches. Cognitions, or thoughts, may become distorted, and in the case of depressed individuals, lead to a vicious cycle of negative emotions, which trigger more distorted thoughts, and so on. Consequently, a major focus of cognitive–behavior therapy is to alter these thoughts through a process known as *cognitive restructuring*. Specific details about how this is achieved may be obtained in the literature (Abramovich, 2006; Sanderson & McGinn, 2001; Stark, Hargrave, & Sander, et al., 2006).

The psychologist taught Ruth how to monitor her thoughts and to record the number of positive thoughts in her daily log. Once Ruth was monitoring her thoughts successfully, baseline data were collected. During Ruth's first week in the hospital, a daily count of positive thoughts was obtained by the psychologist. Also during this first week, the psychologist interviewed Ruth and conducted additional psychological tests to ensure a thorough understanding of her difficulties and to determine the best treatment approach. The daily positive thought scores during the baseline period can be seen in the first, or leftmost panel, of Figure 7.7. Although there is some variability, the positive thought counts are consistently low, as might be expected given Ruth's depressed mood, and do not appear to be increasing or decreasing. Given these baseline data, the psychologist considered it appropriate to institute the treatment phase. Because Ruth was an inpatient, daily therapy sessions were possible. In addition, daily positive thought counts continued to be collected.

As the goal for the first stage of treatment, Ruth was asked to increase her daily positive thought count by approximately two thoughts. Considering that Ruth's positive thoughts during baseline averaged only three a day, a count of five or more was considered a small but measurable improvement. Thus, the first criterion to be reached, five or more positive thoughts, is indicated by the horizontal line in the second panel of Figure 7.7. As can be seen, counts remained consistent with baseline during the first 2 days of treatment but increased substantially during the next 3 days, remaining above criterion throughout the rest of this period.

On Day 9 of treatment, Ruth was asked to once again increase her daily positive thought count, this time adding three additional positive thoughts. This produced a new criterion of 8 total positive daily thoughts. The third panel represents this stage of treatment. Ruth required only 2 days to meet this new criterion, and her count of positive thoughts exceeded the requirement for 4 straight days. The final criterion established for Ruth was a daily positive thought count of 12. The last (far right) panel of the graph in Figure 7.7 depicts this phase of treatment. As can be seen, Ruth appeared to increase her daily positive thought count to a steady state by day 31. Not surprisingly, this increase in positive cognition corresponded to other improvements in Ruth's symptoms and, on the recommendation of the psychologist, Ruth was discharged from the hospital.

It is important at this point to acknowledge the fact that the psychologist's intervention was quite focused, in that it targeted only one category of behavior: positive thoughts. The decision to address this particular behavior was a logical consequence of the clinician's endorsement of a cognitive–behavioral model, but other aspects of client functioning could have been addressed as well. Recall that depression is viewed as a syndrome, having implications for many categories of thought, emotion, and behavior. In fact, some professionals might choose to use

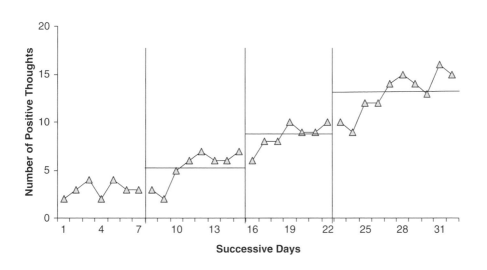

Figure 7.7 Ruth's positive thoughts

a much more global assessment or measurement strategy than to focus on specific classes of behavior. Many clinical psychologists and psychiatrists, for example, would measure depression via a standard scale or survey instrument, such as the Beck Depression Inventory (BDI) (Beck, Steer, & Brown, 1996; Beck, Steer, & Garbin, 1988). The BDI, created by Aaron Beck, is a 21-item self-administered instrument designed to measure such characteristics of depression as sadness, social withdrawal, guilt, loss of weight, low energy level, and suicidal ideation, as well as their degree of severity. Because it is easily administered, takes only a few minutes to complete, and has an extensive history of evaluation, the BDI is used frequently by mental health professionals. Moreover, the BDI has become the measure of choice for depression in clinical trials conducted to evaluate various modes of treatment (Rush, Beck, Kovacs, & Hollon, 1977).

Given that the BDI is a respected and frequently used instrument for measuring depression, you might wonder why Ruth's psychologist would bother having her self-record positive thoughts—or, for that matter, any other specific behavior, such as crying, sleep problems, or suicidal thoughts. In other words, why measure specific behaviors when you have available a global instrument that is assumed to assess the major symptoms of depression? Although there is no one answer to this question, many survey instruments or scales, though easy to administer and score, may prove problematic when used in single-case studies. To understand why this is so, consider that in many large-scale randomized clinical trials, participants would probably complete the BDI both prior to and after intervention. This amounts to a simple between-groups pretest–posttest design, with all participants being administered the BDI twice. However, because single-case designs employ many more measures of the dependent variable than do between-group designs, participants may be completing the BDI many times throughout the course of a study. One potential problem with using such instruments repeatedly is that participants sometimes develop *response sets*; that is, they rapidly fill out the form in nearly automatic fashion, giving little attention to the meaning of the actual questions. Doing so tends to invalidate the instrument, making it difficult to draw meaningful conclusions regarding the actual change in depressive symptoms. In addition, research has shown that scores on the BDI are not stable over time, with significant reductions in scores being observed on a second administration (Hatzenbueler, Parpal, & Matthews, 1983; Zimmerman, 1986). Ahava, Iannone, Grebstein, and Schirling (1998) demonstrated a 40% reduction in reported depressive symptoms among a nonclinical population over an 8-week period. Such a decline strongly suggests substantial measurement error, or a threat to internal validity, such as a response set or regression toward the mean.

There may be ways to combat the problems encountered by the use of such scales in single-case studies. Dahlstrom, Brooks, and Peterson (1990), for instance, recommended that the items on a scale be ordered in a random fashion from one administration to the next in order to reduce the likelihood of response sets. Another option is to utilize different, but conceptually and psychometrically equivalent, scales across multiple administrations. The BDI has been shown to correlate with other measures of depression, so researchers or clinicians could alternate different scales across multiple assessments. Doing so, however, would require researchers to compare numerical ratings that differ across scales, though perhaps indicating similar levels of depression. For instance, a score of 30 to 63 on the BDI indicates "severe depression," whereas only scores of 70 or greater are interpreted as indicative of "severe depression" on the Zung Depression Index (Zung, 1965), a scale known to be strongly correlated with the BDI.

Researchers will undoubtedly resolve the dilemma of direct behavioral measurement versus survey instruments as a function of their training, theoretical orientations, and the logistics of conducting measurement in applied settings. Although there may be reasons for utilizing survey instruments to collect repeated measures, most single-case researchers have opted for direct behavioral measurement as the strategy of choice, and for good reason. So long as the behavior being measured is meaningful and relevant to the client's functioning, changes in this behavior following treatment should reflect clinically significant improvement. In fact, research has shown that the very act of self-monitoring often leads to improvement in the target behavior, even before any systematic treatment is applied (Hayes & Cavior, 1977; Kirby, Fowler, & Baer, 1991). Also, repeated observations of behavior, conducted either by the client him- or herself or by a separate observer, should be relatively free of response sets if the operational definition is clear and if the observer strictly adheres to the observation strategy. Finally, the quantitative properties of observed behavior, such as rate, latency, intensity, and duration, reflect standardized units of measurement recognizable to anyone, and their meaning is universal, not subject to the vagaries of the measuring instrument itself. The numbers reflected in survey instruments tend to be very idiosyncratic—recall that a score of 60 on the BDI and a score of 60 on the Zung Depression Index have entirely different meanings—thus requiring knowledge of the scale and its specific scoring protocol. Standardized measures, such as rate or duration, however, are directly comparable and are universally applicable to any study in which behavior is being observed and measured (Johnston & Pennypacker, 1993b).

A Physical Therapist's Perspective

Physical therapists are critical members of RA treatment teams. The purpose of physical therapy is to decrease pain and allow the patient to continue daily activities. Physical therapy can reduce pain in the soft tissues (e.g., the muscles, ligaments, and tendons), improve ROM in joints, and build muscle strength. A physical therapist provides these treatments as well as providing education, instruction, and support for recovery. Typical techniques used by physical therapists in treating RA may include the following:

Stretching, to reduce stress on joints and improve ROM

Education, to help improve and maintain posture

Exercise, to strengthen muscles.

Manual therapy, including massage, to improve or maintain ROM

Heat therapy, to improve blood circulation to the muscles and other soft tissues

Ice therapy, to reduce swelling and relieve pain

Cycling and limited walking, to promote good physical conditioning

Water exercises, to allow exercise without pressure on the spine

In Ruth's case, the physical therapist was able to meet with Ruth from the start of her hospitalization. Before initiating any treatment, the physical therapist decided on a target behavior and an assessment procedure. One of the most important determinants of treatment success for individuals with RA is how much the RA impacts their daily functioning. Therefore, the physical therapist employed a handheld goniometer (Neistadt & Crepeau, 1998) to measure the ROM in Ruth's wrist. A goniometer measures angles created at joints by the bones of the body. The traditional handheld goniometer (protractor with a movable arm) is frequently used by physical therapists to assess joint movement or range. For the first 5 days, the physical therapist recorded Ruth's scores. Ruth's scores on the goniometer for wrist extension are presented in Figure 7.8. Ruth's ROM was fairly consistent with a range of 10 to 20 degrees. Given this consistent baseline, the physical therapist chose to begin Ruth's treatment by using ice therapy to reduce Ruth's swelling and pain. For the first phase of treatment, the goal was to increase ROM as measured by the goniometer to 0.30 degrees. The second panel in Figure 7.8 indicates Ruth's progression during the next 5 days of treatment; her scores appeared to increase to the desired level. At this point, the physical therapist and Ruth decided to increase the goal to 0.40 degrees. Despite continued treatment, goniometer measurements indicated that Ruth continued to hover around 0.30 degrees. Published accounts of normal wrist extension ROM range from 0.50 degrees to 0.90 degrees (Miller, 1985). In this case, the data collected by the physical therapist allowed a clear demonstration that the selected treatment led to an initial improvement in Ruth's ROM but that improvement stalled after these initial results. Despite continued treatment, Ruth's ROM did not improve past an average of 0.30 degrees.

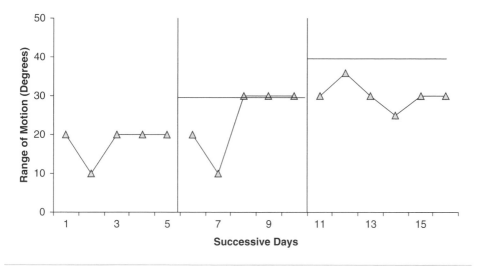

Figure 7.8   Ruth's range of motion

INTERIM SUMMARY

The case of Ruth, the client suffering from RA as well as RA-related depression, demonstrates how both a clinical psychologist and a physical therapist would utilize a changing-criterion design to assess Ruth's response to both psychological and physical therapy interventions. This design allowed for monitoring of the kinds of gradual changes that would be expected to occur in the target behaviors being observed and recorded for Ruth. In Chapter 8, we consider single-case designs that allow researchers to compare the relative effectiveness of two or more treatment strategies.

KEY TERMS GLOSSARY

Changing-criterion design A single-case research design that typically includes one baseline phase followed by several treatment phases in which the target behavior must meet or exceed increasingly challenging prespecified criteria.

Range-bound changing-criterion design (RBCC) A changing-criterion design in which a target behavior must fall within a prespecified range of values within any particular treatment phase.

Distributed-criterion design (DC) A changing-criterion design that integrates features of withdrawal and multiple-baseline designs to evaluate several different target behaviors at the same time.

SUPPLEMENTS

Review Questions

1. In what way does the changing-criterion design differ from withdrawal designs and multiple-baseline designs?

2. Why is the changing-criterion design especially well suited to evaluating gradual changes in a target behavior?

3. Why does the range-bound changing-criterion design allow for somewhat stronger inferences about interventions than the traditional changing-criterion design?

4. What is the primary distinguishing feature of the distributed-criterion design? Describe an example in which its use would be appropriate.

5. What dimensions of behavior change are evaluated in determining the internal validity of a changing-criterion design? Does this differ depending on whether it is a traditional changing-criterion design, a range-bound changing-criterion design, or a distributed-changing criterion design?

Suggested Readings/Helpful Web Sites

http://www.medicinenet.com/rheumatoid_arthritis/article.htm
This Web site provides detailed information about rheumatoid arthritis (RA), including illustrations of joints, causal factors, diagnostic criteria, and treatments. There are numerous links to other RA-related Web sites, research centers, physicians, and RA patients who describe their management of RA.

http://www.hshsl.umaryland.edu/resources/physicaltherapy.html
This Web site maintains links to various Web sites relevant to education, research, and practice of physical therapy. Included are links to relevant physical therapy journals, professional organizations, clinical-trials research, training information, and evidence-based practice issues.

Chapter 8

COMPARING TREATMENTS
The Alternating-Treatments Designs

Paul, a 37-year-old white man, first appeared at his doctor's office after reading a magazine article about diabetes. Over the previous summer he had gained 30 pounds, was "thirsty all the time," and was "running to the bathroom all night long." Getting Paul to the doctor took his wife almost 6 months. Since Paul was a child, he had experienced an aversion to doctors, blood, and needles. His fear began as a child, after he fainted while getting stitches for a cut on his forehead. Over the next few years, he fainted several times during blood tests, vaccinations, and other situations involving needles. As a teenager, he avoided any situation in which he or his friends might injure themselves because he was afraid that he might have to look at the resulting blood, which disgusted him. Eventually, he started avoiding doctors completely. Since becoming a father, he has fainted twice when his children bloodied their knees or cut themselves.

In an effort to help Paul, his doctor used a topical anesthetic cream containing prilocaine and lidocaine, which would reduce the pain of obtaining a blood sample. Unfortunately, although the cream reduced the pain, Paul fainted when he saw his blood. The blood sample allowed Paul's doctor to test the level of blood glucose/sugar in his blood and found Paul's reading to be 360 g/dl. A subsequent test confirmed this high reading, with the second test showing a reading of 340g/dl. Normal fasting blood glucose/sugar level varies between 70 and 110 g/dl.

THE LOGIC OF ALTERNATING TREATMENTS DESIGNS

As we discussed in Chapter 1 of this book, health care practitioners are increasingly expected to utilize clinical interventions that have been demonstrated effective in research, a development largely fueled by the growth of managed care. This is, expectedly, a very tall order to fill, particularly when you consider the array of clinical strategies used by such varied professionals as psychologists, physical and occupational therapists, nurses, and social workers. Moreover, the delivery of empirically supported treatments (ESTs) is rendered even more complex when one considers the large population of target behaviors or clinical symptoms to which interventions are applied, the varying characteristics of the clients involved, and the many kinds of settings in which interventions are delivered. Naturally, any practicing health care worker would greatly appreciate a cookbook that described, in detail, clinical strategies known to be effective in treating all manner of clinical symptoms. No such cookbook exists at present, although some disciplines have made considerable progress in identifying effective treatment modalities for specific kinds of problems. For instance, many decades of psychological research on therapy effectiveness have resulted in some well-established treatment regimens for particular kinds of psychological or behavioral problems.

A good deal of controversy swirls around the process of identifying ESTs, especially in psychology (Castonguay & Beutler, 2006; Chambless & Ollendick, 2001; Hunsley, 2007; Hunsley & Lee, 2006; Nathan & Gorman, 2002; Stirman, DeRubeis, Crits-Christoph, & Rothman, 2005). Consequently, attempts at generating lists of effective therapies have proven similarly frustrating. In part, this is because some kinds of therapies and the problems to which they are applied have been the focus of considerable research, whereas others have received relatively less attention. For instance, although ESTs have existed for some time for phobias and other anxiety disorders, as well as clinical depression, these maladies hardly exhaust the problems encountered by people in the real world. Much less is known about the effectiveness of treatments for personality disorders, eating disorders, and other problems that may occur in smaller numbers yet remain troublesome to those encountering them.

Moreover, even the research that has established EST has come under criticism, much of it quite valid. Much of this research has been purposefully conducted under conditions that are not typical of clinical settings. The gold standard for much of this research is the *randomized clinical (controlled) trial*, in which subjects must be randomly assigned to control or experimental groups, client symptoms must fit diagnostic criteria very specifically, and interventions must be standardized and delivered according to very strict guidelines, usually adhering to manualized descriptions. Clearly, these conditions are seldom met in the normal course of clinical practice. No two clients are ever completely alike. Even those receiving the same diagnosis may differ along numerous dimensions, including age, gender, severity and duration of symptoms, and other factors likely to influence treatment effectiveness. Nor do professional health care practitioners deliver their interventions in a standardized fashion across clients. Instead, interventions tend to be highly individualized and responsive to personal characteristics of the client and to the client's ongoing response to the intervention. In short, the growing research literature on evidence-based practice is a necessary and important development within health care, but the specific products of such research may have limited utility to the individual practitioner considering an intervention for a specific client. Any practicing physician recognizes, for example, that established treatments (e.g., antibiotics for infections) may work most of the time for most patients but be counterindicated for others (e.g., those who may be allergic to conventional antibiotics). No amount of research in the nomothetic tradition can effectively reveal the likelihood of successful treatment in an individual case.

The kind of group research that has contributed to empirically supported interventions has been important in establishing guidelines for clinical practice, but the questionable external validity of such research has not gone unnoticed (Jacobson & Christensen, 1996; Rothwell, 2005; Ruscio & Holohan, 2006). Recall that the sample statistics generated in large-group studies are used primarily to draw inferences about similar population parameters. Thus, comparisons are being made between groups, or collectivities. Inferences about individual subjects or clients are not supported by group data. Individual practitioners, however, bear the somewhat different burden of delivering effective interventions to individual clients, not groups of clients. The practitioner is not interested in whether the average or mean response of a group of clients receiving treatment differed from the average response of a control group not receiving treatment. Instead, the relevant comparison in an applied setting is the individual client's response to the intervention, and this can be accomplished only by way of an intrasubject, time-series comparison. It is precisely this kind of comparison that is made possible by a single-case analysis.

If a trip to your family physician reveals an inner ear infection, you likely will be prescribed one of several widely used antibiotic medications. Of course, there is no guarantee that the medication will effectively eliminate your infection. People respond in sometimes idiosyncratic ways to medication, and what works for one patient may not work for another. Any well-trained physician will tell you that medicine is part science and part art. Sometimes standard treatments do not work, and when this happens the only logical response is to try something different—in essence, to experiment until you find an effective treatment. Naturally, the medical community does not exactly advertise the fact that physicians sometimes fly by the seat of their pants in treating illness, but the fact remains that discovering the right course of action often comes down to pitting one treatment against another until one emerges as the clear victor.

Identifying effective interventions in the behavioral and health sciences often requires a comparative strategy as well. When a professional has identified the target behavior to be treated, more than one potential intervention may come to mind. In fact, in some cases there may be sizable professional literatures attesting to the effectiveness of each type of intervention. In such cases, the professional may find it prudent to utilize both treatments for a particular client in an effort to discover which treatment is most effective in this particular case. Pitting two or more treatments against one another to identify the most effective intervention can be undertaken through the use of an **alternating-treatments design**. As the name implies, such a design involves systematically alternating the treatments across some reasonable time frame and comparing the relative response of the target behavior to each treatment. The manner in which the competing treatments will be alternated depends on the details of the behavior being targeted and the setting in which the treatments will be employed. The design, first described by Barlow and Hayes (1979), has become one of the more common single-case designs employed by applied health care workers.

The alternating-treatments design was derived from a family of experimental designs developed by laboratory scientists studying operant behavior. These designs, including the *multiple schedule design* (Hersen & Barlow, 1976), *simultaneous treatment design* (Kazdin & Hartmann, 1978), and *multi-element design* (Ulman & Sulzer-Azaroff, 1975), were used for the purpose of identifying functional relationships between behavior and programmed stimulus events in basic learning experiments. In general, these designs shared the feature of rapidly changing experimental conditions, with salient stimuli associated with different conditions. Barlow and Hayes (1979) suggested that these particular conditions are not always replicated in applied settings in which the objective is to compare clinical treatments. They recommended, therefore, that applied studies in which treatments are compared within a given client be referred to as *alternating-treatments designs*. As we will see, the design is capable of considerable adaptation and flexibility, as are other single-case designs, particularly when serving the goals of applied researchers. In many respects, the alternating-treatments design shares many features with the other single-case designs discussed throughout this book. Although not an absolute requirement in alternating-treatments designs, baseline data collected prior to any intervention serve the important purpose of identifying the natural rate and patterning of the target behavior. Because of clinical or practical concerns, baseline data may not always be collected, but when they are they serve the same comparative function as in other designs.

The inferences about treatment effectiveness in the alternating-treatments design result from the rapid phase changes that occur as interventions are alternated. Remember that the comparison of target behaviors under different experimental conditions is what supports all conclusions in single-case designs. This feature is elevated to an even higher degree of importance in alternating-treatments designs because phase changes occur frequently and sometimes unpredictably. You may recall from Chapter 2 that the internal validity of any experiment depends on the researcher's confidence that changes in the dependent variable are attributable to the independent variable (treatment) and not to other, uncontrolled factors. In the alternating-treatments design, behavior change that tracks the rapid phase changes (baseline to treatment, or Treatment A to Treatment B) strongly suggests a treatment effect. We would consider the probability to be very low that changes in behavior or clinical symptoms just happen to coincide with changes in treatment, particularly when this pattern repeats itself.

The basic elements of the alternating-treatments design can be described in the hypothetical example of an elderly man who, though living independently, is on a complex medical regimen involving multiple medications. Wilbur, an 84-year-old World War II veteran, has been widowed for 3 years and still lives in the same house he and his wife bought 42 years ago. He walks in his neighborhood several times a week, does all of his own cooking and cleaning, and in general enjoys good health for a man his age. However, Wilbur is required by his physician to take four different medications daily, all of them three times per day. Recently, Wilbur has become forgetful with respect to his medical regimen, and his daughter, who lives in the same town, has become concerned that his health may be compromised because of inconsistent or incorrect use of medication. She does not wish to place her father in a nursing home or assisted care facility because she believes he is happy in his home and that, with the exception of forgetting to take his medication consistently, he is in good health and remains self-sufficient.

Wilbur's daughter contacts his physician to discuss her father's increasing forgetfulness and her concerns for his health. The physician recommends that a visiting home nurse be employed to establish a program for monitoring and enhancing Wilbur's medical compliance. Together, the nurse and Wilbur's daughter discuss the options available to them in helping Wilbur to take his medication consistently. The nurse informs Wilbur's daughter that medication noncompliance is a common and serious problem in the elderly, who are likely to be on more complex medical regimens than people in other age groups (Kendrick & Bayne, 1982; Richardson, 1986). The nurse also explains that little is known about techniques for enhancing compliance because no intervention has been shown to be effective in all cases. On the basis of her knowledge of the literature, the nurse proposes two possible solutions. Because she is close by and has frequent contact with him, one option is for Wilbur's daughter to give him a quick phone call each time he is to take a particular medication. Although this strategy would be inconvenient for many people, Wilbur's daughter works from her home and is on the telephone a good deal anyway. She agrees to make the phone calls at the appropriate interval on days that this intervention will be used. The nurse suggests that the other intervention would involve placing a large-type instruction placard on the kitchen wall in Wilbur's house. This placard describes each medication, its primary therapeutic effect, and the times of day that Wilbur was to take the medication. In this condition, Wilbur's daughter will make one phone call at 7:00 a.m. to tell Wilbur to place the placard on the kitchen wall. A picture hanger will be placed on the wall, so Wilbur can easily hang or remove the placard on the wall himself. At 8:00 p.m., Wilbur's daughter will call to tell him to remove the placard and put it back in a drawer in the kitchen. During days on which the placard is to be displayed, Wilbur's daughter will make no phone calls to remind Wilbur to take his medication; the only calls to be made are to remind him to hang up and then remove the placard each day.

Before contacting her father's physician, Wilbur's daughter had attempted to informally assess Wilbur's compliance by calling him on the phone at the end of the day to ask which medications he had taken. Because his physician had prescribed four different medications, each to be taken three times a day, Wilbur should have been taking 12 pills per day. These data, collected for 5 days prior to the meeting with the nurse, are of somewhat questionable reliability because they are self-reports from Wilbur, but they are also characteristic of baseline measures frequently encountered in applied settings. Direct observation of Wilbur's medical compliance, by his daughter or the home nurse, would clearly have been preferable and more scientifically valid, but such measures are not always available to applied researchers. Despite the lack of rigor in collection of these baseline data, the nurse and Wilbur's daughter decided to use the five self-reports from Wilbur as baseline data against which to compare compliance during the alternating-treatments conditions.

The baseline level of compliance for Wilbur is depicted in the first (left) panel of Figure 8.1. During this 5-day period, Wilbur's reported compliance fluctuated, as is common of most behaviors observed over time, but it remained alarmingly low, hovering around three to five pills per day. This was understandably disconcerting to the nurse and Wilbur's daughter, because Wilbur should have been taking 12 pills each day.

After this 5-day baseline period, and beginning on a Monday, the two intervention strategies were delivered, on alternating days, in order to enhance Wilbur's compliance to his prescribed medical regimen. The primary feature of an alternating-

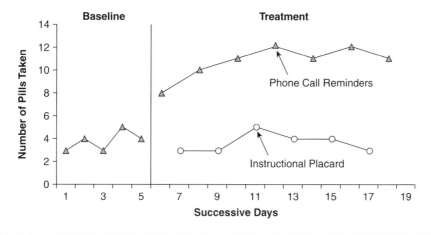

Figure 8.1   Wilbur's medical compliance

treatments design is the rapid change from one treatment to another, but the specific way in which this strategy is implemented differs depending on the setting and target behavior of interest. In Wilbur's case, the nurse and his daughter decided that a simple way to alternate the two treatments (phone call reminders vs. instruction placard) was to deliver the treatments on alternating days, beginning on a Monday of the first week of intervention. Because the dependent measure, number of pills taken, was to be assessed at the end of each day, this strategy allowed for a clean separation of the treatments, with a new treatment beginning each day. On Monday of the first week, Wilbur's daughter, in possession of an information sheet describing his medicine regimen, called Wilbur on the phone each time he was scheduled to take a pill. On Tuesday, the second treatment was delivered for the first time. Wilbur's daughter made one phone call at 7:00 a.m., reminding Wilbur to hang the medication instruction placard on his kitchen wall. The only other phone call made that day was at 8:00 p.m., at which time she informed Wilbur to remove the placard and place it in a kitchen drawer. These two conditions (phone call reminders vs. instructional placard) were then alternated daily for a 2-week period.

The second panel of Figure 8.1 demonstrates Wilbur's level of medical compliance during the period of alternating treatments (phone call reminders vs. instruction placard). Note that, unlike other graphs we have discussed throughout this book, Figure 8.1 contains two function lines during the treatment phase. Each line depicts Wilbur's medical compliance (pills taken per day) under a specific treatment condition. In this particular case, triangles represent pills taken during the phone call reminder condition, and circles represent pills taken during the instructional placard condition. Notice also that data points for each function occur only every other day. This represents the fact that the two treatments were alternated across days. It is quite clear that Wilbur's compliance was considerably greater under the phone call reminder condition than during the instructional placard condition. In fact, the number of pills Wilbur took during the instructional placard condition does not appear to be any different from the low level of compliance observed during the 5-day baseline period. For Wilbur, at least, this would seem to indicate that simple verbal reminders are sufficient to enhance his compliance. Thus, the alternating-treatments design allowed for a quick assessment of two treatments pitted against one another; in this particular case, one treatment was decidedly superior. In most cases, such a clear differentiation between treatment results would lead to an immediate implementation of the more effective treatment and termination of the less effective treatment.

Multitreatment Interference in the Alternating-Treatments Design

Despite its ease of use and inherent flexibility, the alternating-treatments design possesses one substantial shortcoming: **multitreatment interference**. You may recall from earlier chapters that because they involve repeated measures of behavior from the same client, single-case data contain **serial dependence**; that is, the data collected at one moment in time can be assumed to be influenced to some degree by earlier measures. This is even true of data collected under different phases or experimental conditions. In the alternating-treatments design, two different interventions are alternated, sometimes quite rapidly, over time. The possibility exists that some effects of a treatment may carry over into a subsequent phase. This means that only the very first treatment phase is interpretable as a "pure" treatment effect, unaffected by earlier treatments.

Let's take a look at the hypothetical data for Wilbur, our forgetful World War II veteran. The data in Figure 8.1 would seem to be make a strong case for greater effectiveness of the daily phone call intervention for Wilbur. Wilbur's medical compliance was always much greater on these days than on days when he was relying on an instructional placard to remind him to take his medication. However, remember that the daily phone call reminders were the very first treatment Wilbur received following baseline. The very next day, in keeping with the rapid treatment alternations typical of this design, Wilbur relied on a wall placard instead of his daughter's frequent phone calls. It is important to keep in mind that this treatment condition (instructional placard) *follows* a day in which a different treatment (frequent phone calls from his daughter) was in effect. When we evaluate the effects of the placard treatment, we are not necessarily seeing the effect of this treatment compared just with baseline (as would be the case in a standard withdrawal design) but *following* both a baseline and a preceding treatment condition. In other words, it may be that the instructional placard treatment has a different effect when it follows another treatment (in this case, phone calls) than if it were delivered without any preceding treatment. In the case of Wilbur's compliance, we cannot help but wonder what would have happened if the instructional placard treatment had been delivered first (Monday), then followed by the frequent phone calls from his daughter on Tuesday. In other words, might the order or sequencing of the conditions have something to do with their effects on compliance?

The problem of multiple treatment interference (Barlow & Hayes, 1979) poses a potential problem for any study in which two or more treatments are delivered at different times. Fortunately, there are a number of ways to respond to the problem of treatment interference, the specific response depending on whether one is primarily interested in the clinical/practical or the scientific merits of the outcome data. For instance, the nurse confronted with the data from Figure 8.1 could choose to continue the frequent phone calls intervention for several days, without alternating this treatment with the instructional placard treatment. If Wilbur's medical compliance continues at the high rate seen during previous implementation of this treatment, this would serve as additional replications of this treatment's effectiveness. Such data would not clearly indicate the effects of this treatment uncontaminated by the instructional placard intervention, but this may not be the most critical issue, at least from the nurse's perspective or the perspective of Wilbur or his daughter. Although this strategy cannot unequivocally demonstrate that the instructional placard intervention was ineffective, the argument for maintaining the frequent phone calls is strong. Because of the applied nature of the data, all parties involved would likely endorse the continuation of the phone calls. In other words, in this particular case the clinical or applied considerations trump the scientific considerations.

On the other hand, if we wished, as scientists, to be absolutely clear about the effects of the phone call and instructional placard interventions *by themselves*, and uncontaminated by one another, we could implement additional experimental design strategies. One such strategy would be to **counterbalance** the order of treatments, and this would ordinarily require that we use another client or clients. For example, if Wilbur is exposed to the frequent phone calls intervention first, followed by the instructional placard condition, we might want to observe another, similar client who is exposed first to the instructional placard and then to frequent phone call reminders. This method of equalizing the order of treatment effects across more than one subject or client is a common strategy in group studies in which different independent variable conditions are studied. We can also deliver the treatment conditions in a random order, as opposed to the day-to-day alternation that characterized Wilbur's treatment. In such a randomized condition, Wilbur may actually be exposed to one condition for several days in a row, meaning that there would be no systematic treatment interference effects influencing the outcome data. Such a strategy would require, however, that the two treatments alternate, though randomly, many times during the course of the study. Unlike counterbalancing, which requires the use of more than one subject or client, this **randomization design** is a useful method of evaluating two treatments within a single client, and the results can be assessed using available statistical analyses (Edgington, 1972).

The alternating-treatments design is of considerable value to practitioners who face the dilemma of deciding which treatment to deliver to a specific client presenting with a particular problem. Consequently, examples of alternating-treatments designs within the applied literature are common. Anderson and Goldstein (2004) studied the effects of three different methods of frequency modulation of speech delivered to children experiencing mild to severe hearing loss. Eight children, ranging in age from 9 to 12 years, received electronically controlled sentence lists in a standard kindergarten classroom. All of the children wore hearing aids that had been calibrated to match their specific hearing loss profile. Dependent measures included the number of correct sentence words repeated by the child. The children were first given practice sessions responding to the electronically presented sentences; during all experimental conditions the children wore their standard hearing aids. After 10 baseline sentence lists, children were exposed to the following three interventions, in counterbalanced order: (1) an infrared sound field system in which sentences were presented through speakers mounted at the juncture of the ceiling and wall; (2) a personal sound field system, in which sentences were presented through speakers placed directly on the student's desk; and (3) a personal FM system that transmitted messages directly through the student's hearing aid.

The results for all eight children can be seen in Figure 8.2. Baseline data are represented as closed circles in the first panel of the figure. The three different sound amplification conditions are depicted by separate data points (open circles = personal FM system, open triangles = desktop speaker, and open squares = infrared ceiling/wall speaker) in the second panel. The final panel in the figure represents a replication condition in which each child was presented with the intervention that produced the greatest enhancement in word repetition during the previous alternating-treatments condition. For all 8 of the children, the ceiling/wall-mounted speaker condition provided no benefits beyond those provided by the hearing-aid-alone baseline condition. Both the desktop and personal FM sound systems, however, produced greater accuracy in word recall than the hearing-aid-alone condition, although children differed in terms of which of the remaining conditions (personal FM vs. desktop speaker) produced the most benefit.

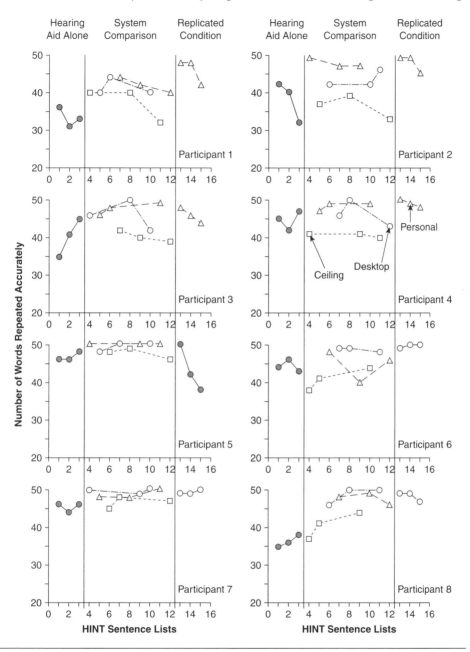

Figure 8.2 Speech recognition accuracy scores in an alternating treatments design for 8 participants. Filled circles represent hearing aids alone, open squares represent the addition of the infrared sound field system in the ceiling, open triangles represent the addition of the desktop sound field system, and open circles represent the addition of the personal FM systems.

Source: Anderson, K. L., & Goldstein, H. (2004). Reprinted with permission of the American Speech-Language-Hearing Association.

Wambaugh (2003) used a combination alternating treatments and multiple-baseline design to compare the effects of two different lexical cueing treatments in a 44-year-old aphasic patient. After having a stroke, the patient experienced chronic anomic aphasia, meaning he frequently had difficulty finding the right words when structuring sentences or trying to name objects. Previous research had indicated that patients exhibiting anomic aphasia could benefit from two types of word retrieval treatments, one based on word sounds (phonetic cueing), the other on word meaning (semantic cueing). Because little work had shown one treatment to be superior to the other, the researcher decided to pit a phonetic cueing treatment against a semantic cueing treatment, using the alternating-treatments design strategy to assess relative effectiveness. The patient was shown line drawings of objects which he had had previous difficulty in naming. Four separate stimulus lists were created. Initial baseline measures of correct naming for Stimulus Sets 1 and 2 were obtained for the first three probe sessions, and baseline data for Sets 3 and 4 were collected throughout 10 probe sessions. This aspect of the study represented the multiple-baseline aspect of the design. During treatment, the two lexical cueing methods (semantic vs. phonetic) alternated throughout the day, with 10- to 20-minute rests separating treatment periods. Following treatment on Sets 1 and 2, and during the treatment on Sets 3 and 4, maintenance probes of naming accuracy were conducted on the List 1 and 2 stimuli. Also, long-term follow-up probes were taken 2 and 6 weeks following treatment for all stimuli. The results demonstrated that, for this particular aphasic patient, both methods of lexical cueing increased accuracy of word retrieval, although semantic cueing appeared to have been slightly more effective than phonetic cueing.

Farrenkopf, McGregor, Nes, and Koenig (1997) assessed the effects of two kinds of prompts (verbal vs. physical) on the independent drinking skills of a 17-year-old female with cortical visual impairment. In cortical visual impairment, damage to the brain's visual cortex or visual pathways produces functional impairment due to problems interpreting information sent by the eyes, which respond normally to light stimulation. This particular client, like many patients with cortical visual impairment, exhibited multiple other disabilities as well, including partial deafness and frequent epileptic seizures. She was, however, enrolled in a regular high school, and the alternating-treatments study was conducted in this natural environment as well as in her home. Although both her vision and hearing were impaired, the client could fixate on and track moving objects and could hear others well enough to respond to the treatment strategies. During baseline, correct drinking responses, which involved visual fixation and movement toward the drinking cup, were measured in response to the cup simply being placed in front of the client. During treatment, placement of the cup was followed by either a verbal prompt, such as "Your drink is in front of you, _____. Drink it," or a physical prompt, such as touching of the client's head, which allowed the client to fixate on the cup. A session was defined as 10 opportunities for natural drinking responses to occur during daily meals. Type of prompt was alternated after 5 successive drinking opportunities, with the order of prompts counterbalanced across sessions. For this client, physical prompting proved more effective than the verbal prompt in enhancing independent drinking skills. Moreover, once the effectiveness of the physical prompt had been demonstrated in the school setting, this treatment was replicated in the home setting, with similar success.

Yuen and Garrett (2001) used an alternating-treatments design to evaluate the effectiveness of three different wheelchair cushions in relieving pressure in a 19-year-old male who had sustained a spinal cord injury (SCI) in a recent automobile accident. Patients with spinal cord injury who spend much of their time in wheelchairs are especially susceptible to pressure ulcers, and wheelchair cushion manufacturers all make claims about the pressure-relieving benefits of their products. Consequently, the researchers used a mapping pressure system that reported the number of sensors at the buttock–cushion interface that were exerting enough pressure to be potentially harmful with continued exposure. Pressure readings were taken after a 5-minute acclimation period for each cushion tested. Initial baseline pressure readings were taken three times a day for 3 days while the patient sat in the cushion originally designed for his wheelchair (Jay Extreme cushion; Sunrise Medical, Longmont, CO). During the alternating-treatments phase of the study, two separate cushions (Roho Enhancer [Crown Therapeutics, Belleville, IL] and Pindot Ulti-Mate [Invacare, Elyria, OH]) were presented once per day for several days. Because the cushions were covered with a uniform material and because cushion style was counterbalanced each day, the patient could not detect which cushion was being used during the alternating-treatments phase of the study.

The results of this study are depicted in Figure 8.3. Data display the amount of pressure being exerted by each cushion during baseline (far left panel), the alternating-treatments (middle panel) phase, and the follow-up phase (far right panel). For this patient, the Roho Enhancer cushion appeared to have exerted the least amount of pressure, as indicated in the middle panel of the figure. As a result of this finding, the Roho Enhancer cushion was used again during the follow-up phase. The data in this phase serve as a replication of the prior alternating-treatments condition, and levels of pressure exhibited during this phase are consistent with those seen in the previous phase. On the basis of these data, the researchers recommended continued use of the Roho Enhancer cushion for this particular patient.

An alternating-treatments design was also used by Dufrene, Watson, and Weaver (2005) to evaluate the effects of a behavioral treatment for an elementary student engaging in public masturbation. The child, a 7-year-old African-American girl,

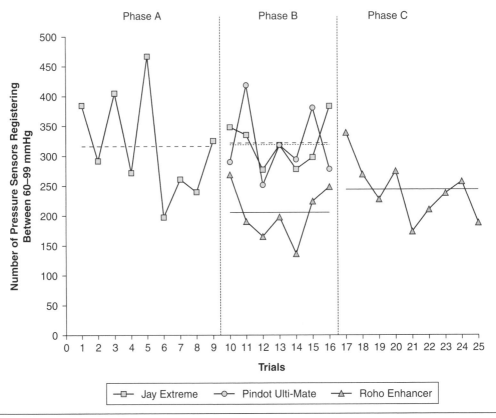

Figure 8.3   Pressure readings across study phases

Source: Yuen, H. K., & Garrett, D. (2001). Reprinted with permission of the American Occupational Therapy Association.

had suffered a traumatic brain injury at age 2, resulting in numerous developmental delays in speech and cognitive ability, as well as spasticity. The child was referred for treatment because a special education teacher had reported frequent instances of the child masturbating while in the classroom. These incidents had also been observed by the student's classmates and were proving disruptive. Using a partial interval scoring procedure, the researchers measured the percentage of intervals in which masturbation occurred as well as the percentage of intervals during which the child exhibited on-task academic behavior. One intervention, called *Response Blocking and Guided Compliance*, entailed the teacher responding to instances of masturbation by saying "No" and physically guiding the student's hand to a pencil while prompting the student to engage in a writing assignment. A second intervention (*Reinforcement*) called for the teacher to verbally praise the child any time the child had engaged in on-task scholastic behavior for a period of 30 consecutive seconds.

Reinforcement alone for on-task behavior did not produce immediate reductions in masturbation, but the combined treatment (Response Blocking and Guided Compliance plus Reinforcement) did eventually reduce and eliminate instances of masturbation. Follow-up measures at 1 and 6 months revealed that treatment gains had been maintained. On-task behavior was much more variable, however, and although increases in appropriate scholastic behavior were demonstrated during the combined treatment, consistently high levels of on-task behavior were not observed.

INTERIM SUMMARY

Alternating-treatments designs are of particular use when a researcher wishes to compare two or more potentially effective treatments with one another for the same client. Rapidly alternating the treatments allows for multiple comparisons of the target behavior under each treatment. Although interpretation of the design can be complicated by multitreatment interference, this threat to internal validity can be neutralized by counterbalancing across clients, or through random presentation of treatment conditions.

THE CASE OF PAUL

It has been estimated that 17 million Americans have diabetes. This represents an increase of nearly 1.5 million in the past couple of years. Of these individuals, nearly 6 million are undiagnosed, yet the disease is silently working to damage blood vessels, hearts, eyes, kidneys, legs, and feet. With type 2 diabetes, which affects almost 95% of persons diagnosed with diabetes, either the body does not produce enough insulin, the hormone necessary to convert sugar and other food into energy, or the body's cells do not use insulin properly.

Once diagnosed with diabetes, the typical first choice for treatment involves lifestyle changes. Dietary changes leading to weight loss and increased daily exercise are the first recommendations. If modifying these lifestyle factors does not reduce blood glucose/sugar levels, then medication is added to the treatment regimen. Oral medications do not contain insulin but help in other ways. Often, oral medications may increase production of insulin by stimulating the pancreas, reducing the body's insulin resistance, slowing the liver's output of extra sugars into the bloodstream, and slowing digestion of sugars and carbohydrates in the intestines or stomach. For some people, injecting insulin may be necessary for short periods of time or when the less invasive treatments are not effective.

Regardless of treatment, one of the daily routines that individuals with diabetes must endure is self-monitoring of their blood glucose/sugar levels. Self-monitoring is very important in the management of diabetes, because maintaining normal blood sugar levels is a necessary step in controlling the negative impacts of the disease. Self-monitoring is accomplished by pricking the skin to obtain a blood sample. This blood sample is placed on a test strip, which is then read by a glucose monitor.

A Clinical Psychologist's Perspective

Many people have a tendency to be somewhat squeamish at the sight of blood or needles. Intense fear, to a phobic level, is less common, affecting an estimated 2% to 4% of children and adults. Onset of Blood–Injection–Injury (BII) phobia usually occurs at a younger age than most other types of phobias. In well over half the documented cases of this type of phobia, a family member has a similar problem. This is between three and six times higher than for the incidence of phobia in the families of people with agoraphobia, social phobia, and animal phobias. Most likely, there is a genetically inherited physiological response to the sight of blood or injury, involving a drop in blood pressure. This leads to sweating, nausea, pallor and, often, fainting. People with BII phobia are the only phobic individuals who actually faint at the sight of their stimuli—the rate of fainting is 70% among people with blood phobias and 56% among people with injection phobias (Öst, 1992). Other phobic individuals may believe they will faint, or they may faint in response to heat or overcrowding, but not to the actual feared stimulus or feared situation.

BII phobias may prevent some people, such as Paul in the present case, from seeking medical care, ultimately jeopardizing their health. Such phobias can be especially problematic for people who must self-inject medication, including people with diabetes or multiple sclerosis. If they are unable to self-inject and rely on others to administer injections, they are more likely to discontinue the medication (Mohr, Boudewyn, & Likosky, 2001).

Treating BII phobias is not the same as treating other types of phobias. One of the most successful treatments for specific phobias involves a procedure known as *systematic desensitization*. Systematic desensitization involves muscle relaxation and exposure—through imagination, virtual reality, or *in vivo*—to a hierarchy of the feared stimuli. Unfortunately, conjuring up images of needle procedures can evoke fainting in people with BII phobia.

Instead, an alternative procedure has been found to be quite effective with people who have BII phobia and to work well in medical situations. This procedure is known as *applied muscle tension*. This technique is used specifically to treat people with blood and needle phobias who have a history of fainting in the situation and would seem to be a good match for the concerns raised by the case of Paul presented in this chapter. The procedure combines exposure to blood and needles with exercises that involve tensing all of the muscles of the body, which temporarily raises the person's blood pressure and prevents fainting. Applied tension is a behavioral treatment approach that has been demonstrated in several controlled trials to be an effective and inexpensive treatment. The combination of applied tension and repeated, graduated exposure results in the eventual extinction of the vasovagal syncope reaction (fainting). Believing that this method would be helpful in Paul's case, the clinical psychologist recommended use of the applied muscle tension treatment to reduce Paul's reluctance to monitor his blood glucose levels.

A Nurse's Perspective

Patients diagnosed with diabetes have many different learning needs relating to diet, self-monitoring, and treatments. In many health care systems, nurses provide many of these needs, usually aiming to empower patients to self-manage their diabetes. For patients presenting with diabetes and BII phobia, the challenges are magnified. In the present case, Paul presents with both a fear of needles and fear of blood. Because of his relatively high blood glucose/sugar level, Paul has been asked to self-monitor five times a day. Although Paul's wife could potentially conduct the test for Paul in the morning and in the evening, Paul must self-monitor during the day. In addition, it would be preferable if Paul were able to engage in complete self-monitoring without the assistance of his wife, because she has a career that requires her to travel out of town several times a month.

Most commonly, nurses provide education and personal training with patients. During this education and personal training process, it became clear that Paul would need additional assistance to be able to self-monitor. Consideration was given to two distinct treatments. First, the topical anesthetic cream containing prilocaine and lidocaine that would reduce the pain of obtaining a blood sample was considered. Paul's physician reported that this cream successfully reduced Paul's pain associated with the needle; however, the cream was not successful in preventing Paul from fainting at the sight of his blood. An alternative might be to apply ice at the injection site. Because the self-monitoring equipment requires only a pin-size drop of blood rather than the larger amounts obtained in the physician's office, it may be that by numbing the fingers by applying ice, Paul might be able to successfully manage the self-monitoring.

As a result, the nurse recommended trying the ice approach as a simple but possibly effective method of helping Paul. The clinical psychologist, on the other hand, believed that Paul's problem might be best addressed through the applied muscle tension approach. When two potentially effective treatments are being considered, the alternating-treatments design becomes a valuable method for assessing their relative effectiveness. Consequently, the nurse and psychologist decided to use such a design to evaluate both the muscle tension intervention and the numbing by ice approach in enhancing Paul's willingness to engage in the critical practice of monitoring his own blood glucose levels.

The frequency with which Paul monitored his blood glucose levels while at home is depicted in Figure 8.4. Not surprisingly, Paul engaged in virtually no self-monitoring during the few days of baseline data that were collected. In fact, on most of these days Paul's wife actually took care of the procedure because of Paul's reluctance to do so. Although only 3 days of baseline data were collected, Paul's nearly nonexistent self-monitoring was clearly unacceptable, and both he and his wife reported that this low level of monitoring was, in fact, quite representative. In other words, there would seem to be little scientific benefit in carrying out baseline measurement for a longer period, because no change in this low level of self-monitoring would be expected. Moreover, the need to intervene promptly was supported by both ethical and clinical considerations. Recall that Paul's blood sugar levels were substantially outside the normal range. Because these levels pose health risks for Paul, the need to bring his self-monitoring into compliance was urgent. Consequently, the nurse and psychologist agreed to begin alternating the ice and muscle tension treatments after only three baseline data points were collected.

The nature of the two treatments makes alternating them on a day-by-day basis quite manageable, and so this method was chosen for evaluating the effects of the interventions on Paul's self-monitoring. As the result of a simple coin toss, the two professionals agreed to begin Paul's ice treatment on the Monday following baseline. This treatment required Paul to hold a small ice cube on the finger he would be testing for blood for a period of 1 minute. Immediately after removing the ice, Paul was to use his testing instrument to collect and measure blood glucose levels. This procedure was to be followed a minimum of five times a day: when Paul awoke in the morning, after each of three meals, and just before going to bed. Thus, for Paul to be in complete compliance with the self-monitoring requirement, he would need to take readings five times each day.

On alternating days, beginning with Tuesday, Paul was asked to practice the muscle tension exercises taught to him by the psychologist for a period of 1 minute just prior to testing his blood sugar levels. On these days, Paul did not apply ice to his finger before he used the monitoring instrument. Paul was expected, however, to monitor his blood sugar level five times a day, just as he was expected to do during the ice treatment condition.

The data for Paul both during the brief (3-day) baseline period and during the 10-day treatment period, in which the two interventions alternated across days, are depicted in Figure 8.4. Although both the ice treatment and the muscle tension treatment appear to have improved Paul's willingness to self-monitor, over time,

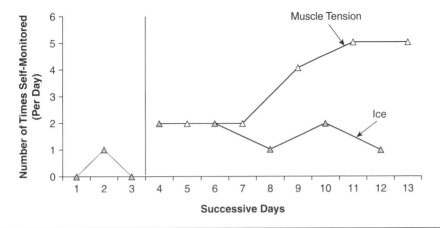

Figure 8.4 Paul's glucose self-monitoring

the muscle tension treatment produced greater improvement than the ice treatment. During the first 3 days of intervention, neither treatment appeared superior to the other. By the end of the first week, however, the muscle tension treatment had raised Paul's self-monitoring frequency to the level recommended by his physician. Compliance under the ice treatment remained at a level above baseline but consistently lower than desired. In this particular case, the muscle tension strategy seems to have clear advantages, at least for Paul, in bringing about self-monitoring compliance.

INTERIM SUMMARY

An alternating-treatments design can be a powerful tool for quickly assessing the relative effectiveness of two potentially useful treatments. In many areas of behavioral and health care, multiple treatments might be indicated for a specific problem, as suggested by large-group research, such as randomized clinical trials. However, because the external validity of such research is often questionable, large-scale studies are of little help to individual health care professionals charged with deciding on the most efficacious treatment for a specific client. The alternating-treatments design allows for a rapid, data-based decision to be made with respect to an individual client. In the case of Paul, two treatments for a phobia related to self-monitoring blood sugar levels were delivered on alternating days. Separation of data patterns under the two treatments provided clear inferences regarding relative effectiveness.

KEY TERMS GLOSSARY

Alternating-treatments design Single-case experimental design in which two or more interventions (or independent variables) are alternated rapidly to compare relative effectiveness.

Serial dependence When data collected at one moment in time are influenced to some degree by earlier measures.

Multitreatment interference A potential threat to the internal validity of an alternating-treatments design in which the effects of one treatment interact with subsequent treatments.

Counterbalance A method of experimental control in which the order of treatments in an alternating-treatments design is varied (counterbalanced) across experimental phases to eliminate order effects.

Randomization A method of experimental control in which the alternating of treatments is not predictable but occurs randomly during intervention phases.

SUPPLEMENTS

Review Questions

1. What are some of the criticisms that have been leveled at research on empirically supported treatments?

2. Why is the alternating-treatments design especially useful to clinicians working in applied settings?

3. What is *multitreatment interference*, and how might it affect interpretation of the data from an alternating-treatments design?

4. How does counterbalancing control for the threats posed by multitreatment interference in an alternating-treatments design? Also, how does counter-balancing differ from randomization as a control strategy in this kind of research?

5. What kind of interpretation would you give for the data from Paul presented in Figure 8.4? Also, why are there so few baseline data points for Paul? Is this problematic? Why or why not?

Suggested Readings/Helpful Web Sites

http://www.anxietytreatment.ca
This Web site describes the symptoms, theorized causes, and treatments for various specific phobias, including blood phobia, as depicted in the case of Paul in this chapter. There are also suggested readings for both lay and professional audiences.

http://www.diabetes.org/home.jsp
This is the official Web site of the American Diabetes Association. It has numerous links to information about prevention, research, exercise and diet recommendations, parent advice, books, and message boards.

Chapter 9

DATA ANALYSIS IN SINGLE-CASE RESEARCH

Single-case research designs utilize observational and measurement strategies common to any scientific endeavor. The idiographic or single-case data are generated under conditions that are as rigorous and controlled as possible and are evaluated and interpreted for the purpose of drawing reasonable conclusions. As we have discussed throughout this book, data collected in single-case studies are in important ways different from the nomothetic data generated in traditional group designs. Consequently, interpretation and analysis of single-case data usually involve a different set of analytic and decision criteria. In this chapter, we discuss the traditional conventions of visual inspection used by researchers for decades to evaluate single-case data, as well as the controversial topic of statistical analysis of single-case data. A growing methodological literature has addressed the advantages and disadvantages of submitting single-case data to tests of statistical inference, although a consensus has been difficult to achieve in this area. Finally, we will explore the differing criteria used by researchers and clinicians in evaluating the effects of interventions. This is of particular concern to applied professionals conducting research in clinical settings, not the laboratory.

INTERPRETING BEHAVIOR CHANGE

In most research in the behavioral and health sciences, the primary dependent variable is some measured property of a subject or participant's behavior or subjective experience. This may be number of suicidal thoughts in a depressed patient in a given day, frequency of testing blood sugar levels in a person with diabetes, or mileage walked by a recovering heart attack victim. The independent variable is ordinarily implemented or manipulated intentionally by the clinician or researcher. In applied research this variable is usually a treatment regimen of some sort, be it a course of psychotherapy or physical therapy or a social work intervention. The purpose of single-case research is to observe, measure, and track the clinically or socially relevant behavior over time and to determine whether important changes in the behavior occur in response to the treatment or intervention. Thus, the applied researcher must draw conclusions about the effects of a treatment program, and this can be done only if certain established conditions are met.

Experimental Logic: Eliminating Alternative Hypotheses

The logic of single-case experimentation is no different from that which applies to experimental research in any discipline, be it psychology, biology, or chemistry. The purpose of any well-conducted experiment is to isolate causal relationships between independent and dependent variables. By systematically delivering the treatment (independent variable) and continuously measuring the relevant target behavior (dependent variable), changes in the behavior can be monitored and conclusions drawn about determinants of this change. A methodologically sound study allows the researcher to conclude that changes in the client's or subject's behavior occurred in response to the treatment or independent variable and not for some other reason. All experiments exhibit this essential decision-making logic, regardless of differences in subject matter, settings, or variables of interest.

Internal Validity

The **internal validity** of the study refers to how confident the researcher can be that changes in the dependent variable are due to introduction of the independent variable and not to some other factor. Thus, researchers go to considerable lengths to design studies that allow for such causal inferences. You may recall the group study described in Chapter 2 in which researchers evaluated the effectiveness of an Internet-delivered psychoeducational program on measures of eating-disorder risk among college women (Zabinski, Wilfley, Calfas, & Winzelberg, 2004). In this study, students found to be at risk for developing an eating disorder were randomly assigned to experimental and control groups. In a group study, random assignment is an important strategy for ensuring equivalent groups prior to independent variable manipulation. After exposure to the Internet treatment, experimental participants were compared with the control participants, who had not been exposed to the Internet treatment, and differences in risk levels between the groups were compared for statistical significance. So long as group differences on eating-disorder risk could not be attributable to any other factor, the most plausible explanation for this difference would be the independent variable, the Internet psychoeducational program.

Although single-case designs employ a different set of data collection and analysis strategies, the logic of experimental comparison is similar to that characterizing group designs. A subject's behavior is observed, measured, and recorded under both baseline (no treatment) and treatment conditions, and comparison of the target behavior under these different conditions leads to conclusions about the effects of the independent variable. As with group studies, the strength of the single-case design lies in its ability to eliminate alternative explanations for behavior change, that is, changes due to factors other than the explicitly manipulated independent variable or treatment. The study's internal validity will be evaluated by how well the researcher has eliminated these alternative explanations.

So what stands in the way of asserting a study's internal validity? As is true of any experiment, single-case research designs are potentially affected by a number of threats to internal validity, or explanations for behavior change during treatment that are not directly due to the treatment itself. For instance, you may recall from Chapter 7 the case of Ruth, who was being treated for both depression and rheumatoid arthritis. Ruth received a standard cognitive–behavioral treatment for her depression, and data collected during her treatment indicated an increase in Ruth's daily number of positive thoughts. However, might Ruth's positive thoughts have been influenced by some variable other than the cognitive–behavioral treatment? Perhaps, unbeknownst to the researcher, Ruth had been prescribed an antidepressant medication at about the same time she began receiving cognitive–behavioral therapy. If so, we would be reluctant, as researchers, to conclude that Ruth's increased positive thoughts were due to the cognitive–behavioral therapy, as there is another plausible explanation. In this example, the antidepressant medication represents a *confound variable* because it confounds, or renders difficult, any strong conclusions about the manipulated independent variable.

Another threat to internal validity is referred to as a *maturation effect*, because changes in the dependent variable over time are due to normal developmental or maturational factors, not to the manipulated independent variable. Maturation is a more likely threat to internal validity in studies of infants or young children, particularly if the study unfolds over a long time span, such as months or years. For example, suppose we were evaluating a program designed to teach preschool-age children how to respond assertively to strangers who might attempt to abduct or harm them. If the program is delivered throughout the entirety of a school year and measures of abduction vulnerability are taken at the beginning of the year and then again at the end of the year, we would want to determine how likely such changes might be due to the treatment program. If, however, such changes may be attributable simply to the normative amount of "growing up" we would expect preschoolers to experience during a year, then conclusions about the assertiveness training program might be suspect. Clearly, maturation is not a reasonable threat to internal validity in studies that are conducted on adults or those that are conducted on children over relatively short time spans.

Internal validity may also be compromised by a *history effect*, in which some variable outside the experimental environment, and therefore uncontrolled by the researcher, influences the dependent variable. In the example of teaching children to respond more assertively to potentially harmful strangers, a recent child abduction in the local community may have sensitized children in the targeted school system to the dangers of interactions with strangers. If so, conclusions about the effects of the assertiveness training program may be untenable because of the history variable that has occurred at this local level.

Finally, sometimes changes in a dependent variable may be due to a mathematical phenomenon known as *statistical regression* or *regression toward the mean*. In the case of Ruth, positive thoughts occurred initially at very low levels during baseline. Very low or very high scores on any behavioral measure are, by definition, statistically rare, and upon further measurement such scores often move toward more normative or typical values, even in the absence of any treatment or independent variable. What this means in the case of Ruth is that we might expect her rate of positive thoughts to increase some over time, regardless of whether she receives any kind of therapy for depression. This statistical regression toward more common or average values is typical, especially when initial measures of a dependent variable are extreme. Researchers may unintentionally evaluate change in the dependent variable as resulting from the manipulated independent variable.

On the basis of the preceding description of threats to internal validity, it may seem that all studies are irreparably flawed and that no solid conclusions can be drawn from them. Fortunately, both group and single-case researchers have at their disposal a number of procedures commonly used to control these threats. In single-case research, threats to internal validity are controlled primarily through two strategies: (1) replication and (2) repeated measurement of the dependent variable. The importance of replication, as described in Chapter 4, is that each replication allows for a comparison between the subject's behavior during baseline (no treatment) and during treatment. In a standard reversal design, this involves at least three phase changes, with the first being from an initial baseline to an initial treatment condition, the second being from the initial treatment condition back to baseline (frequently termed the *return-to-baseline* phase), and the third being from the return-to-baseline phase to reinstituting the treatment condition. If changes in behavior during initial treatment are due to some other variable, such as a confound, then we would not expect behavior to (1) return to levels observed when the initial baseline condition was established and (2) demonstrate another change when phases shift again, from the return-to-baseline phase to the reinstituting the treatment condition. In other words, each phase change is an opportunity to observe changes in the target behavior, and it is quite improbable that this change would coincide each time with a confound variable. Moreover, the more replications built into the design, the better, because the likelihood of a coincidental confound variable decreases with each phase change. In addition, intersubject replications add to the study's internal validity in much the same way that such replications serve this function in many scientific disciplines. Indeed, when any experiment produces an important result, whether in physics, biology, or psychology, one can expect other researchers to replicate the study in order to ascertain whether the original findings were valid. This is, in essence, a check on the original study's internal validity; such checks are quite easily conducted in single-case research by simply repeating the experiment with another subject or participant.

In addition to replication, single-case research establishes internal validity through the repeated measures strategy that characterizes the family of single-case designs. As we discussed in Chapter 2, this is an extremely critical and unique feature of single-case research. Being in constant contact with the relevant target behavior is necessary to observing and measuring the continuous nature of behavioral phenomena. This practice also provides for an important control over many potential threats to internal validity. For instance, if Ruth's baseline positive thoughts are so rare that we would expect them to increase simply as a function of statistical regression, we would expect this to happen after the first observation of this target behavior. In a single-case design, these scores are taken numerous times *before* the introduction of treatment; thus, statistical regression should be apparent in these early baseline scores, before treatment is actually applied. If no such change in positive thoughts is observed during the multiple baseline measures, then we can be confident that statistical regression is not a threat to internal validity and that any changes occurring during treatment are not reflective of this particular threat. The repeated measurement of the dependent variable also counters the threat of maturation, because developmental changes would be expected to occur during baseline measures, not just, coincidentally, during treatment.

Single-case researchers, then, have specific strategies for handling the potential threats to internal validity that would otherwise compromise the conclusions drawn from such studies. In most cases, both replication and repeated measurement of the dependent variable are utilized in an effort to strengthen the inferences drawn from single-case studies, although how these strategies are employed depends on the nature of the relevant target behaviors, settings, and restrictions that might be in place in the applied environment.

External Validity

In addition to being concerned with conclusions that can be drawn about the effects of the independent variable on the dependent variable, single-case researchers also may be interested in whether their findings might be applicable to subjects and/or settings beyond their own research study. The extent to which a particular study's findings can be extended to subject populations or settings beyond the original study is a measure of the study's **external validity**. It is important to understand that the value of external validity to single-case researchers, particularly those delivering health services to individual clients, is very different from the value of external validity in basic research. Much research in the behavioral and health sciences is conducted in well-controlled laboratory environments for the purpose of identifying specific behavioral principles or even generalizable laws. This research is often also theory driven, in that it is conducted for the purpose of testing aspects of a formal theory. Such research is being done not so much to show the effect of a variable for a particular subject but to demonstrate the general applicability or effect of the variable at the level of the population. In such research, external validity takes on an importance commensurate with that of internal validity. The researcher is interested in identifying an effect or phenomenon that can be extended to or applied to a much larger domain than entailed by the particular study.

Some single-case research is conducted in controlled laboratory environments and meets the criteria for basic research. This kind of research may in fact be done for the purpose of identifying general laws or principles, and clearly the external validity of such research is a common goal of researchers. We have been more interested, however, in single-case research that is conducted by health care professionals in applied settings. The predominant goal of such research is to establish the effectiveness of a clinical intervention for a particular client. Within the confines of such a study external validity may not emerge as an important goal, although intersubject replications would serve the purpose of establishing whether the intervention may be applicable or extended to other clients. Whether establishing the external validity of a treatment is a useful or meaningful goal is an individual decision left to the discretion of the researcher. It is important to note that although this may be an objective of single-case research, external validity quite obviously takes something of a backseat to internal validity in most single-case research.

INTERIM SUMMARY

Single-case researchers wish to draw conclusions about the effects of an intervention (independent variable) on a subject's relevant target behavior (dependent variable), and this means being able to determine causes of behavior change across different phases of a study. In doing so, researchers attempt to control for various threats to internal validity, the extent to which changes in the target behavior can be confidently attributed to the intervention and not to other factors. Single-case researchers employ both replication and repeated dependent variable measurement to achieve control of threats to internal validity. In addition, though less common, single-case researchers may be interested in establishing the external validity of their study, which refers to whether their specific findings apply or generalize to other subjects and/or settings.

VISUAL ANALYSIS OF SINGLE-CASE DATA

The primary data available to single-case researchers, as discussed in Chapter 4, are multiple measures of a client's target behavior both prior to and during a clinical intervention. These data are most frequently presented via line graphs, time-series graphs, or Standard Celeration Charts, also as described in earlier chapters. The task facing the single-case researcher, then, is to evaluate changes in the target behavior by comparing dimensions of the behavior during baseline with these same dimensions during treatment. Although numerous methods for evaluating and interpreting behavior change have been proposed over the years, visual inspection of single-case data remains a viable and long-practiced strategy (Baer, 1977; Parsonson & Baer, 1986). Although this strategy has its critics (Franklin, Gorman, Beasley, & Allison, 1997; Ottenbacher, 1990b, 1992), visual analysis continues to enjoy considerable support by methodologists, and its long history in the behavioral sciences warrants attention. In this section, we explore the dimensions of target behavior as well as the criteria used by researchers to evaluate and make decisions about behavior change based on visual inspection of data.

Differences in Level

In evaluating single-case data, the comparison of interest is between the data observed during baseline and those observed during treatment. One method of making this comparison is to evaluate the level of the two phases of data: (1) baseline and (2) treatment. Figure 9.1 shows data for John Doe, first presented in Chapter 4 (as Figure 4.5). John Doe was the client diagnosed with obsessive–compulsive disorder who washed his hands dozens of times a day because of a fear of contamination. You may recall that he received a behavioral treatment known as *exposure and response prevention* during this phase of the study. Comparison of the levels of hand washing across phases would seem to indicate that hand washing was reduced substantially during treatment relative to baseline levels.

Thus, using level alone as a criterion for assessing change, we would be inclined to conclude that behavior change was evident in this study. Keep in mind that we are simply discussing whether changes in behavior are apparent when moving from the nontreatment condition to the treatment condition. Deciding that the levels of behavior are in fact different does not automatically allow us to declare the change is due to the treatment. This inference requires that we be confident that threats to internal validity have been sufficiently controlled, and this is a research design issue, not strictly a data analysis issue.

Although the data in Figure 9.1 seem to support a fairly strong inference about the effects of the behavioral treatment (assuming adequate control over threats to internal validity), actual data from single-case studies are not always clear. Differences in level between baseline and treatment data are often not as apparent, and this adds a measure of ambiguity to the interpretation process. How best to resolve this ambiguity is the subject of a growing literature, and we explore some of these issues in a later section of this chapter.

Changes in Trend or Slope

One of the advantages of single-case data is the ability to monitor and evaluate moment-to-moment changes or fluctuations in behavior. Indeed, we have discussed this data collection strategy as among the most powerful advantages of single-case research design, relative to group designs, which seldom allow for ongoing, continuous behavioral measurement. The continuous measurement of behavior allows

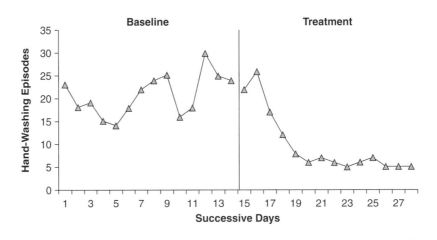

Figure 9.1   John Doe's hand-washing behavior during baseline and treatment

researchers to see, at a level of resolution unavailable to most group researchers, the transitions that occur in behavior over time, particularly in response to interventions. Both the magnitude and rapidity of these behavioral transitions can be easily observed in the repeated measures of single-case data. These transitions can also be evaluated for evidence of behavior change in response to treatment introduction.

Unfortunately, transitions in behavior can occur in the absence of any kind of formal intervention, and such trends can render interpretation of treatment effects difficult. The problem with interpreting the effects of an independent variable against the backdrop of changes in behavior slope or trend can be seen in Figure 9.2. Data in the graph represent number of minutes a bank president spends riding an exercise bike both during baseline and during a physician-recommended exercise regimen. The number of minutes spent bike riding clearly exhibits a steady ascending trend during the baseline phase. This upward trend continues during the treatment condition. Thus, one cannot conclude that the intervention is responsible for the change in the target behavior because the upward trend from the baseline phase is simply continuing during the treatment phase. In fact, if you envision this graph without the vertical line indicating the phase change from baseline to treatment, the continuous nature of the upward trend becomes even more obvious. There is nothing in the data to suggest that any variable has been manipulated. Thus, trends in baseline data, whether upward or downward, pose problems for researchers who are trying to account for behavior changes across phase changes.

A more subtle trend in baseline data is also evident in the hand-washing behavior of John Doe, as seen in Figure 9.1. Although this upward trend could prove

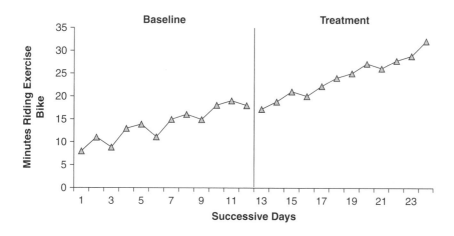

Figure 9.2 Bank president's exercise regimen

problematic to the interpretation of a treatment effect, in John Doe's case this upward trend reverses itself during treatment, as incidents of hand washing reduce substantially, eventually reaching normal levels. Thus, the trend in John Doe's baseline hand washing, although far from optimal, does not pose quite the same difficulty as does the trend in the bank president's exercise regimen during baseline (see Figure 9.2). Baseline measurement ideally should continue until a reasonable degree of stability has occurred, with no obvious upward or downward trend. If a trend is apparent in baseline behavior and that trend is in the same direction intended by the intervention, then changes that occur during the treatment phase are difficult to interpret. However, baseline data in real studies often lack the kind of stability we might see in basic research, and applied researchers may not have the luxury of observing for long periods of time until stability ensues. This balancing act between scientific rigor in data collection and the logistic and ethical limitations of the clinical setting is the eternal dilemma of applied health care professionals.

Changes in Variability

In addition to changes in level and trend, researchers may be interested in tracking the changes that the target behavior undergoes with respect to variability, particularly comparisons of baseline and treatment variability. It may very well be, for instance, that the major goal of a treatment program is to reduce or increase variability in the target behavior, not necessarily the overall level of the behavior. Suppose a diabetic patient is being taught to use a new blood sugar monitor and the objective is to have the patient take measures consistently, five times a day. Baseline measures of blood sugar measurement reveal that the patient exhibits considerable inconsistency from day to day in taking the measurements. Figure 9.3 depicts this measurement variability in the baseline phase. On some days, the patient actually takes blood sugar level measures more frequently than is really necessary (six or seven) but on other days fails to take any measures. The goal of a behavioral therapy program might be to bring more consistency to this behavior, not to either eliminate or increase the frequency of the behavior. The data in the treatment condition indicate that the patient is measuring blood sugar levels between four and five times a day, consistently, throughout a 2-week period. As is apparent in the figure, there is not really an overall increase or decrease in frequency of testing because this is not really the purpose of the intervention. What is clear is that the target behavior is exhibiting much less variability; the target behavior has become much more consistent and does not fluctuate between high and low frequencies. The change in behavior is readily seen and in this particular case would represent a clinically relevant change in the target behavior, assuming that threats to internal validity had been adequately controlled by the researcher.

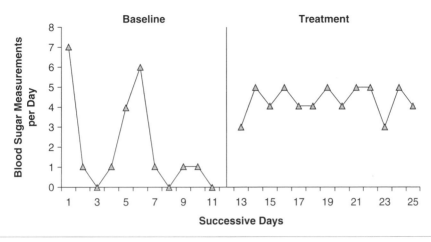

Figure 9.3 Variability in blood sugar level testing

Rationale for Visual Analysis

The practice of interpreting the effects of an independent variable by visually inspecting the data patterns generated under baseline and treatment conditions has a considerable history in the behavioral sciences. Indeed, evaluating response rates over long experimental sessions has been the primary data analysis tool in the field of behavior analysis; it was first developed by B. F. Skinner in the 1930s and 1940s. Behavior analysts (Sidman, 1960; Skinner, 1956) have long argued that changes in responding that occur under independent-variable conditions are ordinarily readily apparent against the backdrop of stable baseline responding. Because moment-to-moment measures of behavior are standard practice in behavior analysis, visual inspection is ordinarily sufficient to reveal systematic changes in behavior. The sensitivity of this data analytic strategy naturally depends on a reliable and valid measurement system, demonstrated stability in baseline responding, and adequate control over extraneous variables.

Early behavior analysts were primarily laboratory scientists conducting basic research into general behavior principles, and the conditions described earlier are not difficult to achieve under such conditions. As we have seen throughout this book, however, the conditions of observation and measurement in applied settings often limit the methodological rigor of research programs in such settings. Stable baselines are not always easily obtained, and control cannot always be adequately exercised over extraneous variables. Nevertheless, applied scientists who have endorsed the use of single-case research have forcefully argued that visual inspection still remains a sufficient data analytic procedure in clinical settings. Indeed,

Baer (1977), Parsonson and Baer (1986), and Kazdin (1982b) have suggested that the kinds of behavior change ordinarily viewed as desirable by health care professionals should be observable to the naked eye, that is, clearly identified through visual inspection of single-case data. In other words, an effect of treatment that would be seen as acceptable, to perhaps client and clinician alike, should be quite large and apparent. Effects that are very small and difficult to discern in graphed data may, arguably, indicate less than a successful treatment outcome. This is a contentious claim, and many contemporary methodologists believe that there are good reasons to become aware of small but reliable treatment effects as well and that such effects may be more easily missed through visual analysis (Ottenbacher, 1990b). The dialogue about data analysis and treatment effect decision criteria is a growing and complex one; we address this topic in the next section.

INTERIM SUMMARY

Inferences about treatment effects in single-case data historically have been drawn on the basis of visual inspection of patterns in graphed data. By attending to overall level differences, upward or downward trends, and magnitude of variability under both baseline and treatment conditions, researchers can draw inferences about the relationship between the dependent variable and the independent variable or treatment. Confidence in such inferences is influenced by the stability of baseline data as well as the researcher's ability to control threats to internal validity. Large between-phase differences are more easily observed, and some researchers believe that only large treatment effects should be considered successful interventions. Others believe that there is value in identifying even small treatment effects, which are more likely to be missed through visual inspection.

THE QUANTITATIVE ANALYSIS OF SINGLE-CASE DATA

For many years, the analysis of single-case data, in both basic and applied studies, entailed visual inspection of graphed data patterns. More recent decades have seen the endorsement of single-case research methodology by health care workers in many disciplines; consequently, the strategies and tactics of single-case research have undergone increased scrutiny. For many researchers, the visual analysis of data has been a weak link in an otherwise flexible and powerful collection of research designs. These researchers have argued that the contemporary focus on evidence-based practice places a greater importance on making decisions about treatment effects that are objective and quantitatively driven. For these researchers, single-case research would benefit immensely from adoption of the kinds of data analytic tools more common to group research in the behavioral and social sciences. Let us consider why these methodologists have endorsed more quantitatively sophisticated single-case research.

Limitations of Visual Inspection

Researchers who have argued for the increased use of quantitative and statistical data analysis of single-case data do so because they believe that visual inspection is characterized by inherent shortcomings as a data analytic strategy. First, they suggest, visual inspection is a highly subjective mode of analysis, influenced by the vagaries of human perceptual biases and capacities and contaminated by individual differences. Moreover, subjective visual analysis offers the researcher no formal or standardized criteria for making judgments about treatment effects (DeProspero & Cohen, 1979; Wolery & Harris, 1982). To their credit, these critics have amassed an impressive amount of empirical evidence to suggest that visual inspection is indeed susceptible to idiosyncratic interpretation and, thus, to error (Furlong & Wampold, 1982, 1981; Ottenbacher, 1990b; Ottenbacher & Cusick, 1991). DeProspero and Cohen (1979), for instance, showed that research participants presented with graphed single-case data often disagree about the presence or absence of treatment effects in such data. This appears to be the case even when the participants are trained professionals (Harbst, Ottenbacher, & Harris, 1991). In addition, research has shown that disagreements in judgments about single-case data are fairly clearly related to particular characteristics of the data, such as amount of trend or magnitude of effect (Bailey, 1984; Ottenbacher, 1990b) and amount of serial dependency or autocorrelation in the data (Bengali & Ottenbacher, 1998). Thus, visual analysis, as the sole means of drawing inferences from single-case data, would seem to be problematic on several grounds. Consequently, much effort has been expended in recent years developing data analytic strategies that could serve to enhance the scientific integrity of single-case methodology.

Advantages of Quantitative Analysis

Researchers who find wanting the visual analysis of single-case data feel that more objective, quantitative data analytic strategies, many of which have been fruitfully utilized by researchers for years, should also be adopted by single-case researchers. Such tools should reduce the idiosyncratic nature of visual inspection and provide single-case researchers with a standardized method of reaching decisions about treatment effects. Many believe that such quantitative analyses should be used in conjunction with more traditional visual analysis, not necessarily as the only method of analyzing single-case data. It is important, at this point, to understand that *quantitative analysis* refers to a large collection of mathematical practices, not just the conventional null hypothesis testing with which social and behavioral scientists are familiar. In the following review of quantitative strategies for analyzing single-case data, we describe methods that are essentially descriptive in nature, as well as methods that borrow from the long-standing social science tradition of statistical inference. We do not attempt an exhaustive review of all quantitative methods developed in recent years, because many articles and book-length documents have been devoted to this topic (Brossart, Parker, Olson, & Mahadevan, 2006; Campbell, 2004; Edgington, 1984; Fisch, 2001; Gottman, 1981, 1995; Hoaglin, Mosteller, & Tukey, 1985; Huitema, 1986; Kazdin, 1984; Scruggs & Mastropieri, 2001). Instead, we will describe methods that have become fairly common strategies of data analysis among those single-case researchers who endorse quantitative analyses of data.

Mean Lines

One of the primary goals of data analysis, in many areas of research, is the summarization of large amounts of data. This practice is quite logical because it can become very difficult for human observers to make sense of large tables filled with dozens, hundreds, or even thousands of numbers. Researchers use *descriptive statistics* to reduce or summarize a large amount of data into more manageable chunks or units of information. You may recall from Chapter 2, in our comparison of group and single-case research, that we described the *arithmetic mean* as a tool for describing a large group of subjects on some measured variable. The mean is a measure of central tendency whose purpose is to provide a representative picture of a large data set. Although single-case researchers are not dealing with groups, they are often dealing with many data points, collected from a subject or client over several different phases of a study. It is possible to calculate a mean for the data in any phase (baseline or intervention) of a study for an individual subject or client. Comparing the means for baseline versus treatment phases permits us to conclude how much differently the subject or client performed, on average, during these respective phases.

Figure 9.4 depicts the data from John Doe that we have discussed throughout this chapter. The horizontal line that runs across both phases of the study (baseline and treatment) represents John's mean response rate under the baseline condition. Although it may be quite easy to interpret John's response patterns during baseline and treatment without this line, the line serves as something of a visual anchor, making more explicit the change in hand washing evidenced over the course of the study. In some sense, the analysis is still heavily visual, but it is aided

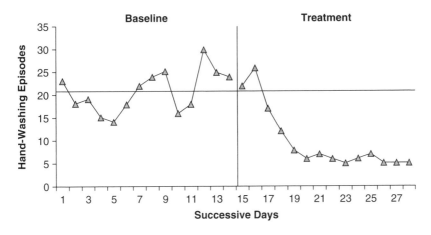

Figure 9.4   John Doe's hand washing, with a horizontal line indicating the mean hand-washing rate during baseline

by a line generated through a standard and simple mathematical procedure. Thus, the use of mean lines in single-case research represents an easy mathematical adjunct to standard visual analysis and an additional piece of information for supporting judgments about treatment effects. In the current example, the mean difference in hand-washing episodes in John Doe's behavior is quite apparent because the level during treatment is well below that exhibited during baseline.

Celeration and Trend Lines

A major strength of single-case research is its capacity to reveal moment-to-moment changes in the target behavior over time. In most applied studies of health care interventions, it is this transition from baseline responding to treatment responding that is of interest. Just as mean lines can be used to describe the overall difference in behavior under baseline and treatment conditions, **celeration and trend lines** can be used to describe the degree and rapidity of change occurring under different conditions. *Celeration* is simply another name for trend, and it is the root of the terms *acceleration* and *deceleration*. Often, a clinical intervention is delivered for the purpose of accelerating a desirable behavior or decelerating an undesirable behavior; thus, celeration or trend lines can be used to describe the effectiveness of the intervention. This fact—that behavior change can almost always be described by acceleration and deceleration—is what led Ogden Lindsley and his colleagues to develop the Standard Celeration Chart, which we described in Chapter 4.

There are several methods for calculating celeration/trend lines, and we will describe the two methods used most frequently within single-case research. Perhaps the easiest and least sophisticated from a mathematical perspective is the *split-middle line of progress,* introduced by White (1971). Calculation of the split-middle line is not terribly difficult, and specific directions for its calculation can be found in Cooper, Heron, and Heward (2007). The method generally involves separating a data phase (either baseline or treatment) into halves, and then identifying the middle, or median, observation in each phase. A vertical line is drawn through this data point, and a second, horizontal line is drawn through this first line at the level of the median value for this half of the data phase. Then a straight line is drawn connecting these two intersecting points. If this line does not divide the phase data in half, then it is adjusted up or down, while remaining parallel to the first line, until it does so.

Interpreting single-case data using the split-middle line is a pretty straightforward process. We assume that this line of celeration observed during baseline would continue along its established course if no treatment effect occurs. In other words, the trend line continued from the baseline condition is our best guess or prognostication about the future pattern and rate of the behavior in the absence of treatment. Consequently, we can extend the baseline trend line into treatment and evaluate whether the treatment data deviate from this line. If the trend line from baseline differs in slope or level from the trend line in treatment, then we would conclude that a treatment effect is likely.

A more sophisticated method of creating trend lines is the use of *linear regression* to produce a *line of best fit* running through each phase of data. For any set of data, there will be one straight line that does the best job of reducing the distance between each data point and the line; this is the *least squares regression line.* We will not describe the detailed procedure for calculating a regression line, but examples can be found in most basic statistics books; regression lines are commonly used in the behavioral and social sciences both for the purpose of describing data sets and for predicting subjects' scores on important dependent variables. In addition, most statistical programs written for computers are capable of calculating and drawing regression lines through data sets. In most cases, the regression line will be very close to the trend line generated through the split-middle method described previously. Also as with the split-middle technique, the regression line for the treatment condition can be compared with the regression line for the baseline condition to determine the presence of a treatment effect. If the treatment regression line differs in slope or intercept from the baseline regression line, a treatment effect can be assumed. Figure 9.5 depicts the data from John Doe with regression lines drawn through both the baseline and treatment data. Keep in mind that celeration lines drawn using the split-middle median split method would be very similar to these regression lines. Interpreting behavior change in Figure 9.5

is straightforward. John Doe's baseline hand-washing rate demonstrates an upward trend during baseline. This trend, however, reverses itself during intervention. Although the data in this figure are not hard to interpret in the absence of celeration lines, the lines offer an additional visual stimulus that highlights the nature of behavior change in this case.

The PND Statistic

Among the most frequently utilized methods for analyzing single-case data in the behavioral literature is the **PND** (percentage of nonoverlapping data) **statistic**, introduced by Scruggs and colleagues (Scruggs & Mastropieri, 2001; Scruggs, Mastropieri, Cook, & Escobar, 1986; Scruggs, Mastropieri, Forness, & Kavale, 1988). The analysis is easy to conduct and the statistic simple to interpret because it requires only that one calculate the percentage of treatment data that overlap with the most "extreme" data point (i.e., either the lowest or highest value) exhibited during baseline. In studies in which the goal of intervention is to reduce maladaptive behavior, the most extreme data point in baseline would be the data point with the lowest numerical value. In cases in which the goal of the intervention is to increase adaptive behavior, the most extreme data point in baseline would be the data point with the highest numerical value.

In Figure 9.6, the data for John Doe are presented with a horizontal line drawn through the most extreme lowest data point in baseline and extended into the treatment phase. In John Doe's case, abnormally frequent hand washing is being

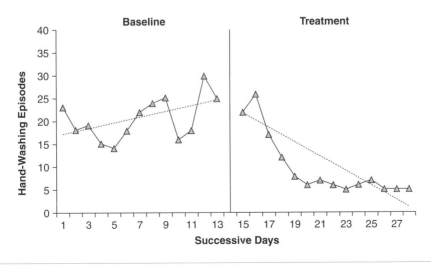

Figure 9.5   John Doe's hand washing with regression lines drawn through both the baseline and treatment data

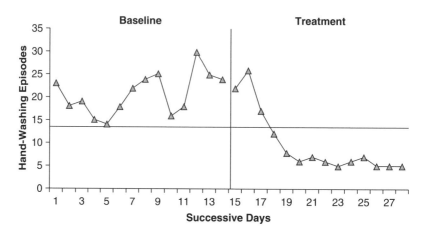

Figure 9.6 John Doe's hand washing with a horizontal line drawn through the most extreme low data point in baseline and extended into the treatment phase

targeted for reduction. Therefore, the data point from Session 5 of baseline is used for drawing the horizontal line that extends into the treatment phase. On Session 5, John exhibited 14 episodes of hand washing. In this case, the PND is the percentage of data points in the treatment phase that do not overlap with (i.e., are less than) the value 14. Looking at the graph, we can see that 11 of 14 (about 79%) of the data points in the intervention phase have values of less than 14. Thus, PND = 79% in this case.

Scruggs and Mastropieri (1998) argued that the PND statistic is easy to evaluate because a percentage measure reflects a fairly intuitive metric. They also offered the following criteria as reasonable judgmental aids for researchers:

PND $\geq$ 90% = Very effective treatment

PND 70%–90% = Effective treatment

PND 50%–70% = Questionable effectiveness

PND < 50% = Ineffective treatment

The use in single-case research of PND as a measure of effect size, or as a single index that purports to quantify intervention effectiveness, is not without its critics. Some researchers have argued that the PND is not sensitive to data in which baseline trends are evident (White, 1987), that its usefulness is compromised by small data sets (Allison & Gorman, 1994), and that the strategy possesses the same limitations of any measure of central tendency, namely, that a single number is often poorly representative of larger data sets (Parker, Hagan-Burke, & Vannest, 2007; Salzberg, Strain, & Baer, 1987). Indeed, the value of PND can fluctuate greatly if just one data point in baseline differs substantially from the other data points in baseline. For example, in Figure 9.6, if John had an unusual day during baseline, wherein he exhibited only four episodes of hand washing, then PND would have equaled 0% (a highly ineffective treatment) instead of 79% (an effective treatment). Despite these limitations, the PND has become a commonly reported statistic in single-case studies, because of its ease of calculation and interpretation. In has been especially popular in summaries of single-case literature in the field of developmental disabilities (Mathur, Kavale, Quinn, Forness, & Rutherford, 1998; Schlosser & Goetze, 1991; Scotti, Evans, Meyer, & Walker, 1991).

Statistical Process Control

A promising development in the quantitative analysis of single-case data has its origin in the manufacturing world, specifically research on quality control of manufactured products (Doty, 1996; Ostle, Turner, Hicks, & McElrath, 1996). Research in manufacturing has used **statistical process control** (SPC) **charts** to ensure that manufactured parts do not deviate substantially from design specifications. Such deviations can be problematic, especially if the manufactured part is being machined to high specifications, as is true of many components found in many kinds of modern technology. Although the use of SPC charts has not been adopted widely within the health and behavioral sciences, some professionals have found this method of analysis both easy to carry out and useful in making clinical decisions. Many social work researchers, for instance, have endorsed the use of SPC charts for analyzing social work interventions (Berman, 1995; Boettcher, 1998; Moore & Kelly, 1996). Rehabilitation workers have also recently embraced both single-case research design and the use of SPC charts as a useful method of analysis (Callahan & Barisa, 2005; Callahan & Griffen, 2003), as have some applied behavior analysts (Pfadt & Wheeler, 1995).

An SPC chart begins with plotting of individual data on a time-series graph in a manner identical to that which we have discussed throughout this book, with a vertical line separating baseline and treatment data. The researcher then calculates the mean score for the baseline data as well as the standard deviation for these data. The *standard deviation* is a measure of variability or dispersion of scores about a mean, and it is calculated using the following formula:

$$SD = \sqrt{\frac{\Sigma(x - \bar{x})^2}{n - 1}},$$

where the first x is a single data point or raw score, the second x is the mean of all the data points, and n is the total number of data points that figure into the calculation.

This formula is telling us to subtract the mean from each individual data point, square this deviation score, and then add together all of the squared deviation scores. Then we divide the sum of the squared deviation scores by the number of scores in the phase minus 1. Finally, we calculate the square root of this number. The standard deviation is a commonly used statistic that tells us how much scores in a group deviate from the mean score of that group. Because of properties of the normal curve, which we discussed in Chapter 2, we can draw some conclusions about data in our study relative to the standard deviation. The standard deviation quantifies how much the individual scores in a data set deviate, on average or typically, from the mean of that data set. In a normally distributed data set we can calculate the percentage of scores in the data set that would be expected to deviate by 1, 2, or more standard deviations from the mean. In normally distributed data sets, if we move 2 standard deviations both above and below the mean, we will capture 95% of all the scores in the data set. This means that any score that lies more than 2 standard deviations away, either above or below, the mean, is a very rare score indeed. Its probability of occurrence is 5% or less.

After calculating the mean and standard deviation of the baseline data, the researcher creates horizontal lines that encompass 2 standard deviations both above and below the mean. These lines can then be extended from the baseline into the treatment phase to serve as a guideline for interpreting data under treatment. These lines are often referred to as *confidence interval lines* because they describe an interval of scores within which any score would be expected to fall at a probability of 95%. What this means is that scores falling outside the confidence interval lines are very unusual (5% or less) and thus would not seem to be representative of the data obtained during baseline. If treatment data lie outside this confidence interval, a treatment effect is suggested. Researchers suggest that at least two consecutive data points need to fall outside the confidence interval lines for a treatment effect to be determined (Orme & Cox, 2001). Obviously, this line of argument suggests that some kind of decision rule must accompany the use of the confidence interval lines in SPC charts, although different researchers may choose different criteria for doing so. No standard rule for identifying a treatment effect seems to have been agreed on by researchers who use SPC charts to analyze single-case data (Orme & Cox, 2001; Pfadt & Wheeler, 1995).

This is, in fact, also true of the size of the confidence interval itself. As developed within manufacturing research, SPC charts often use 3 standard deviations as the confidence interval (Doty, 1996). This is an even more stringent criterion because 3 standard deviations capture 99.7% of the scores in a set of scores.

Researchers in the health and behavioral sciences may view this as an overly stringent and unnecessary criterion, hence the adoption of a 2-standard deviation band in evaluating the effects of clinical interventions. This 95% confidence interval is also consistent with the criteria used by group researchers who submit their data to tests of statistical inference, so it would seem to be more than sufficient as a criterion for identifying applied intervention effects.

Figure 9.7 depicts the data for John Doe, with a 95% confidence interval line (also referred to as the *two standard-deviation band method*) beginning in the baseline phase and extending into the treatment phase. It is clear in this particular example that a treatment effect is apparent because more than two successive data points during treatment are below the lower band of this interval. Because the goal of the behavioral treatment in this case is to reduce the number of hand-washing episodes per day, we would wish to see data falling below the lower confidence line, and this is clearly the case. Remember that these data points are statistically rare (less than 5% chance of occurrence), and this rarity is what leads us to suggest that the data are not consistent with, or predictable from, the pattern seen in baseline. Thus, the change seen in the treatment condition data meet the quantitative criterion required in the use of SPC chart analysis.

Dual-Criteria Analysis

An approach that combines the calculation of trend lines with the confidence intervals of SPC charts is referred to as *dual-criteria analysis* and was introduced by Fisher, Kelley, and Lomas (2003). The term *dual criteria* refers to the fact that

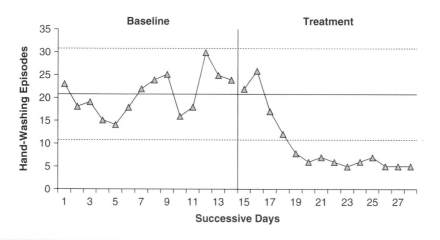

Figure 9.7   John Doe's hand washing with a 95% confidence interval line

data are interpreted relative to two separate mathematically derived criteria, one representing the mean of the baseline data and the other representing a celeration line generated from these same data. Calculation of the mean line is straightforward and follows the procedure described earlier in this chapter. The celeration line is actually a regression line calculated using the standard least squares regression procedure, also alluded to earlier in this chapter. At first, Fisher et al. suggested the use of these lines in a manner similar to the confidence interval or control limit lines of SPC charts. Data falling outside the lines and in a direction consistent with expected treatment effects would be considered rare and, consequently, likely to be due to the intervention. Although the use of this dual-criteria method proved quite useful in controlling for common errors in data analysis, Fisher et al. argued that an even more rigorous decision criterion might better serve applied researchers. Thus, they extended the logic of the dual-criteria method by moving the celeration line (up or down, depending on expected treatment effects) by 0.25 standard deviation. Because this adjustment results in a more conservative decision criterion, the authors referred to this analytic method as the *conservative dual-criteria* method.

In a series of statistical evaluations of the dual-criteria methods, Fisher et al. (2003) demonstrated that both strategies support strong inferences and were powerful in detecting effects, with low observed rates of both Type I (concluding that the intervention had an effect when it did not) and Type II (concluding that the intervention had no effect when it did) errors. In addition, the researchers reported that the conservative dual-criteria method was useful even under conditions of relatively high autocorrelation, a frequent occurrence in single-case data. Finally, the dual-criteria strategy was shown to produce reliable researcher conclusions following explicit training in the method. Although fairly new, the dual-criteria analytic strategy represents a fairly simple yet rigorous and promising tool for single-case researchers who wish to submit data to objective and conservative analytic procedures.

Tests of Statistical Significance

Most of the quantitative methods of data analysis that we have discussed thus far have been primarily descriptive in that summary measures such as means and standard deviations are calculated on data, and decisions about treatment effects are rendered on the basis of these calculations, often with the addition of level or trend lines consistent with the calculations. In most instances, the decision criteria in these examples have not involved tests of statistical significance, which, as we discussed in Chapter 2, are a standard part of the machinery of null hypothesis testing. This is not to say that statistical inference has been ignored by single-case researchers; in fact, recent years have seen a tremendous increase in the development and use of tests of significance for evaluating single-case data. Nevertheless, the practice of using statistical inference to evaluate single-case data remains highly controversial, and little consensus exists regarding how best to statistically analyze such data. We will not attempt an exhaustive review and critique of this growing issue, largely because no consensus has been reached among scientists who continue to pursue the matter of single-case data analysis. However, in the following section we attempt to address some of the more global issues from which this controversy arises and hazard something of a recommendation for those who face the task of analyzing single-case data.

In considering the issues confronting the analysis of single-case data, readers may benefit from a rereading of Chapter 2 or the introductory chapters of any good beginning statistics textbook. The data analytic armamentarium of most behavioral and social scientists consists of a battery of statistical tests designed to identify significant differences between data values, usually values representing descriptive statistics generated by groups of subjects. In evaluating these differences, we want to know whether the group difference is large enough that it would be unlikely to occur by chance, thus leading us to attribute the difference to an independent variable. The exact probability of the difference obtained can be evaluated using the descriptive properties of our group data and mathematical properties of the normal curve. If the difference is determined to be very unlikely (usually 5% or less), then the group difference is called *statistically significant* and the null hypothesis (i.e., the assumption that there is no difference between the groups at the population level) is rejected.

There are dozens of tests of statistical inference that can be used by researchers to evaluate data, and their appropriateness in any particular study is influenced by a number of factors, including the manner in which the data are measured, the number of independent and dependent variables used, and so on. Many of the most commonly used tests, however, are valid only if certain conditions of observation or measurement are met. One of the most important assumptions characterizing many statistical tests is the condition of *independent observation*. This term refers to the fact that each measurement of a variable is independent of, or unaffected by, other measures of that variable. This condition is ordinarily met sufficiently in group research because measuring a variable in one subject is an event independent from measuring that variable in another subject. This condition is not met, however, in single-case research, because all measures of the dependent variable are collected from the same subject over time. There is a good deal of dependence in single-case data, and we would expect this, because behavior is a continuous phenomenon exhibiting considerable serial dependency. In data analysis, this serial dependency is called *autocorrelation*, and such autocorrelation proves problematic for traditional significance tests (Gottman, 1981; Gottman & Rushe, 1994; Matyas & Greenwood, 1991). Although a number of researchers have developed methods of analyzing time-series data possessing autocorrelation, the validity of these methods remains questionable even today (Huitema, 2004; Huitema & McKean, 2000), and the general relevance of statistical inference to single-case data remains a highly controversial topic (Ator, 1999; Baron, 1999; Fisch, 2001). There is no doubt that the final chapters of this ongoing dialogue remain yet to be written.

Perhaps the most substantial shortcoming of tests of statistical inference for single-case data comes from the very moniker given such tests: *inference*. You may recall from Chapter 2 that we call such tests *inferential statistics* because the overriding goal of much research is to draw conclusions about a larger population from which the sample data were actually collected; that is, researchers, particularly those conducting basic research to identify general behavior principles or test substantive theories, are seldom interested in results generated by their subject sample. They wish instead to draw larger conclusions about the effects of an independent variable at the population level; thus, they wish to *infer* something about the population from their sample data.

We have suggested throughout this book that single-case researchers, especially those working in applied health care settings, seldom have as their goal the drawing of inferences to larger populations. Instead, these researchers are almost exclusively concerned with the effects of an independent variable (a clinical treatment) on a particular client, and questions about generality often do not even arise. Should the question of generality or external validity become important, single-case research already contains the necessary tools for pursuing the applicability of demonstrated effects. The conduct of intersubject replication studies, a long-standing staple of research strategy in the natural sciences, is the method of choice adopted by single-case researchers who wish to extend the validity of their findings to other clients and/or settings (Cohen, 1990; Sidman, 1960). Indeed, Jacob Cohen, a respected methodologist and statistician, has frequently argued that external validity was best served through good replication research, not through statistical inference or the use of large subject samples:

> A successful piece of research doesn't conclusively settle an issue, it just makes some theoretical propositions to some degree more likely. Only successful future replication in the same and different settings (as might be found through meta-analysis) provides an approach to settling the issue. (Cohen, 2003b, p. 422)

So, given the current disagreement characterizing the dialogue about data analysis for single-case research, what should one do? This is a legitimate question, particularly from an applied scientist operating in a managed care environment and being asked to provide empirical evidence for the effectiveness of his or her clinical interventions. We would suggest, along with many of those contributing to the recent dialogue on single-case data analysis (Bloom, Fischer, & Orme, 2006; Franklin et al., 1997; Nourbakhsh & Ottenbacher, 1994), that researchers utilize both traditional **visual analysis** and some form of **quantitative analysis** in evaluating single-case data. In addition to visually noting such things as trend, level, and data overlap in baseline and treatment data, the use of trend or celeration lines, or the confidence intervals utilized in SPC charts and Fisher et al.'s (2003) **dual-criteria analysis**, appear to be reasonable adjuncts in supporting clinical decisions. We make this recommendation largely on the grounds that the use of celeration/trend lines and conventional confidence intervals remains a largely descriptive, though quantitative, practice, unaffected by the requirements and assumptions of statistical inference. In addition, these data analytic methods are not terribly cumbersome, are likely to be more easily understood and utilized by practitioners, and add a more objective and quantitative component to the analysis. Although decision criteria still need to be adopted for this purpose (e.g., confidence interval size, number of data points required to be outside the confidence interval), this is also true of traditional null hypothesis testing research as well. Group researchers in the Fisherian tradition have for many decades used a 95% confidence interval as the criterion for rejecting the null hypothesis. We see no overwhelming reason to deviate from this standard and, as we mentioned earlier in this chapter, this practice has become somewhat common in many empirical studies by social workers, physical therapists, and other health care workers.

INTERIM SUMMARY

Several scholars have argued that the visual inspection of single-case data, a long-standing tradition in this area of research, is an inherently biased and poor method of data analysis. These scholars have called for single-case researchers to adopt the quantitative data analysis strategies common in the behavioral and health sciences. These strategies include both unsophisticated descriptive techniques, such as the use of mean level and celeration lines, and more complex tests of statistical significance. Although no consensus exists regarding the relative advantages and disadvantages of statistical treatment of single-case data, we recommend the combined use of both visual inspection and some quantitative treatment of data for applied scientists increasingly called on to meet evidence-based practice mandates.

KEY TERMS GLOSSARY

Internal validity How confident the researcher can be that changes in the dependent variable are due to introduction of the independent variable and not to some other factor.

External validity The extent to which a particular study's findings can be extended to subject populations or settings beyond the original study.

Celeration/trend lines Lines of best fit, calculated by least squares regression or the split-middle technique, that portray phase trends in single-subject graphs.

PND analysis A quantitative assessment of the amount of overlap, expressed in a percentage, between baseline and treatment data.

Statistical process control chart A method of data analysis that uses confidence intervals about a mean level line to evaluate treatment effects in single-subject data.

Visual analysis Traditional, nonquantitative method of inspection of level, trend, and overlap of data to evaluate treatment effects in single-subject data.

Quantitative analysis Methods of data analysis relying on descriptive and inferential statistics in evaluating treatment effects in single-subject data.

Dual-criteria analysis Data analytic method employing both a mean and regression line generated by baseline data against which to evaluate treatment data.

SUPPLEMENTS

Review Questions

1. What is the difference between internal and external validity, and why might single-case researchers be more interested in the former than the latter?

2. In visual analysis of single-case research, why is an upward or downward trend in baseline data problematic to interpretation?

3. Why do proponents of visual analysis believe that visual inspection is a sufficient method of analyzing single-case data?

4. According to critics of visual analysis, what are the drawbacks of relying on visual inspection of single-case data? What do these researchers see as the major advantages of quantitative and statistical analysis of such data?

5. How are computed trend/celeration lines used to make judgments about treatment effects in single-case data?

6. What kind of decision criterion is used in evaluating data in SPC charts?

7. Suppose you were a therapist charged with helping the bank president (see Figure 9.2) increase his level of exercise. Using the data in figure 9.2, calculate the PND using the appropriate data point in the baseline phase. What is the PND? Is this an appropriate analysis technique for these data? Why or why not?

Suggested Readings/Helpful Web Sites

http://www.asq.org/learn-about-quality/statistical-process-control/overview/overview.html

This Web site, maintained by the American Society for Quality, describes the history of statistical process control and its contribution to the quality-control movement in industry. There are links to articles and software developed for use in many applications.

Callahan, C. D., & Barisa, M. T. (2005). Statistical process control and rehabilitation outcome: The single-subject design revisited. *Rehabilitation Psychology, 50,* 24–33.

This is a very readable introduction to statistical process control as applied to rehabilitation psychology. The authors do a laudable job of describing the unique characteristics of SPC to single-case data and the advantages of this type of analysis for health care researchers.

Sidman, M. (1960). *Tactics of scientific research*. New York: Basic Books.

This is a classic book on experimental design by one of the pioneers of single-case research design. Sidman's treatment of such topics as experimental replication and the difference between group (nomothetic) and single-case (idiographic) study should be required reading for behavioral and health care researchers.

Chapter 10

CONTEMPORARY THEMES AND FUTURE DIRECTIONS IN SINGLE-CASE RESEARCH

The purpose of this book has been to introduce the reader to the fundamental logic and strategies of single-case research as it is practiced by professionals in various behavioral and health care disciplines. Because of recent managed-care mandates for demonstrating treatment effectiveness and recommendations for innovation by leading methodologists, applied scientists are particularly well situated to bringing alternative research strategies, among them single-case designs, to the clinical setting. Fortunately, many of the issues that practicing professionals encounter in this effort have also received attention by researchers pursuing the potential of single-case designs. In this chapter, we explore some of the recent developments in single-case research as well as the many methodological and clinical issues sure to confront future **scientist–practitioners**. More specifically, we discuss such topics as the increasing use of meta-analysis in the summary and interpretation of single-case studies. We also consider the single-case implications of the dialogue on statistical and clinical significance and external validity. Finally, we consider the theoretical neutrality of single-case research and its consequent potential for widespread adoption in applied health care environments.

STATISTICAL VERSUS CLINICAL SIGNIFICANCE

We have argued throughout this book that the strategies and tactics of single-case research are unique in their easy importability to applied clinical settings. This

233

means that applied scientists are in an enviable position not only to deliver interventions to real clients but also to do so in a way consistent with the objectives of scientific research. Although professional training programs profess commitment to the ideal of science-informed practice, practitioners report an altogether different reality. Psychologist Joseph Matarazzo, a recognized scientist and clinician, claimed some time ago that "few of my research findings affect my practice. Psychological science per se doesn't guide me one bit" (Bergin & Strupp, 1972, p. 340). Such a statement is an alarming claim coming from such a notable scientist–practitioner, but it sheds important light on the contentious nature of the science–practice relationship and confirms what has become a widespread concern among professionals (Barlow, 1981; Stricker, 1992; Stricker & Trierweiler, 2006).

The well-documented disconnect between science and practice is likely attributable to a number of factors, the most salient being the research training received by behavioral and health care professionals. As has already been demonstrated, this training has been dominated by the conventions of null hypothesis significance testing (NHST) and statistical inference. Of particular value to those professionals in training who will be delivering services to clients in applied settings is the distinction between **statistical and clinical significance**. *Statistical significance*, as we discussed in Chapter 2, refers to a specific probability that a calculated value of a test statistic, such as reflected in the difference between two group means on a dependent variable, is due to chance. If this probability is very low (usually 5% or less) and the study was conducted in a methodologically sound manner, then the results are said to be statistically significant, leading to the inference that the group difference was due to the independent variable. However, a number of factors influence the likelihood of achieving a statistically significant result, many of which have nothing to do with the variables of interest in the study. For instance, as every group researcher knows and appreciates, the likelihood of obtaining a statistically significant result increases with larger sample sizes; that is, everything else being equal, increasing the number of subjects in a study will increase the probability of rejecting the null hypothesis, thus producing a statistically significant result.

The fact that larger samples are more likely to render statistically significant results is not, in and of itself, problematic. What is troubling is the tendency for behavioral scientists to overemphasize the act of rejecting or failing to reject the null hypothesis and treating this binary decision as THE standard by which the quality of a research study should be assessed. There is, in fact, little reason to rejoice at the prospects of rejecting the null hypothesis, given that it is invariably false to begin with (Cohen, 1994, 1990; Loftus, 1993, 1996; Meehl, 1978). In addition, misinterpretations of the kinds of inferences supported by tests of statistical significance are common among researchers. As Cohen (1994, 1990) has pointed out, significance levels, reported as alpha (α) in published studies, are often depicted as if they are reflective of the strength or size of an effect when in fact they are not properly interpreted in this way. A study producing significance at an alpha level of .001 is not somehow more important or more clinically relevant than a study producing significance at an alpha level of .05.

Fortunately, research methodologists, having acknowledged the relative poverty of the null hypothesis, have increasingly endorsed alternative data analytic strategies, including the measurement of effect sizes. Numerous effect size measures are available to researchers, but they all share the same measurement objective. Instead of merely asking whether an independent variable or intervention had an effect on the dependent variable, effect size measures offer a quantitative statement about the size or magnitude of the effect. Such measures offer the potential for bridging the previously discussed gap that exists between basic science and professional practice (Barlow, 1981; Kanfer, 1990; Peterson, 2006; Stricker, 1992; Stricker & Trierweiler, 2006). For many practicing professionals, an intervention is significant, or important, to the extent that it produces a noticeable, real-world change in functioning for the client. This standard, known as *clinical* or *practical significance*, has been recommended as a more relevant criterion for evaluating change than the purely mathematical criterion of statistical significance.

Single-case researchers have been frequent contributors to the dialogue on statistical versus clinical significance (Barlow & Hersen, 1984; Hayes, 1981). Recall from Chapter 4 that evaluation of data from a single-case research study involves assessment of change exhibited in repeatedly measured target behavior across two or more phase changes. This assessment can be done visually, as has been the long-running practice in behavior analysis, or it can be aided by quantitative criteria, as has been more recently recommended by a host of researchers (Franklin, Gorman, Beasley, & Allison, 1997; Ottenbacher, 1990b, 1992). Regardless of what kind of data analysis ensues, establishing the clinical significance of target behavior change revolves around the criteria identified by either the researcher or others who may have a vested interest in the client's behavior. Within behavior analysis, one influential proposal for assessing clinical significance has emerged under the banner of **social validation**, which refers to whether an intervention is perceived as being relevant or effective by the client or individuals involved in the client's life, such as spouses, siblings, parents, friends, teachers, or coworkers (Kazdin, 1977; Wolf, 1978). Social validation data can be collected and assessed in a number of ways, such as through questionnaires or through either structured or open-ended interviews (Kennedy, 1992). The method employed will depend on the goals of the specific intervention program.

Social validation boasts several dimensions, only some of which may be pertinent to a particular study. For example, a researcher may simply be interested in whether the behaviors or symptoms being targeted by an intervention are the ones that the client believes to be most appropriate. It may seem odd, but there is no guarantee that the professional and the client will automatically identify the same problem areas or behaviors as needing intervention. Achieving a consensus on this issue is not necessarily difficult, and doing so before developing the intervention enhances the study's social validity. On the other hand, the focus may be on the actual procedures to be carried out and their acceptability to clients or other indirectly affected individuals. Some interventions or behavior change strategies are more preferable than others to particular clients (often for very idiosyncratic reasons), and the professional who dismisses the preferences or values of the client in determining details of the intervention risks both poor outcomes and low social validity. In some studies, it may be relevant to compare a client's level of functioning following an intervention with a group of peers who serve as models of appropriate behavior. For example, an autistic child being mainstreamed in a normal classroom may be evaluated on the basis of how closely certain aspects of his or her academic repertoire resemble, or are indistinguishable from, those of classmates. In such a study, reduced disparities between the client and the peer comparison group may be among the best indicators of program effectiveness.

Finally, and most relevant to the topic of clinical significance, researchers may wish to know whether the client or invested others view the change brought about by the intervention as useful or sufficient; that is, does the intervention lead to behavior change that translates into more effective and/or meaningful activity at home, school, the workplace, or other real-world setting? Because the client is considered to be in the best position to render this judgment, his or her interpretation may very well take precedence over the judgment of the applied scientist, even when the latter's judgments are provoked by quantitative analyses of the client's behavior. The general mentality behind social validation, then, is that behavior change must be sufficient to be noticeable to the individuals who are actually receiving, or otherwise benefiting from, services, regardless of how objective or scientifically credible such changes may be.

Meta-Analysis in Single-Case Research

Within the behavioral sciences, **meta-analysis**—a statistical procedure for comparing and evaluating the effect sizes generated by multiple studies—has emerged as an influential data analysis strategy, particularly as used to make sense of large numbers of studies conducted on the same phenomenon (Lipsey & Wilson, 2001). As we discussed in the previous section, an effect size is a statistic that depicts the size of a difference between two group means or the strength of a relationship between two variables in a correlational study; that is, an effect size tells the researcher something quite different than does the p value (alpha level) in a study.

Instead of indicating the probability of obtaining a test statistic of a particular value given the null hypothesis, effect size measures actually depict the magnitude of effect produced by the independent variable or, in applied settings, an intervention. Because an effect size measure is a descriptive statistic, not an inferential statistic, its use is not constrained by the kinds of assumptions (e.g., normally distributed variables, independent observations) that apply to tests of statistical significance. Although different kinds of effect size measures can be used depending on the type of data being analyzed, all such measures reflect the proportion of variance in a dependent variable (target behavior) accounted for by an independent variable (intervention). A standard effect size (ES) statistic is calculated in the following way:

$$ES = \frac{(Mean_1 - Mean_2)}{Pooled\ Standard\ Deviation}$$

This formula simply states that the effect size measure is a ratio of the difference between two group means divided by a weighted average of the standard deviations for the two groups. This equation is best interpreted as a conceptual description of an effect size rather than a precise mathematical formula for calculating an effect size. In practice, dozens of effect size measures exist, and researchers utilize different specific calculations based on both quantitative features of the original studies and particular goals of the meta-analysis itself.

As you may have surmised, in single-case experiments the means in the numerator of this equation represent not group means but mean response characteristics from a single client generated under baseline and treatment conditions. Similarly, the pooled standard deviation is the weighted average of the baseline and treatment standard deviations. Although conventional group researchers have been utilizing effect size measures for several decades, this method of data analysis is a relatively recent development within single-case research designs. Consequently, the use of effect size measures, and meta-analytic techniques in general, exhibit considerable variability within the single-case literature, and researchers are not in complete agreement regarding how to calculate effect sizes for the data from individual subjects or clients (Busk & Serlin, 1992; Campbell, 2004; Dunst, Hamby, & Trivette, 2004; Faith, Allison, & Gorman, 1997; Kromrey & Foster-Johnson, 1996; Robey, Schultz, Crawford, & Sinner, 1999). A number of characteristics of single-case data can complicate decisions regarding how to calculate and interpret the results of effect size measures, including extreme data points, or outliers; trends in baseline data; and degree of overlap or variability between baseline and treatment data. In addition, Dunst et al. (2004) suggested that comparison of effect size measures depends to a large extent on the data having been generated by similar research designs.

Regardless of the contentious nature of calculating effect sizes for single-case data, numerous benefits follow from being able to conduct meta-analyses of such studies. Most important, because effect size measures are expressed in standardized units, meta-analysis allows researchers to directly compare findings from dozens, even hundreds, of studies, despite substantial differences in methods, variables measured, subject characteristics, and so on. This kind of research integration is an essential feature of the cumulative nature of science, because it allows one to identify patterns of results in large bodies of research that might otherwise be viewed as inconsistent or difficult to interpret. Indeed, Vogt (2007) argued that meta-analysis is now the gold standard for conducting any formal review of a sizable literature and that conventional qualitative literature reviews are of limited value in the contemporary research landscape.

An additional benefit of meta-analysis, particularly for single-case studies, is the opportunity for enhancing the **external validity** of any particular finding. *External validity* refers to whether results can be generalized or applied to different subjects or settings beyond that of a specific study. Indeed, single-case research has been historically criticized on the grounds that results from one or very few subjects cannot be assumed to be representative of larger groups or populations. As it turns out, this criticism is only partly true, and in the next section we discuss how the external validity of single-case designs can be convincingly established. Nevertheless, to the extent that a meta-analysis of single-case studies demonstrates similar effect sizes for interventions across multiple subjects and settings, the external validity of that intervention would seem to be strengthened. Even more optimistically, Dunst and colleagues (Dunst et al., 2004; Dunst, Trivette, & Cutspec, 2002) have demonstrated that effect size measures are capable of identifying specific strategies or treatment components responsible for effective interventions.

INTERIM SUMMARY

The distinction between statistical and clinical significance is of considerable import to professionals delivering interventions in applied settings. Assessment of clinical significance may be achieved through various means, including collection of social validity data and the use of effect size measures. The increasing application of meta-analysis also represents an important development in the interpretation of single-case research. Although historically considered a shortcoming of the method, the external validity or generality of effects produced in single-case studies can be demonstrated through strategic use of direct and systematic replication.

EXTERNAL VALIDITY AND SINGLE-CASE RESEARCH

Researchers are usually interested in whether their specific findings are applicable to, or can be generalized, outside the confines of their study. This characteristic of a study, known as *external validity*, is often described as a particularly strong feature of group designs in which hundreds or even thousands of participants take part in the study. Single-case designs, on the other hand, are often criticized on the grounds that they contain very little, if any, external validity. As is often the case in research methodology, the issue is actually quite a bit more complex than this. Think for a moment about the phenomenon to which the phrase *external validity* usually refers. A standard textbook definition of the concept is "the extent to which the results of a particular study generalize to other people, places, or conditions" (Graziano & Raulin, 2004, p. 181). Such a definition actually suggests that external validity contains several dimensions. One of these dimensions is the population from which the study sample was obtained. One might, for instance, be primarily concerned about whether the results of a study conducted on college students at an Ivy League school should be taken as representative of the college population at large. On an even larger scale, what can the reader of such a study conclude about the much larger population of same-aged but noncollege adults throughout the country? The question of whether specific results generalize beyond the study sample is a pervasive issue in research, and the burden of arguing for the external validity of a study, of course, lies with the researcher. In most large-group research, considerable time and energy are focused on obtaining a sample of subjects that will be representative of the identified population. To a large extent, the results of a study are believed to generalize best when a large sample of participants is randomly selected from the relevant population.

The question of whether a study's results will generalize to a population is, however, only one dimension of external validity. Notice that the preceding definition also refers to whether the results can be applied to other "places" or "conditions." Although the precise referents of these words are not clear, the authors are most likely alluding to such things as the procedures used by the researchers (independent variables manipulated or interventions delivered) and actual setting of the study (laboratory, school, workplace, etc.). Questions about whether results will generalize across particular procedures and settings are not the same as those regarding subject generality, and yet they may be of considerable importance to a particular study. For instance, it would certainly make sense for a therapist delivering an intensive behavioral intervention to an autistic child to know whether the behavior changes produced by the intervention carry over, or generalize, to the child's home. In fact, it would be even more helpful to know whether the intervention is effective in any of a number of environments in which the child might find him- or herself. Unless the study was conducted to assess for generality of the intervention across settings, however, conclusions about this dimension of external validity would be inappropriate. Thus, researchers would be well advised to consider seriously the dimensions of generality, if any, that are important in a particular study, and devise specific methods for evaluating those dimensions (Johnston, 1979).

What the preceding discussion has highlighted is the fact that the external validity of a given study is difficult to assess without knowing the relevant dimensions across which generality is being evaluated. Not all dimensions may be relevant, and it would be unfair to criticize a study for possessing poor external validity unless the study was intentionally designed to assess for one or more aspects of generality. This issue is of special pertinence as it applies to single-case research designs. As we mentioned in Chapter 9, most single-case research is not conducted for the purpose of generalizing results to a population. In most cases, conclusions provoked by such studies are highly localized, being interpreted only at the level of the particular client. In fact, this was precisely the reason that traditional statistical inference was argued to be of limited utility in the analysis of single-case data. Because most single-case researchers are not interested in testing formal theories or uncovering universal laws of behavior, tests of statistical inference are of questionable value in interpreting the results of such research.

This is not to say that questions about generality, be it across subjects or procedures or settings, do not arise in single-case research. In fact, such concerns are sometimes a focus of such research. However, single-case researchers argue that questions of generality are best approached through replication, not through sampling strategies and the logic of statistical inference. This different take on generality represents a crucial disparity in the epistemologies of large-group and single-case researchers. The establishment of generality through experimental replication rather than statistical inference is a time-honored practice in the natural sciences and has been endorsed as well by many behavior analysts. The point was persuasively made by Murray Sidman (1960), a pioneer in the development of single-case research in psychology:

> Once the experimenter has pointed out those features of the data with which he is particularly concerned, how does he go about determining their generality? . . . We cannot dispose of the problem of subject generality by employing large groups of subjects and using statistical measures, such as the mean and variance of the groups. It is not true that the larger the group, the greater is the generality of the data. Representativeness is an actuarial problem to which the currently prevalent statistical design is not applicable. (1960, p. 47)

The generality of any particular finding from large-group research cannot be assumed except under conditions that are in fact seldom met in such research. Subject samples, for instance, are often not acquired through true random sampling from the relevant population but through methods primarily convenient to the researcher. Such samples are often characterized by considerable heterogeneity. It is for this reason that authors of such studies frequently admit that the external validity of the study's findings is limited and that future research should be conducted on additional samples in order to enhance generality. However, this somewhat obligatory call for replication usually goes unheeded because the practicalities of repeating a study with large numbers of subjects can be prohibitive. In actuality, replication studies are uncommon in many areas of research in the behavioral sciences, a situation long lamented by methodologists (Cohen, 1990).

Fortunately, this is not true of single-case research. Among the advantages of this research strategy is the ability to readily conduct replications, both within the same subject (**intrasubject**) and across subjects (**intersubject**). In fact, many of the single-case designs we have discussed, such as the withdrawal, multiple-baseline, and changing-criterion designs, are partly defined by intrasubject and intersubject replications of the independent variable or intervention. In addition, single-case researchers have described the important distinction between *direct replication* and *systematic replication* (Sidman, 1960). **Direct replication** involves the exact duplication of experimental procedures with different subjects. The primary purpose of direct replication is to establish not the generality of the finding but its reliability, or reproducibility. **Systematic replication**, on the other hand, involves repetition of the experiment but with some specified difference from the original experiment. For example, delivering an intervention to a client first in a hospital setting, then repeating the same intervention in the client's home, would represent a systematic replication. Because different variables might be expected to impact behavior in these two settings, reproducing the effects of the intervention would provide especially convincing support for the robustness of the intervention. As Sidman (1960) suggested, systematic replication is an extremely important tool in establishing the generality, or external validity, of a particular effect. Indeed, many single-case studies are designed from the beginning to allow for such systematic replications. Because the logistic requirements of replicating an effect at the level of individual subjects are not foreboding, single-case designs are quite powerful in their capacity for establishing generality across subjects, procedures, and settings. This is, of course, somewhat ironic, given that single-case studies are often criticized on the grounds that they possess little external validity.

Future Directions in Single-Case Research

In Chapter 2 of this book, we described some of the conceptual and historical factors influencing research design in the behavioral and health sciences, including some recent developments of alternative methods. Much has been written about the shortcomings of conventional NHST research. In fact, in 1995, the American Psychological Association charged a task force with looking into the time-honored practices of null hypothesis testing and statistical inference. Among the recommendations made by this group to behavioral scientists was that researchers make more frequent and effective use of graphing techniques to present data and that they report effect sizes and confidence intervals for computed statistics (Wilkinson & The Task Force on Statistical Inference, 1999). In addition to these recommendations, alternative research tactics have been championed on several fronts. Qualitative research methods, for instance, have witnessed an explosive growth in popularity, as many social scientists have touted the rich and highly informative nature of data that are not easily quantified, such as verbal utterances and narrative records (Berg, 2001; Chi, 1997).

Single-case research design represents yet another alternative to conventional NHST and large group designs, and the advantages of this methodology appear to have been recognized by many professionals, particularly those involved in delivering health care interventions. As we have seen throughout this book, single-case research strategies are easily implemented in settings that would pose formidable challenges to researchers requiring large client samples. Because clinical interventions are delivered, almost without exception, to individuals, research designs that utilize observation, measurement, and data analysis at the level of the individual are inherently superior to nomothetic strategies. Moreover, because intervention effectiveness is being considered only at this "local" level, questions of statistical inference and population parameters do not arise. When subjects or clients serve as their own controls and phase changes reveal reliable effects on continuously measured dependent variables, the resulting data support strong causal inferences. Finally, because single-case research methods allow for ongoing and immediate assessment of relevant dependent measures, rapid and appropriate adjustments in interventions can be made. This kind of design flexibility, an inherent strength of single-case methodology, would be inconceivable in large sample group studies.

It is our contention that a confluence of circumstances, including current managed care mandates and an emphasis on evidence-based practice, has placed an unprecedented premium on empirical research in health care disciplines. In many of these disciplines, the conduct of large sample studies, including randomized clinical trials, is unwieldy because of the restraints of conventional research practices.

Single-case research designs, on the other hand, are ready-made for precisely this kind of research environment and boast an impressive track record in such fields as behavior analysis (Bailey & Burch, 2002), special education (Horner et al., 2005), and rehabilitation (Callahan & Barisa, 2005; Zhan & Ottenbacher, 2001). Researchers' reluctance to utilize this family of designs may largely be due to lack of training in the methods, although there are clearly other candidates as well. As we described in Chapter 2, single-case methodology was strongly endorsed by proponents of behavior analysis within psychology, especially Murray Sidman (1960) and B. F. Skinner (1956). Hayes (1981) claimed, probably correctly, that many researchers have rejected single-case designs because of their association with behaviorism:

> This is unfortunate, however, because the methodology is theory free. One can use time series experimentation to answer questions about self-disclosure as readily as behavioral indicants of anxiety, and about insight-oriented procedures as successfully as assertiveness training. (p. 194)

We would like to think that the climate has changed markedly since Hayes's (1981) observation. Because of their theoretically neutral status, single-case designs are easily imported to applied health care settings, as demonstrated by the extent to which nurses, physical and occupational therapists, social workers, and rehabilitation workers have embraced their use in divergent ways. We have, in fact, seen the strategies and tactics of single-case design applied to an enormous array of client problems, intervention practices, and target behaviors and across a considerable spectrum of health care disciplines. The combination of more innovative research training of professionals and increased mandates from managed care to demonstrate treatment effectiveness should serve as powerful catalysts for researchers to adopt and use single-case research designs in applied health care settings.

INTERIM SUMMARY

Single-case researchers pursue external validity through both direct and systematic replication instead of through statistical inference. Replication has been strongly endorsed by methodologists as an important but insufficiently utilized strategy to demonstrate the reliability and generalizability of research findings. The shortcomings of conventional group research, managed care pressures to empirically validate interventions, and an increased tolerance for innovation in research design all serve to highlight the promise of single-case research for applied professionals. Its theoretical neutrality and flexible design features render single-case methodology an appealing alternative to large group NHST designs. As documented throughout this book, many researchers in applied health settings have come to endorse the use of single-case designs in studies evaluating the effectiveness of interventions.

KEY TERMS GLOSSARY

Scientist–practitioner A practitioner (e.g., psychologist, nurse, social worker) who adheres to methods, procedures, and research in his or her day-to-day practice.

Statistical significance A result is said to be statistically significant when the result would occur less than 5% of the time if the populations were really identical.

Clinical or practical significance When a noticeable, real-world change in a client's symptoms or behavior is produced.

Social validation Whether an intervention is perceived as being relevant or effective by the client or individuals involved in the client's life, such as a spouse, siblings, parents, friends, teachers, or coworkers.

Meta-analysis A statistical procedure for comparing and evaluating the effect size generated by multiple studies.

Intrasubject Within a single subject.

Intersubject Across more than one subject.

External validity The extent to which the results of a particular study are applicable to subjects, settings, or behaviors beyond that specific study.

Direct replication Repeating a study by exactly duplicating the experimental procedures with different subjects.

Systematic replication Repetition of an experiment but with some specified difference from the original experiment (variable manipulated or setting of study, etc.).

SUPPLEMENTS

Review Questions

1. What is the difference between statistical and clinical significance, and how is the concept of social validation related to this issue?

2. What is meta-analysis, and how is it related to the concept of clinical significance?

3. Why have researchers been critical of the external validity of single-case research studies?

4. What strategy is used by single-case researchers to demonstrate the external validity of a study?

5. What is the difference between direct and systematic replication?

6. Why do the book authors argue that single-case designs are well suited to and easily imported into applied settings?

Suggested Readings

Cohen, J. (1990). Some things I have learned (so far). *American Psychologist, 45,* 1304–1312.

One of psychology's leading methodologists discusses, in engaging and often humorous fashion, the problems inherent in the null hypothesis testing tradition.

Peterson, D. R. (2006). Connection and disconnection of research and practice in the education of professional psychologists. *Training and Education in Professional Psychology, S*(1), 47–57.

The gap separating science and practice has long been lamented by health care professionals in many disciplines. Peterson's article aptly describes how this issue has been conceptualized and handled within the training of professional psychologists.

Wolf, M. M. (1978). Social validity: The case for subjective measurement, or how applied behavior analysis is finding its heart. *Journal of Applied Behavior Analysis, 11,* 203–214.

This article, a classic in the field of behavior analysis, describes a method for collecting and presenting data bearing on the topic of clinical significance.

REFERENCES

Abramovich, E. (2006). Application of CBT in an inpatient setting: Case illustration of an adult male with anxiety, depression, and Axis II symptoms. *Clinical Case Studies, 5,* 305–330.

Ackerman, S. J., Benjamin, L. S., Beutler, L. E., Gelso, C. J., Goldfried, M. R., Hill, C., et al. (2001). Empirically supported therapy relationships: Conclusions and recommendations of the Division 29 Task Force. *Psychotherapy: Theory, Research, Practice, Training, 38,* 495–497.

Aeschleman, S. R. (1991). Single-subject research designs: Some misconceptions. *Rehabilitation Psychology, 36,* 43–49.

Ahava, G. W., Iannone, C., Grebstein, L., & Schirling, J. (1998). Is the Beck Depression Inventory reliable over time? An evaluation of multiple test–retest reliability in a nonclinical college student sample. *Journal of Personality Assessment, 70,* 222–231.

Allen, K. D., & Evans, J. H. (2001). Exposure-based treatment to control excessive blood glucose monitoring. *Journal of Applied Behavior Analysis, 34,* 497–500.

Allison, D. B., & Gorman, B. S. (1994). "Make things as simple as possible, but no simpler": A rejoinder to Scruggs and Mastropieri. *Behavioral Research and Therapy, 32,* 885–890.

American Medical Association Evidence-Based Practice Working Group. (1992). Evidence-based medicine: A new approach to teaching the practice of medicine. *Journal of the American Medical Association, 268,* 2420–2425.

American Psychiatric Association. (1994). *Diagnostic and statistical manual of mental disorders* (4th ed.). Washington, DC: Author.

American Psychiatric Association. (2000). *Diagnostic and statistical manual of mental disorders* (4th ed., text rev.). Washington, DC: Author.

Anderson, K. L., & Goldstein, H. (2004). Speech perception benefits of FM and infrared devices to children with hearing aids in a typical classroom. *Language, Speech, and Hearing Services in Schools, 35,* 169–184.

Apple, A. L., Billingsley, F., & Schwartz, I. S. (2005). Effects of video modeling alone and with self-management on compliment-giving behaviors of children with high-functioning ASD. *Journal of Positive Behavior Interventions, 7,* 33–46.

Åsenlöf, P., Denison, E., & Lindberg, P. (2005). Individually tailored treatment targeting motor behavior, cognition, and disability: 2 experimental single-case studies of patients with recurrent and persistent musculoskeletal pain in primary health care. *Physical Therapy, 85,* 1061–1077.

Ator, N. A. (1999). Statistical inference in behavior analysis: Environmental determinants. *The Behavior Analyst, 22,* 93–97.

Baer, D. M. (1977). Perhaps it would be better not to know everything. *Journal of Applied Behavior Analysis, 10,* 167–172.

Bailey, D. B. (1984). Effects of lines of progress and semilogarithmic charts on ratings of charted data. *Journal of Applied Behavior Analysis, 17,* 359–365.

Bailey, J. S., & Burch, M. R. (2002). *Research methods in applied behavior analysis.* Thousand Oaks, CA: Sage.

Barlow, D. H. (1981). On the relation of clinical research to clinical practice: Current issues, new directions. *Journal of Consulting and Clinical Psychology, 49,* 147–155.

Barlow, D. H., & Hayes, S. C. (1979). Alternating treatments design: One strategy for comparing the effects of two treatments in a single subject. *Journal of Applied Behavior Analysis, 12,* 199–210.

Barlow, D. H., & Hersen, M. (1984). Single-case experimental designs: Strategies for studying behavior change (2nd ed.). New York: Pergamon Press.

Baron, A. (1999). Statistical inference in behavior analysis: Friend or foe? *The Behavior Analyst, 22,* 83–85.

Beasley, T. M., Allison, D. B., & Gorman, B. S. (1997). The potentially confounding effects of cyclicity: Identification, prevention, and control. In R. D. Franklin, D. B. Allison, & B. S. Gorman (Eds.), *Design and analysis of single-case research* (pp. 279–332). Mahwah, NJ: Lawrence Erlbaum.

Beck, A. T., Steer, R. A., & Brown, G. K. (1996). *BDI–II manual.* New York: Psychological Corporation.

Beck, A. T., Steer, R. A., & Garbin, M. G. (1988). Psychometric properties of the Beck Depression Inventory: Twenty-five years of evaluation. *Clinical Psychology Review, 8,* 77–100.

Bengali, M. K., & Ottenbacher, K. J. (1998). The effect of autocorrelation on the results of visually analyzing data from single-subject designs. *American Journal of Occupational Therapy, 52,* 650–655.

Berg, B. L. (2001). *Qualitative research methods for the social sciences* (4th ed.). Boston: Allyn & Bacon.

Bergin, A., & Strupp, H. (1972). *Changing frontiers in the science of psychotherapy.* Chicago: Aldine-Atherton.

Berman, E. M. (1995). Implementing TQM in state welfare agencies. *Administration in Social Work, 19,* 55–72.

Bigelow, K. M., Huynen, K. B., & Lutzker, J. R. (1993). Using a changing criterion design to teach fire escape skills to a child with developmental disabilities. *Journal of Developmental and Physical Disabilities, 5,* 121–128.

Binder, C. (1996). Behavioral fluency: Evolution of a new paradigm. *The Behavior Analyst, 19,* 163–197.

Blampied, N. M. (1999). A legacy neglected: Restating the case for single-case research in cognitive–behaviour therapy. *Behaviour Change, 16,* 89–104.

Blampied, N. M. (2000). Single-case research designs: A neglected alternative. *American Psychologist, 55,* 960.

Blampied, N. M. (2001). The third way: Single-case research, training, and practice in clinical psychology. *Australian Psychologist, 36,* 157–163.

Blampied, N. M., Barabasz, A., & Barabasz, M. (1996). Single-case research designs for the science and practice of neurotherapy. *Journal of Neurotherapy, 1,* 15–26.

Bloom, M., Fischer, J., & Orme, J. G. (2006). *Evaluating practice: Guidelines for the accountable professional* (5th ed.). Boston: Pearson/Allyn & Bacon.

Boettcher, R. E. (1998). A study of quality-managed human service organizations. *Administration in Social Work, 22,* 41–56.

Borckardt, J. J., Nash, M. R., Murphy, M. D., Moore, M., Shaw, D., & O'Neil, P. (2008). Clinical practice as natural laboratory for psychotherapy research: A guide to case-based time-series analysis. *American Psychologist, 63,* 77–95.

Bosch, S., & Fuqua, W. (2001). Behavioral cusps: A model for selecting target behaviors. *Journal of Applied Behavior Analysis, 34,* 123–125.

Broskowski, A. T. (1994). Current mental health care environments: Why managed care is necessary. In R. L. Lowman & R. J. Resnick (Eds.), *The mental health professional's guide to managed care* (pp. 1–18). Washington, DC: American Psychological Association.

Brossart, D. F., Parker, R. I., Olson, E. A., & Mahadevan, L. (2006). The relationship between visual analysis and five statistical analyses in a simple AB single-case research design. *Behavior Modification, 30,* 531–563.

Buning, M. E., & Hanzlik, J. R. (1993). Adaptive computer use for a person with visual impairment. *American Journal of Occupational Therapy, 47,* 998–1008.

Busk, P. L., & Serlin, R. (1992). Meta-analysis for single-case research. In T. R. Kratochwill & J. R. Levin (Eds.), *Single-case research design and analysis: New directions for psychology and education* (pp. 187–212). Hillsdale, NJ: Lawrence Erlbaum.

Callahan, C. D., & Barisa, M. T. (2005). Statistical process control and rehabilitation outcome: The single-case design reconsidered. *Rehabilitation Psychology, 50,* 24–33.

Callahan, C. D., & Griffen, D. L. (2003). Applying statistical process control techniques to emergency medicine: A primer for providers. *Academic Emergency Medicine, 10,* 883–890.

Cameron, M. J., Shapiro, R. L., & Ainsleigh, S. A. (2005). Bicycle riding: Pedaling made possible through positive behavioral interventions. *Journal of Positive Behavior Interventions, 7,* 153–158.

Campbell, J. M. (2004). Statistical comparison of four effect sizes for single-case designs. *Behavior Modification, 28,* 234–246.

Carr, E. G., Austin, J. L., Britton, L. N., Kellum, K. K., & Bailey, J. S. (1999). An assessment of social validity trends in applied behavior analysis. *Behavioral Interventions, 14,* 223–231.

Carr, J. E. (2005). Recommendations for reporting multiple-baseline designs across participants. *Behavioral Interventions, 20,* 219–224.

Carr, J. E., Bailey, J. S., Carr, C. A., & Coggin, A. M. (1996). The role of independent variable integrity in the behavioral management of Tourette syndrome. *Behavioral Interventions, 11,* 35–45.

Castonguay, L. G., & Beutler, L. E. (2006). *Principles of therapeutic change that work.* New York: Oxford University Press.

Chambless, D. L., Baker, M. J., Baucom, D. H., Beutler, L., Calhoun, K. S., Crits-Christoph, P., et al. (1998). Update on empirically validated therapies, II. *The Clinical Psychologist, 51,* 3–16.

Chambless, D. L., & Hollon, S. D. (1998). Defining empirically supported therapies. *Journal of Consulting and Clinical Psychology, 66,* 7–18.

Chambless, D. L., & Ollendick, T. H. (2001). Empirically supported psychological interventions: Controversies and evidence. *Annual Review of Psychology, 52,* 685–716.

Chi, M. T. H. (1997). Quantifying qualitative analyses of verbal data: A practical guide. *Journal of the Learning Sciences, 6,* 271–315.

Clay, R. A. (2000, June). Treatment guidelines: Sorting fact from fiction. *Monitor on Psychology, 31.* Retrieved from www.apa.org/monitor/jun00/guidelines.html

Cleland, J., Hunt, G. C., & Palmer, J. (2004). Effectiveness of neural mobilization in the treatment of a patient with lower extremity neurogenic pain: A single-case design. *Journal of Manual and Manipulative Therapy, 12,* 143–152.

Cohen, J. (1990). Things I have learned (so far). *American Psychologist, 45,* 1304–1312.

Cohen, J. (1994). The Earth is round ($p < .05$). *American Psychologist, 49,* 997–1003.

Cohen, J. (2003). Things I have learned (so far). In A. E. Kazdin (Ed.), *Methodological issues and strategies in clinical research* (3rd ed., pp. 407–424). Washington, DC: American Psychological Association.

Cooper, J. O., Heron, T. E., & Heward, W. L. (2007). *Applied behavior analysis* (2nd ed). Upper Saddle River, NJ: Pearson/Merrill Prentice Hall.

Cosmides, L., & Tooby, J. (1992). Cognitive adaptations for social exchange. In J. H. Barkow, L. Cosmides, & J. Tooby (Eds.), *The adapted mind: Evolutionary psychology and the generation of culture* (pp. 163–228). New York: Oxford University Press.

Dahlstrom, W. G., Brooks, J. D., & Peterson, C. D. (1990). The Beck Depression Inventory: Item order and the impact of response sets. *Journal of Personality Assessment, 55,* 224–233.

DeLuca, R. V., & Holborn, S. W. (1992). Effects of a variable-ratio reinforcement schedule with changing criteria on exercise in obese and nonobese boys. *Journal of Applied Behavior Analysis, 25,* 671–679.

DeProspero, A., & Cohen, S. (1979). Inconsistent visual analysis of intra-subject data. *Journal of Applied Behavior Analysis, 12,* 573–579.

Dickens, C., McGowan, L., Clark-Carter, D., & Creed, F. (2002). Depression in rheumatoid arthritis: A systematic review of the literature with meta-analysis. *Psychosomatic Medicine, 64,* 52–60.

Dixon, M. R. (2003). Creating a portable data-collection system with Microsoft Embedded Visual Tools for the Pocket PC. *Journal of Applied Behavior Analysis, 36,* 271–284.

Doty, L. A. (1996). *Statistical process control* (2nd ed.). New York: Industrial Press.

Dufrene, B. A., Watson, T. S., & Weaver, A. (2005). Response blocking with guided compliance and reinforcement for a habilitative replacement behavior: Effects on public masturbation and on-task behavior. *Child & Family Behavior Therapy, 27*(4), 73–84.

Dunst, C. J., Hamby, D. W., & Trivette, C. M. (2004). Guidelines for calculating effect sizes for practice-based research syntheses. *CenterScope, 3*(1), 1–10.

Dunst, C. J., Trivette, C. M., & Cutspec, P. A. (2002). An evidence-based approach to documenting the characteristics and consequences of early intervention practices. *CenterScope, 1*(2), 1–6.

Ebbinghaus, H. (1913). *Memory* (H. A. Ruger & C. E. Bussenius, Trans.). New York: Teachers College. (Original work published 1885)

Edgington, E. S. (1972). $N = 1$ experiments: Hypothesis testing. *The Canadian Psychologist, 13,* 121–135.

Edgington, E. S. (1984). Statistics and single-case designs. *Progress in Behavior Modification, 16,* 83–119.

Elder, J. H. (1997). Single subject experimentation for psychiatric nursing. *Archives of Psychiatric Nursing, 11*, 133–138.

Ericsson, K. A., & Simon, H. A. (1984). *Protocol analysis: Verbal reports as data.* Cambridge: MIT Press.

Faith, M. S., Allison, D. B., & Gorman, B. S. (1997). Meta-analysis of single-case research. In R. D. Franklin, D. B. Allison, & B. S. Gorman (Eds.), *Design and analysis of single-case research* (pp. 245–277). Mahwah, NJ: Lawrence Erlbaum.

Farrenkopf, C., McGregor, D., Nes, S. L., & Koenig, A. J. (1997). Increasing a functional skill for an adolescent with cortical visual impairment. *Journal of Visual Impairment & Blindness, 91,* 484–493.

Fisch, G. S. (2001). Evaluating data from behavior analysis: Visual inspection or statistical models? *Behavioural Processes, 54,* 137–154.

Fisher, W. W., Kelley, M. E., & Lomas, J. E. (2003). Visual aids and structured criteria for improving visual inspection and interpretation of single-case designs. *Journal of Applied Behavior Analysis, 36,* 387–406.

Foxx, R. M., & Rubinoff, A. (1979). Behavioral treatment of caffeineism: Reducing excessive coffee drinking. *Journal of Applied Behavior Analysis, 12,* 335–344.

Franklin, R. D., Gorman, B. S., Beasley, T. M., & Allison, D. B. (1997). Graphic display and visual analysis. In R. D. Franklin, D. B. Allison, & B. S. Gorman (Eds.), *Design and analysis of single-case research* (pp. 93–117). Mahwah, NJ: Lawrence Erlbaum.

Furlong, M. J., & Wampold, B. (1981). Visual analysis of single-subject studies by school psychologists. *Psychology in the Schools, 18,* 80–86.

Furlong, M. J., & Wampold, B. (1982). Intervention effects and relative variation as dimensions in experts' use of visual inference. *Journal of Applied Behavior Analysis, 15,* 415–421.

Gill, C., Stratford, P., & Sanford, J. (1992). The use of single subject design to evaluate a potential adverse effect. *Physiotherapy Canada, 44*(3), 25–29.

Goldstein, A. P., Glick, B., & Gibbs, J. C. (1998). *Aggression Replacement Training: A comprehensive intervention for aggressive youth* (Rev. ed.). Champaign, IL: Research Press.

Gonnella, C. (1989). Single-case experimental paradigm as a clinical decision tool. *Physical Therapy, 69,* 91–99.

Gottman, J. M. (1981). *Time-series analysis: A comprehensive introduction for social scientists.* New York: Cambridge University Press.

Gottman, J. M. (Ed.). (1995). *The analysis of change.* Mahwah, NJ: Lawrence Erlbaum.

Gottman, J. M., & Rushe, R. H. (1994). The analysis of change: Issues, fallacies, and new ideas. *Journal of Consulting and Clinical Psychology, 61,* 907–910.

Gould, S. J. (1996). *Full house: The spread of excellence from Plato to Darwin.* New York: Three Rivers Press.

Graziano, A. M., & Raulin, M. L. (2004). *Research methods: A process of inquiry.* Boston: Pearson/Allyn & Bacon.

Gresham, F. M. (1997). Treatment integrity in single-subject research. In R. D. Franklin, D. B. Allison, & B. S. Gorman (Eds.), *Design and analysis of single-case research* (pp. 93–117). Mahwah, NJ: Lawrence Erlbaum.

Gresham, F. M., Gansle, K. A., & Noell, G. H. (1993). Treatment integrity in applied behavior analysis with children. *Journal of Applied Behavior Analysis, 26,* 257–263.

Gresham, F. M., Gansle, K. A., Noell, G., Cohen, S., & Rosenblum, S. (1993). Treatment integrity of school-based behavioral intervention studies: 1980–1990. *School Psychology Review, 22,* 254–272.

Gunter, P. L., Venn, M. L., Patrick, J., Miller, K. A., & Kelly, L. (2003). Efficacy of using momentary time samples to determine on-task behavior of students with emotional/behavioral disorders. *Education & Treatment of Children, 26,* 400–412.

Hanley, G. P., Iwata, B. A., & McCord, B. E. (2003). Functional analysis of problem behavior: A review. *Journal of Applied Behavior Analysis, 36,* 147–185.

Harbst, K. B., Ottenbacher, K. J., & Harris, S. R. (1991). Interrater reliability of therapists' judgments of graphed data. *Physical Therapy, 71,* 107–115.

Hartmann, D. P., & Hall, R. V. (1976). The changing criterion design. *Journal of Applied Behavior Analysis, 9,* 527–532.

Hartnedy, S., & Mozzoni, M. P. (2000). Managing environmental stimulation during meal time: Eating problems in children with traumatic brain injury. *Behavioral Interventions, 15,* 261–268.

Harvey, M. T., May, M. E., & Kennedy, C. H. (2004). Nonconcurrent multiple baseline designs and the evaluation of educational systems. *Journal of Behavioral Education, 13,* 267–276.

Harzem, P. (1985). Operationism, smuggled connotations, and the nothing-else clause. *Behavioral and Brain Sciences, 7,* 559.

Hatzenbueler, L. C., Parpal, M., & Matthews, L. (1983). Classifying college students as depressed or nondepressed using the Beck Depression Inventory: An empirical analysis. *Journal of Consulting and Clinical Psychology, 51,* 360–366.

Hayes, S. C. (1981). Single case experimental design and empirical clinical practice. *Journal of Consulting and Clinical Psychology, 49,* 193–211.

Hayes, S. C., & Cavior, N. (1977). Multiple tracking and the reactivity of self-monitoring: I. Negative behaviors. *Behavior Therapy, 8,* 819–831.

Haynes, S. N., & Horn, W. F. (1982). Reactivity in behavioral observation: A methodological and conceptual critique. *Behavioral Assessment, 4,* 369–385.

Hendricks, R. L. (1993). *A model for health care: The history of Kaiser Permanente.* New Brunswick, NJ: Rutgers University Press.

Henry, G. T. (1995). *Graphing data: Techniques for display and analysis.* Thousand Oaks, CA: Sage.

Hersch, L. (1995). Adapting to health care reform and managed care: Three strategies for survival and growth. *Professional Psychology: Research and Practice, 26,* 16–26.

Hersen, M., & Barlow, D. H. (1976). *Single case experimental designs: Strategies for studying behavior change.* New York: Pergamon.

Himle, M. B., Miltenberger, R. G., Flessner, C., & Gatheridge, B. (2004). Teaching safety skills to children to prevent gun play. *Journal of Applied Behavior Analysis, 37,* 1–9.

Hinderer, S. R., & Liberty, K. (1996). Effects of baclofen on oral counting, arithmetic, and symbol decoding: An explorative multiple-baseline design across subjects. *International Journal of Rehabilitation and Health, 2,* 41–55.

Hoaglin, D. C, Mosteller, F., & Tukey, J. W. (Eds.). (1985). *Exploring data tables, trends, and shapes.* New York: Wiley.

Hoerster, L., Hickey, E. M., & Bourgeois, M. S. (2001). Effects of memory aids on conversations between home residents with dementia and nursing assistants. *Neuropsychological Rehabilitation, 11,* 399–427.

Horner, R. D., & Baer, D. M. (1978). Multiple-probe technique: A variation of the multiple baseline. *Journal of Applied Behavior Analysis, 11,* 189–196.

Horner, R. H., Carr, E. G., Halle, J., McGee, G., Odom, S., & Wolery, M. (2005). The use of single-case research to identify evidence-based practice in special education. *Exceptional Children, 71,* 165–179.

Horner, R. H., Dunlap, G., & Koegel, R. L. (Eds.). (1988). *Generalization and maintenance: Life-style changes in applied settings.* Baltimore: Paul Brookes.

Huitema, B. E. (1986). Statistical analysis and single-subject designs. In A. Poling & R. W. Fuqua (Eds.), *Research methods in applied behavior analysis: Issues and advances* (pp. 209–232). New York: Plenum Press.

Huitema, B. E. (2004). Analysis of interrupted time-series experiments using ITSE: A critique. *Understanding Statistics, 3,* 27–46.

Huitema, B. E., & McKean, J. W. (2000). Design specification issues in time-series intervention models. *Educational and Psychological Measurement, 60,* 38–58.

Hunsley, J. (2007). Addressing key challenges in evidence-based practice in psychology. *Professional Psychology: Research and Practice, 38,* 113–121.

Hunsley, J., & Lee, C. M. (2006). *Introduction to clinical psychology: An evidence-based approach.* Toronto, Ontario, Canada: Wiley.

Ingersoll, B., Dvortcsak, A., Whalen, C., & Sikora, D. (2005). The effects of a developmental, social-pragmatic language intervention on rate of expressive language production in young children with autistic spectrum disorders. *Focus on Autism and Other Developmental Disabilities, 20,* 213–222.

Iwata, B. A., Dorsey, M. F., Slifer, K. J., Bauman, K. E., & Richman, G. S. (1994). Toward a functional analysis of self-injury. *Journal of Applied Behavior Analysis, 27,* 197–209.

Iwata, B. A., Pace, G. M., Dorsey, M. F., Zarcone, J. R., Vollmer, T. R., Smith, R. G., et al. (1994). The functions of self-injurious behavior: An experimental–epidemiological analysis. *Journal of Applied Behavior Analysis, 27,* 215–240.

Jacobson, N. S., & Christensen, A. (1996). Studying the effectiveness of psychotherapy: How well can clinical trials do the job? *American Psychologist, 51,* 1031–1039.

Jacobson, N. S., Dobson, K. S., & Truax, P. A. (1996). A component analysis of cognitive–behavioral treatment for depression. *Journal of Consulting and Clinical Psychology, 64,* 295–304.

Johnson, J. W., McDonnell, J., Holzwarth, V. N., & Hunter, K. (2004). The efficacy of embedded instruction for students with developmental disabilities enrolled in general education classes. *Journal of Positive Behavior Interventions, 6,* 214–227.

Johnston, J. M. (1979). On the relation between generality and generalization. *The Behavior Analyst, 2*(2), 1–6.

Johnston, J. M., & Pennypacker, H. S. (1993a). Generalization and generality. In J. M. Johnston & H. S. Pennypacker (Eds.), *Readings for strategies and tactics of behavioral research* (2nd ed., pp. 173–180). Hillsdale, NJ: Lawrence Erlbaum.

Johnston, J. M., & Pennypacker, H. S. (1993b). *Strategies and tactics of behavioral research* (2nd ed.). Hillsdale, NJ: Lawrence Erlbaum.

Jones, R. R., Vaught, R. S., & Reid, J. B. (1975). Time series analysis as a substitute for single subject analysis of variance designs. In G. R. Patterson, I. M. Marks, J. D. Matarazzo, R. A. Myers, G. E. Schwartz, & H. H. Strupp (Eds.), *Behavior change 1974* (pp. 164–169). Hawthorne, NY: Aldine.

Kahng, S., & Iwata, B. A. (1998). Computerized systems for collecting real-time observational data. *Journal of Applied Behavior Analysis, 31,* 253–261.

Kanfer, F. H. (1990). The scientist–practitioner connection: A bridge in need of constant attention. *Professional Psychology: Research and Practice, 21,* 264–270.

Kay, S., Harchik, A. E., & Luiselli, J. K. (2006). Elimination of drooling by an adolescent student with autism attending public high school. *Journal of Positive Behavioral Interventions, 8,* 24–28.

Kazdin, A. E. (1976). Statistical analyses for single-case experimental designs. In M. Hersen & D. H. Barlow (Eds.), *Single-case experimental designs: Strategies for studying behavior change* (pp. 265–313). New York: Pergamon.

Kazdin, A. E. (1977). Assessing the clinical or applied significance of behavior change through social validation. *Behavior Modification, 1,* 427–452.

Kazdin, A. E. (1981). Drawing valid inferences from case studies. *Journal of Consulting and Clinical Psychology, 49,* 183–192.

Kazdin, A. E. (1982a). History of behavior modification. In A. S. Bellack, M. Hersen, & A. E. Kazdin (Eds.), *International handbook of behavior modification and therapy* (pp. 3–32). New York: Plenum Press.

Kazdin, A. E. (1982b). *Single-case research designs: Methods for clinical and applied settings.* New York: Oxford University Press.

Kazdin, A. E. (1984). Statistical analyses for single-case experimental designs. In D. H. Barlow & M. Hersen (Eds.), *Single case experimental designs: Strategies for studying behavior change* (pp. 285–321). New York: Pergamon.

Kazdin, A. E. (1994). *Behavior modification in applied settings* (5th ed.). Pacific Grove, CA: Brooks/Cole.

Kazdin, A. E., & Hartmann, D. P. (1978). The simultaneous-treatment design. *Behavioral Therapy, 9,* 912–922.

Kendrick, R., & Bayne, R. (1982). Compliance with prescribed medication by elderly patients. *Canadian Medical Association Journal, 11,* 961–962.

Kennedy, C. H. (1992). Trends in the measurement of social validity. *The Behavior Analyst, 15,* 147–156.

Kennedy, C. H. (2002). The maintenance of behavior as an indicator of social validity. *Behavior Modification, 26,* 594–606.

Kent, R. N., O'Leary, D. K., Dretz, A., & Diament, C. (1979). Comparison of observational recordings in view, via mirror and via television. *Journal of Applied Behavior Analysis, 12,* 517–522.

Kirby, K. C., Fowler, S. A., & Baer, D. M. (1991). Reactivity in self-recording: Obtrusiveness of recording procedure and peer comments. *Journal of Applied Behavior Analysis, 24,* 487–498.

Kollen, B. J., Rietberg, M. B., Kwakkel, G., & Emmelot, C. H. (2000). Effects of overloading of the lower hemiparetic extremity on walking speed in chronic stroke patients: A pilot study. *NeuroRehabilitation, 14,* 159–164.

Kromrey, J. D., & Foster-Johnson, L. (1996). Determining the efficacy of interventions: The use of effect sizes for data analysis in single-case research. *Journal of Experimental Education, 65,* 73–93.

Kuentzel, J. G., Henderson, M. J., Zambo, J. J., Stine, S. M., & Schuster, C. R. (2003). Motivational interviewing and fluoxetine for pathological gambling disorder: A single case study. *North American Journal of Psychology, 5,* 229–248.

Landrum, T. J., & Lloyd, J. W. (1992). Generalization in social behavior research with children and youth who have emotional or behavioral problems. *Behavior Modification, 16,* 593–616.

Leary, M. R. (2004). *Introduction to behavioral research methods* (4th ed.). Boston: Pearson/Allyn & Bacon.

Lejuez, C. W., Zvolensky, M. J., & Eifert, G. H. (1999). Using a single-subject design to assess the development of anxiety in humans. *Journal of Behavior Therapy and Experimental Psychiatry, 30,* 15–20.

Levant, R. F. (2005, February). Evidence-based practice in psychology. *APA Monitor, 36,* 5.

Levinson, S., Kopari, J., & Fredstrom, J. (2002). *Helping kids change their behavior: The helper's guide to the MotivAider method.* Thief River Falls, MN: Behavioral Dynamics.

Lindsley, O. R. (1956). Operant conditioning methods applied to research in chronic schizophrenia. *Psychiatric Research Reports, 5,* 118–139.

Lindsley, O. R. (1960). Characteristics of the behavior of chronic psychotics as revealed by free-operant conditioning methods. *Diseases of the Nervous System* (Monograph Suppl.), *21,* 66–78.

Lipsey, M. W., & Wilson, D. B. (2001). *Practical meta-analysis.* Thousand Oaks, CA: Sage.

Loftus, G. R. (1993). A picture is worth a thousand p values: On the irrelevance of hypothesis testing in the microcomputer age. *Behavior Research Methods, Instrumentation, & Computers, 25,* 250–256.

Loftus, G. R. (1996). Psychology will be a much better science when we change the way we analyze data. *Current Directions in Psychological Science, 5,* 161–171.

Logue, A. W. (1988). Research on self-control: An integrating framework. *Behavioral and Brain Sciences, 11,* 665–709.

Ludwig, T. D., & Geller, E. S. (1991). Improving the driving practices of pizza deliverers: Response generalization and moderating effects of driving history. *Journal of Applied Behavior Analysis, 24,* 31–44.

Mandel, U., Bigelow, K. M., & Lutzker, J. R. (1998). Using video to reduce home safety hazards with parents reported for child abuse and neglect. *Journal of Family Violence, 13,* 147–162.

Marshall, R. C., Capilouto, G. J., & McBride, J. M. (2007). Treatment of problem solving in Alzheimer's disease: A short report. *Aphasiology, 21,* 235–247.

Marshall, R. C., Karow, C. M., Morelli, C. A., Iden, K. K., & Dixon, J. (2003). A clinical measure for the assessment of problem solving in brain-injured adults. *American Journal of Speech-Language Pathology, 12,* 333–348.

Mathur, S. R., Kavale, K. A., Quinn, M. M., Forness, S. R., & Rutherford, R. B. (1998). Social skills interventions with students with emotional and behavioral problems. *Behavioral Disorders, 23,* 193–201.

Mattacola, C. G., & Lloyd, J. W. (1997). Effects of a 6-week strength and proprioception training program on measures of dynamic balance: A single-case design. *Journal of Athletic Training, 32,* 127–135.

Matyas, T. A., & Greenwood, K. M. (1991). Problems in the estimation of autocorrelation in brief time series and some implications for behavioral data. *Behavioral Assessment, 13,* 137–157.

McDonell, M., Rodgers, M., Short, R., Norell, D., Pinter, L., & Dyck, D. (2007). Clinician integrity in multiple family groups: Psychometric properties and relationship with schizophrenia client and caregiver outcomes. *Cognitive Therapy & Research, 31,* 785–803.

McDougall, D. (2005). The range-bound changing criterion design. *Behavioral Interventions, 20(2),* 129–137.

McDougall, D. (2006, December). The distributed criterion design. Journal of Behavioral Education, 15, 236–246.

McDougall, D., Hawkins, J., Brady, M., & Jenkins, A. (2006). Recent innovations in the changing criterion design: Implications for research and practice in special education. *Journal of Special Education, 40,* 2–15.

McDougall, D., Skouge, J., Farrell, C.A., & Hoff, K. (2006, Summer). Research on self-management techniques used by students with disabilities in general education settings: A promise fulfilled? *Journal of the American Academy of Special Education Professionals,* 36–73.

McDougall, D., & Smith, D. (2006). Recent innovations in small-*N* designs for research and practice in professional school counseling. *Professional School Counseling, 9,* 392–400.

McGlinchey, J. B., & Dobson, K. S. (2003). Treatment integrity concerns in cognitive therapy for depression. *Journal of Cognitive Psychotherapy, 17,* 299–318.

Meehl, P. (1978). Theoretical risks and tabular asterisks: Sir Karl, Sir Ronald, and the slow progress of soft psychology. *Journal of Consulting and Clinical Psychology, 46,* 806–834.

Meza, C. V., Powell, N. J., & Covington, C. (1998). The influence of olfactory intervention on nonnutritive sucking skills in a premature infant. *Occupational Therapy Journal of Research, 18,* 71–83.

Michael, J. (1974). Statistical inference for individual organism research: Mixed blessing or curse? *Journal of Applied Behavior Analysis, 7,* 647–653.

Miller, L. K. (1997). *Principles of everyday behavior analysis* (3rd ed.). Pacific Grove, CA: Brooks/Cole.

Miller, P. J. (1985). Assessment of joint motion. In J. M. Rothstein (Ed.), *Measurement in physical therapy* (pp. 103–136). New York: Churchill Livingstone.

Miltenberger, R. G., Rapp, J. T., & Long, E. S. (1999). A low-tech method for conducting real-time recording. *Journal of Applied Behavior Analysis, 32,* 119–120.

Mischel, H. N., & Mischel, W. (1983). The development of children's knowledge of self-control strategies. *Child Development, 54,* 603–619.

Misdrahi, D., Llorca, J. P., Lancon, C., & Bayle, F. J. (2002). Compliance in schizophrenia: Predictive factors, therapeutic considerations and research implications. *Encephale, 28,* 266–272.

Mohr, D. C., Boudewyn, A. C., & Likosky, W. (2001). Injectable medication for the treatment of multiple sclerosis: The influence of self-efficacy expectations and injection anxiety on adherence and ability to self-inject. *Annals of Behavioral Medicine, 23,* 125–132.

Moncher, F., & Prinz, R. (1991). Treatment fidelity in outcome studies. *Clinical Psychology Review, 11,* 247–266.

Moore, S. T., & Kelly, M. J. (1996). Quality now: Moving human service organizations toward a consumer orientation to service quality. *Social Work, 41,* 33–40.

Morgan, D. L., & Morgan, R. K. (2001). Single-participant research design: Bringing science to managed care. *American Psychologist, 56,* 119–127.

Nathan, P. E., & Gorman, J. M. (Eds.). (2002). *A guide to treatments that work* (2nd ed.). New York: Oxford University Press.

Neef, N. A. (1995). Research on training trainers in program implementation: An introduction and future directions. *Journal of Applied Behavior Analysis, 28,* 297–299.

Neistadt, M. E., & Crepeau, E. B. (1998). *Willard & Spackman's occupational therapy* (9th ed.). Philadelphia: Lippincott Williams & Wilkins.

Newell, A., & Simon, H. A. (1972). *Human problem solving*. Englewood Cliffs, NJ: Prentice Hall.

Nezu, A. M., & Nezu, C. M. (2005). Comments on "Evidence-based behavioral medicine: What is it and how do we achieve it?": The interventionist does not always equal the intervention—The role of therapist competence. *Annals of Behavioral Medicine, 29,* 80.

Nourbachsh, M. R., & Ottenbacher, K. J. (1994). The statistical analysis of single-subject data: A comparative examination. *Physical Therapy, 74,* 768–776.

Nuehring, E. M., & Pascone, A. B. (1986). Single-subject evaluation: A tool for quality assurance. *Social Work, 31,* 359–365.

Orme, J. G., & Cox, M. E. (2001). Analyzing single-subject design data using statistical process control charts. *Social Work Research, 25,* 115–127.

Öst, L. (1992). Blood and injection phobia: Background and cognitive, physiological, and behavioral variables. *Journal of Abnormal Psychology, 101,* 68–74.

Ostle, B., Turner, K. V., Jr., Hicks, C. R., & McElrath, G. W. (1996). *Engineering statistics*. Belmont, CA: Dusbury Press.

Ottenbacher, K. J. (1990a). Clinically relevant designs for rehabilitation research: The idiographic model. *American Journal of Physical Medicine & Rehabilitation, 69,* 286–292.

Ottenbacher, K. J. (1990b). Visual analysis of single-subject data: An empirical analysis. *Mental Retardation, 28,* 283–290.

Ottenbacher, K. (1992). Analysis of data in idiographic research: Issues and trends. *American Journal of Physical Medicine & Rehabilitation, 71,* 202–208.

Ottenbacher, K. J., & Cusick, A. (1991). An empirical investigation of inter-rater agreement for single-subject data using graphs with and without trendlines. *Journal of the Association for Persons With Severe Handicaps, 16,* 48–55.

Pace, G. M., & Toyer, E. A. (2000). The effects of a vitamin supplement on the pica of a child with severe mental retardation. *Journal of Applied Behavior Analysis, 33,* 619–622.

Padgett, L. S., Strickland, D., & Coles, C. D. (2006). Case study: Using a virtual reality computer game to teach fire safety skills to children with fetal alcohol syndrome. *Journal of Pediatric Psychology, 31,* 65–70.

Parker, R. I., Hagan-Burke, S., & Vannest, K. (2007). Percentage of all non-overlapping data (PAND): An alternative to PND. *Journal of Special Education, 40,* 194–204.

Parrish, J. M., Cataldo, M. F., Kolko, D. J., Neef, N. A., & Egel, A. L. (1986). Experimental analysis of response covariation among compliant and inappropriate behaviors. *Journal of Applied Behavior Analysis, 19,* 241–254.

Parsonson, B. S., & Baer, D. M. (1986). The graphic analysis of data. In A. Poling & R. W. Fuqua (Eds.), *Research methods in applied behavior analysis: Issues and advances* (pp. 157–186). New York: Plenum Press.

Perepletchikova, F., & Kazdin, A. E. (2005). Treatment integrity and therapeutic change: Issues and research recommendations. *Clinical Psychology: Science and Practice, 12,* 365–383.

Peterson, D. R. (2006). Connection and disconnection of research and practice in the education of professional psychologists. *Training and Education in Professional Psychology, S*(1), 47–57.

Peterson, L., Homer, A., & Wonderlich, S. (1982). The integrity of independent variables in behavior analysis. *Journal of Applied Behavior Analysis, 15,* 477–492.

Pfadt, A., & Wheeler, D. J. (1995). Using statistical process control to make data-based clinical decisions. *Journal of Applied Behavior Analysis, 28,* 349–370.

Phelps, R., Eisman, E. J., & Kohout, J. (1998). Psychological practice and managed care: Results of the CAPP practitioner's survey. *Professional Psychology: Research and Practice, 29,* 31–36.

Pinker, S. (1997). *How the mind works.* New York: W. W. Norton.

Pipal, J. E. (1995). Managed care: Is it the corpse in the living room? An expose. *Psychotherapy, 32,* 323–332.

Porr, S. M., & Rainville, E. B. (1999). *Pediatric therapy: A systems approach.* Philadelphia: F. A. Davis.

Powell, J., Martindale, A., & Kulp, S. (1975). An evaluation of time-sample measures of behavior. *Journal of Applied Behavior Analysis, 8,* 463–469.

Random House Webster's college dictionary. (1997). New York: Random House.

Reiss, S., Peterson, R. A., Gursky, D. M., & McNally, R. J. (1986). Anxiety sensitivity, anxiety frequency, and the prediction of fearfulness. *Behaviour Research and Therapy, 24,* 1–8.

Richardson, J. L. (1986). Perspectives on compliance with drug regimens among the elderly. *Journal of Compliance in Health Care, 1,* 33–42.

Rickel, A. U., & Wise, T. N. (1999). *Understanding managed care: An introduction for health care professionals.* New York: Karger.

Robey, R. R., Schultz, M. C., Crawford, A. B., & Sinner, C. A. (1999). Single-subject clinical-outcome research: Designs, data, effect sizes, and analyses. *Aphasiology, 13,* 445–473.

Rosales-Ruiz, J., & Baer, D. M. (1997). Behavioral cusps: A developmental and pragmatic concept for behavior analysis. *Journal of Applied Behavior Analysis, 30,* 533–544.

Rothwell, P. M. (2005). External validity of randomized controlled trials: "To whom do the results of this trial apply?" *The Lancet, 365,* 82–93.

Ruscio, A. M., & Holohan, D. R. (2006). Applying empirically supported treatments to complex cases: Ethical, empirical, and practical considerations. *Clinical Psychology: Science and Practice, 13,* 146–162.

Rush, A. J., Beck, A. T., Kovacs, M., & Hollon, S. (1977). Comparative efficacy of cognitive therapy and pharmacotherapy in the treatment of depressed outpatients. *Cognitive Therapy and Research, 1,* 17–37.

Sagan, C. (1980). *Cosmos.* New York: Random House.

Salzberg, C. L., Strain, P. S., & Baer, D. M. (1987). Meta-analysis for single-subject research: When does it clarify, when does it obscure? *Remedial and Special Education, 8,* 43–48.

Sanderson, W. C., & McGinn, L. K. (2001). Cognitive–behavioral therapy of depression. In M. M. Weissman (Ed.), *Treatment of depression: Bridging the 21st century.* Washington, DC: American Psychiatric Press.

Saudargas, R. A., & Zanolli, K. (1990). Momentary time sampling as an estimate of percentage time: A field validation. *Journal of Applied Behavior Analysis, 23,* 533–537.

Schlosser, R. W. (2002). On the importance of being earnest about treatment integrity. *Augmentative & Alternative Communication, 18,* 36–44.

Schlosser, R. W., & Goetze, H. (1991). Effectiveness and treatment validity of interventions addressing self-injurious behavior: From narrative reviews to meta-analyses. In T. E. Scruggs & M. A. Mastropieri (Eds.), *Advances in learning and behavioral disabilities* (Vol. 7, pp. 135–176). Greenwich, CT: JAI Press.

Scotti, J. R., Evans, I. M., Meyer, L. H., & Walker, P. (1991). A meta-analysis of intervention research with problem behavior: Treatment validity and standards of practice. *American Journal on Mental Retardation, 96,* 233–256.

Scruggs, T. E., & Mastropieri, M. A. (1998). Synthesizing single-subject research: Issues and applications. *Behavior Modification, 22,* 221–242.

Scruggs, T. E., & Mastropieri, M. A. (2001). How to summarize single-participant research: Ideas and applications. *Exceptionality, 9,* 227–244.

Scruggs, T. E., Mastropieri, M. A., Cook, S., & Escobar, C. (1986). Early intervention for children with conduct disorders: A quantitative synthesis of single-subject research. *Behavioral Disorders, 11,* 260–271.

Scruggs, T. E., Mastropieri, M. A., Forness, S. R., & Kavale, K. A. (1988). Early language intervention: A quantitative synthesis of single-subject research. *Journal of Special Education, 22,* 259–283.

Shabani, D. B., Wilder, D. A., & Flood, W. A. (2001). Reducing stereotypic behavior through discrimination training, differential reinforcement of other behavior, and self-monitoring. *Behavioral Interventions, 16,* 279–286.

Shepherd, M., Watt, D., Falloon, L., & Smeeton, N. (1989). The natural history of schizophrenia: A five-year follow-up in a representative sample of schizophrenia. *Psychological Medicine, Monograph Supplement 15,* 1–45.

Sidman, M. (1960). *Tactics of scientific research: Evaluating experimental data in psychology.* New York: Basic Books.

Siris, S. G. (2001). Suicide and schizophrenia. *Journal of Psychopharmacology, 15,* 127–135.

Skinner, B. F. (1953). *Science and human behavior.* New York: Free Press.

Skinner, B. F. (1956). A case history in scientific method. *American Psychologist, 11,* 221–233.

Smith, G. J., McDougall, D., & Edelen-Smith, P. (2006). Behavioral cusps: A person-centered concept for establishing pivotal individual, family, and community behaviors and repertoires. *Focus on Autism and Developmental Disorders, 21,* 223–229.

Song, F. (1997). Risperidone in the treatment of schizophrenia: A meta-analysis of randomized controlled trials. *Journal of Psychopharmacology, 11,* 65–71.

Spidle, J. (1999). The historical roots of managed care. In D. A. Bennahum (Ed.), *Managed care: Financial, legal, and ethical issues* (pp. 11–20). Cleveland, OH: Pilgrim Press.

Sprague, J. R., & Horner, R. H. (1992). Covariation within functional response classes: Implications for treatment of severe problem behavior. *Journal of Applied Behavior Analysis, 25,* 735–745.

Stark, K. D., Hargrave, J., Sander, J., Custer, G., Schnoebelen, S., Simpson, J., & Molnar, J. (2006). Treatment of childhood depression: The ACTION treatment program. In P. C. Kendall (Ed.), *Child and adolescent therapy: Cognitive–behavioral procedures* (3rd ed., pp. 169–216). New York: Guilford Press.

Sterling, Y. M., & McNally, J. A. (1992). Single-subject research for nursing practice. *Clinical Nurse Specialist, 6,* 21–26.

Stirman, S. W., DeRubeis, R. J., Crits-Christoph, P., & Rothman, A. (2005). Can the randomized controlled trial literature generalize to nonrandomized patients? *Journal of Consulting and Clinical Psychology, 73,* 127–135.

Stokes, T. F., & Baer, D. M. (1977). An implicit technology of generalization. *Journal of Applied Behavior Analysis, 10,* 349–367.

Stokes, T. F., & Osnes, P. G. (1989). An operant pursuit of generalization. *Behavior Therapy, 20,* 337–355.

Stricker, G. (1992). The relationship of research to clinical practice. *American Psychologist, 47,* 543–549.

Stricker, G., & Trierweiler, S. J. (1995). The local clinical scientist. *American Psychologist, 50,* 995–1002.

Stricker, G., & Trierweiler, S. J. (2006). The local clinical scientist: A bridge between science and practice. *Training and Education in Professional Psychology, 1,* 37–46.

Tertinger, D. A., Greene, B. F., & Lutzker, J. R. (1984). Home safety: Development and validation of one component of an ecobehavioral treatment program for abused and neglected children. *Journal of Applied Behavior Analysis, 17,* 159–174.

Thompson, R. H., McKerchar, P. M., & Dancho, K. A. (2004). The effects of delayed physical prompts and reinforcement on infant sign language acquisition. *Journal of Applied Behavior Analysis, 37,* 379–383.

Tiger, J. H., Bouxsein, K. J., & Fisher, W. W. (2007). Treating excessively slow responding of a young man with Asperger syndrome using differential reinforcement of short response latencies. *Journal of Applied Behavior Analysis, 40,* 559–563.

Tufte, E. R. (2001). *The visual display of quantitative information* (2nd ed.). Cheshire, CT: Graphics Press.

Ullman, J. D., & Sulzer-Azaroff, B. (1975). Multielement baseline design in educational research. In E. Ramp & G. Semb (Eds.), *Behavioral analysis: Areas of research and application* (pp. 371–391). Upper Saddle River, NJ: Prentice Hall.

Vernon, D. S., Schumaker, J. B., & Deshler, D. D. (1996). *The SCORE skills: Social skills for cooperative groups* (2nd ed.). Lawrence, KS: Edge Enterprises.

Vogt, W. P. (2007). *Quantitative research methods for professionals.* Boston: Pearson/Allyn & Bacon.

Wambaugh, J. L. (2003). A comparison of the relative effects of phonologic and semantic cueing treatments. *Aphasiology, 17,* 433–441.

Ward, P., & Carnes, M. (2002). Effects of posting self-set goals on collegiate football players' skill execution during practice and games. *Journal of Applied Behavior Analysis, 35,* 1–12.

Warnes, E., & Allen, K. D. (2005). Biofeedback treatment of paradoxical vocal fold motion and respiratory distress in an adolescent girl. *Journal of Applied Behavior Analysis, 38,* 529–532.

Watson, P. J., & Workman, E. A. (1981). The nonconcurrent multiple baseline across-individuals design: An extension of the traditional multiple baseline design. *Journal of Behavior Therapy and Experimental Psychiatry, 12,* 257–259.

Weiden, P. J., & Zygmunt, A. (1997, March). Medication noncompliance in schizophrenia: Part I. Assessment. *Journal of Practical Psychiatry and Behavioral Health, 3,* 106–110.

White, O. R. (1971). *The "split-middle": A "quickie" method of trend estimation* (Working Paper No. 1). Eugene: University of Oregon, Regional Center for Handicapped Children.

White, O. R. (1987). Some comments concerning "the quantitative synthesis of single-subject research." *Remedial and Special Education, 8,* 34–39.

Wilkinson, L., & The Task Force on Statistical Inference. (1999). Statistical methods in psychology: Guidelines and explanations. *American Psychologist, 54,* 594–604.

Wolery, M., & Harris, S. R. (1982). Interpreting results of single-subject research designs. *Physical Therapy, 62,* 445–452.

Wolf, M. M. (1978). Social validity: The case for subjective measurement, or how applied behavior analysis is finding its heart. *Journal of Applied Behavior Analysis, 11,* 203–214.

Woods, D. W., Miltenberger, R. G., & Lumley, V. A. (1996). Sequential application of major habit-reversal components to treat motor tics in children. *Journal of Applied Behavior Analysis, 29,* 483–493.

Wren, C. S. (1999, August 17). Harnessing the powerful secrets of a dog's nose. *The New York Times.* Retrieved March 18, 2008, from http://query.nytimes.com/gst/fullpage.html?res=9C0DE4D 81139F934A2575BC0A96F958260.

Wu, H., & Miller, L. K. (2007). A tutoring package to teach pronunciation of Mandarin Chinese characters. *Journal of Applied Behavior Analysis, 40,* 583–586.

Wu, S., Huang, H., Lin, C., & Chen, M. (1996). Effects of a program on symmetrical posture in patients with hemiplegia: A single-subject design. *American Journal of Occupational Therapy, 50,* 17–23.

Yuen, H. K. (1993). Improved productivity through purposeful use of additional template for a woman with cortical blindness. *American Journal of Occupational Therapy, 47,* 105–110.

Yuen, H. K., & Garrett, D. (2001). Case report: Comparison of three wheelchair cushions for effectiveness of pressure relief. *American Journal of Occupational Therapy, 55,* 470–475.

Zabinski, M. F., Wilfley, D. E., Calfas, K. J., & Winzelberg, A. J. (2004). An interactive psychoeducational intervention for women at risk of developing an eating disorder. *Journal of Consulting and Clinical Psychology, 72,* 914–919.

Zhan, S., Ottenbacher, K. J. (2001). Single-subject experimental designs for disability research. *Disability and Rehabilitation, 23,* 1–8.

Zieman, G. (1998). *Handbook of managed behavioral healthcare: A complete and up-to-date guide for students and practitioners.* San Francisco: Jossey-Bass.

Zimmerman, M. (1986). The stability of the Revised Beck Depression Inventory in college students: Relationship with life events. *Cognitive Therapy and Research, 10,* 37–43.

Zung, W. W. K. (1965). A self-rating depression scale. *Archives of General Psychiatry, 12,* 63–70.

INDEX

ABOUT THE AUTHORS

David L. Morgan obtained his PhD in experimental psychology, with an emphasis in human operant behavior, from Auburn University in 1988. He is currently a professor in the School of Professional Psychology at Spalding University in Louisville, Kentucky, where he has been teaching since 1990. Dr. Morgan has published research articles in numerous behavioral journals and has taught research methodology courses at both the undergraduate and graduate levels at several institutions, including Spalding University. He is the author of *Essentials of Learning and Cognition*.

Robin K. Morgan obtained her PhD in clinical psychology from Auburn University in 1988. She is currently a professor at Indiana University Southeast in New Albany, Indiana, where she has been teaching since 1988. Dr. Morgan has worked in both inpatient psychiatric and medical settings as well as outpatient settings, including private practice, with child, adolescent, and adult clients running the gamut of psychological disorders. Dr. Morgan has published articles in several journals and has been recognized for her excellence in teaching. She is the author of *Case Studies in Child and Adolescent Psychopathology* and has written and edited several additional books related to college teaching.